Study Guide

to Accompany

West's Paralegal Today
The Legal Team at Work
Second Edition

ROGER LeROY MILLER
Institute for University Studies
Arlington, Texas

MARY MEINZINGER URISKO
Madonna University
Missouri

Prepared by
Celia C. Elwell

WEST LEGAL STUDIES
Thomson Learning™

Africa • Australia • Canada • Denmark • Japan • Mexico • New Zealand • Philippines
Puerto Rico • Singapore • Spain • United Kingdom • United States

Printed in the United States of America
4 5 6 7 8 9 10 XXX 05 04 03 02

For more information, contact:
Delmar, 3 Columbia Circle, PO Box 15015, Albany, NY 12212-0515;
or find us on the World Wide Web at http://www.westlegalstudies.com

ISBN 0-7668-1011-9

Library of Congress Catalog Card Number: 99–29176

TABLE OF CONTENTS

Study Skills	iv
CHAPTER 1: Today's Professional Paralegal	1
CHAPTER 2: Careers in the Legal Community	11
CHAPTER 3: Ethics and Professional Responsibility	23
CHAPTER 4: The Legal Workplace	35
CHAPTER 5: Sources of American Law	45
CHAPTER 6: The Court System and Alternative Dispute Resolution	57
CHAPTER 7: Substantive Law I	69
CHAPTER 8: Substantive Law II	83
CHAPTER 9: Administrative Law and Government Regulation	95
CHAPTER 10: Civil Litigation—Before the Trial	111
CHAPTER 11: Trial Procedures	123
CHAPTER 12: Criminal Law and Procedures	135
CHAPTER 13: Conducting Interviews and Investigations	149
CHAPTER 14: Legal Research	161
CHAPTER 15: Computer-Assisted Legal Research	173
CHAPTER 16: Legal Analysis and Writing	187

STUDY SKILLS FOR *WEST'S PARALEGAL TODAY: THE LEGAL TEAM AT WORK*

Every student has a different way to study. We give several study hints below that we think will help any student to better master the textbook *West's Paralegal Today: The Legal Team at Work, Second Edition.* These skills involve outlining, marking, taking notes, and summarizing. You may not need to use all of these skills. Nonetheless, if you do improve your ability to use them, you will be able to understand more easily the information in *West's Paralegal Today: The Legal Team at Work, Second Edition.* Remember, though, that sometimes forgotten in the activity of studying are the reasons for studying in the first place. You may find it helpful, from time to time, to remind yourself of your own reasons for studying—you may be studying, for example, to be ready for tomorrow's class, to be prepared for the final examination, to attain a certain grade, to be awarded a degree, and to ultimately obtain a position in an occupational field that you believe you will enjoy.

MAKING AN OUTLINE

An outline is simply a method for organizing information. The reason an outline can be helpful is that it shows how concepts relate to each other. Outlining can be done as part of your reading, at the end of your reading, or as a rereading of each section within a chapter before you go on to the next section. Even if you do not believe that you need an outline, our experience has been that the act of *physically* writing an outline for a chapter helps most students to improve greatly their ability to retain the material in *West's Paralegal Today: The Legal Team at Work, Second Edition* and master it, thereby obtaining a higher grade in the class, with less effort.

To make an effective outline, you have to be selective. Outlines that contain all the information in the text are not very useful. Your objective in outlining is to identify main concepts and to subordinate details to those main concepts. Therefore, your first goal is to *identify the main concepts in each section.* Often the large first-level headings within your textbook are sufficient as identifiers of the major concepts within each section. You may decide, however, that you want to phrase an identifier in a way that is more meaningful to you. In any event, your outline should consist of several levels written in a standard outline format. The most important concepts are assigned a roman numeral, the second most important are assigned a capital letter; the third most important are assigned numbers; and the fourth most important are assigned lower-case letters. Even if you make an outline that is no more than the headings in the text, you will be studying more efficiently than you would be otherwise. As we stated above, the process of physically writing the words will help you master the material.

MARKING A TEXT

Why Marking is Important Marking is important for the same reason that outlining is—it helps you to organize better the information in the text. It allows you to become an *active* participant in the mastery of the material. Researchers have shown that the physical act of marking, just like the physical act of outlining, helps you better retain the material. The better the material is organized in your mind, the more you will remember. There are two types of readers—passive and active. The active reader outlines and/or marks. Active readers typically do better on exams. Perhaps one of the reasons that active readers retain more is because the physical act of outlining and/or marking requires greater concentration. It is through greater concentration that more is remembered.

Different Ways of Marking The most commonly used form of marking is to underline important points. The second most commonly used method is to use a felt-tipped highlighter, or marker, in yellow or some other transparent color. Marking also includes circling, numbering, using arrows, brief notes, or any other method that allows you to remember things when you go back to skim the pages in your textbook prior to an exam.

Points to Remember When Marking

1. **Read one section at a time before you do any extensive marking.** You cannot mark a section until you know what is important, and you cannot know what is important until you read the whole section.
2. **Don't over mark.** Just as an outline cannot contain everything that is in a text (or in a lecture), marking cannot be of the whole book. Do not fool yourself into thinking you have done a good job just because each page is filled up with arrows, asterisks, circles, and underlines. When you go back to review the material, you will not remember what was important. The key is *selective* activity. Mark each page in a way that allows you to see the most important points at a glance. You can follow up your marking by writing out more in your subject outline.

Summarizing the Material

Even if a certain chapter has a concept summary, it is still worthwhile for you to make your own summary points. The reason is that the more active you are as a reader, the better you will understand the material.

Summarization helps you in your reading comprehension. It is the final step in reviewing the book. There is probably nothing else you can do that works as well to help you remember what your textbook has to say.

The importance of summarizations is that the notes you make are in your own words, not in the words of the author. Writing down a summary in your own words is the most effective use of your time. This allows you to process the information into your own memory by being required to think about it. You also have to make it part of your vocabulary. Whenever you cannot state important legal concepts in your own words, you probably have not understood the concepts necessary to master the material. Indeed, summary notes are a good way to determine whether you have actually understood something. Do not simply make a mechanical listing of quotes taken right out of the textbook. Rather, you should make summary notes using complete sentences with correct grammar. This forces you to develop your ideas logically and clearly. Also, summary notes written in this manner can be more easily remembered.

Be Brief. Your notes should condense the information in the text into statements that summarize the concepts. It is when you force yourself to make the statements brief that you best learn the material. By making only brief summary notes, you have to think about the essence of each concept and present it in a form that is compact enough to remember. You should typically have no more than a one-paragraph summary for each important topic in the chapter.

What Format to Use? The authors find that using 5″ × 8″ cards is the best way to take summary notes. Do not fill up each note card. You need to leave room to make additional notes later, when you are reviewing for the final exam. In other words, leave margins for further notes and study markings. Additionally, if you leave enough room, you can integrate the notes that you take during lectures onto these summary note cards.

Another reason to place your summary notes on 5″ × 8″ cards is to have a set of flash cards that you can use in studying for a final exam.

In taking notes, you may find it helpful to use some of the terms, abbreviations, and symbols that law students, lawyers, and judges use in their note-taking and writing. Symbols that are commonly used include "K," which is used to refer to a contract (and of course "Ks" for "contracts"). To indicate a reference to a plaintiff, the pi symbol (Π) is often used, and a defendant is noted by Δ, a triangle.

Some of the abbreviations that you may find helpful are those that appear in case citations. "S.Ct." is an abbreviation for the United States Supreme Court, for instance. "Aff'd" means "affirmed"—that is, that the decision of a lower court was upheld by a higher court. "J." can be shorthand for "judge" and "JJ." for "judges."

Some of the terms you may run across include those that refer to plots of land. Regardless of the size of an estate, a farm, a suburban yard, or an urban homesite, reference is frequently made to the land as "Blackacre." If two properties are involved, the second is usually called "Whiteacre," and if there are references to three, the third is often "Greenacre."

Other terms that you may run across include Latin words. *Infra,* for example, indicates that its accompanying reference is discussed "below," and *supra* indicates that the topic is discussed "above." *Inter alia* means "among other things." *Inter se* translates as "among or between themselves," which is used to distinguish rights or duties between two or more parties from their rights or duties to others.

How to Study and Take Exams

There is basically one reason why you have purchased *Study Guide to Accompany West's Paralegal Today: The Legal Team at Work, Second Edition*—to improve your exam grades. By using this study guide assiduously, you will have the confidence to take your mid-terms and final examinations and to do well. The study guide, however, should not just be used a day before each exam. Rather, the guide is most helpful if you use it at the time that you read the chapter. That is to say, after you read a chapter in *West's Paralegal Today: The Legal Team at Work, Second Edition,* you should go directly to the appropriate chapter in the study guide. This systematic review technique is the most effective study technique you can use.

Besides learning the concepts in each chapter as well as possible, there are additional strategies for taking exams. You need to know in advance what type of exam you are going to take—essay or objective or both. You need to know which reading materials and lectures will be covered. For both objective and essay exams (but more importantly for the former), you need to know if there is a penalty for guessing incorrectly. If there is, your strategy will be different: you will usually only mark what you are certain is correct. Finally, you need to know how much time will be allowed for the exam.

Following Directions

Students are often in a hurry to start an exam, so they take little time to read the instructions. The instructions can be critical, however. In a multiple-choice exam, for example, if there is no indication that there is a penalty for guessing, then you should never leave a question unanswered. Even if there only remains a few minutes at the end of the exam, you should guess for those questions about which you are uncertain.

Additionally, you need to know the weight given to each section of an exam. In a typical multiple-choice exam, all questions have equal weight. In some exams, particularly those involving essay questions, different parts of the exam carry different weights. You should use these weights to apportion your time accordingly. If an essay part of an exam accounts for only 20 percent of the total points on the exam, you should not spend 60 percent of your time on the essay.

You need to make sure you are answering the question correctly. Some exams require a No. 2 lead pencil to fill in the dots on a machine-graded answer sheet. Other exams require underlining or circling. In short, you have to look at the instructions carefully.

Lastly, check to make sure that you have all the pages of the examination. If you are uncertain, ask the instructor or the exam proctor. It is hard to justify not having done your exam correctly because you failed to answer all the questions. Simply stating that you did not have them will pose a problem for both you and your instructor. Do not take a chance. Double check to make sure.

Taking Objective Examinations

The most important point to discover initially with any objective test is if there is a penalty for guessing. If there is none, you have nothing to lose by guessing. In contrast, if a half-point is subtracted for each incorrect answer, then you probably should not answer any question for which you are purely guessing.

Students usually commit one of two errors when they read objective-exam questions: (1) they read things into the question that do not exist, or (2) they skip over words or phrases.

Most test questions include key words such as:

- All.
- Always.
- Never.
- Only.

If you miss these key words, you will be missing the "trick" part of the question. Also, you must look for questions that are only *partly* correct, particularly if you are answering true/false questions.

Never answer a question without reading all of the alternatives. More than one of them may be correct. If more than one of them seems correct, make sure you select the answer that seems the most correct.

Whenever the answer to an objective question is not obvious, start with the process of elimination. Throw out the answers that are clearly incorrect. Even with objective exams in which there is a penalty for guessing, if you can throw out several obviously incorrect answers, then you may wish to guess among the remaining ones. Your probability of choosing the correct answer is high.

Typically, the easiest way to eliminate incorrect answers is to look for those that are meaningless, illogical, or inconsistent. Often test authors put in choices that make perfect sense and are indeed true, but they are not the answer to the question under study.

When taking a multiple-choice examination, you may find the following method to be helpful. First, before reading the entire problem, read the *question* that the problem asks. If the problem is longer than a single sentence—that is, if it involves a set of facts—the question is usually the last sentence. Does the question involve, for example, a contract issue? Does it ask you to evaluate a set of facts, a claim, or a defense? The idea is to get a grasp of the answer toward which the problem is pointing. Always be clear on what is being asked—it may knock out one or two of the answer alternatives. Next, read the facts, paying particular attention to those facts that are directed to the question. If you are allowed to write on the examination, underline relevant facts. Then reread the question. Finally, read the answers. If possible, consider each alternative as a true-false question, and eliminate the false ones. Sometimes, there may be two responses that seem equally correct—choose the "best" right answer.

Writing Essay Exams

To write an essay exam, you should be prepared. One way of being prepared is to practice writing timed essays. In other words, find out in advance how much time you will have for each essay question, then practice writing an answer to a sample essay question during that time period. This is the only way you will develop the skills needed to pace yourself for an essay exam. Since most essay exams are closed book, do your timed essay practice without using the book.

Usually you can anticipate certain essay exam questions. You do this by going over the major concept headings, either in your lecture notes or in your text. Search for the themes that tie the materials together, then think about questions that your instructor might ask. You might even list possible essay questions as a review device; then write a short outline for each of those most likely questions.

As with objective exams, you need to read the directions to the essay questions carefully. It is best to write out a brief outline *before* you start writing. The outline should present your conclusion in one or two sentences, then it should present your supporting argument. It is important to stay on the subject. If the essay question is presented in the form of a hypothetical fact situation to which you are to apply some of the principles that you learned in your class, you may find the following format to be useful in answering the question: Introduction, Principle, Application, Conclusion.

Begin your answer with a short introduction. In this introduction, identify what the question is about—for example, "the main issue in this sales question concerns which party bears the risk of loss." Also state how the question will be answered—for example, "each of the two lawsuits will be discussed."

Next, state the general principle that applies to the situation, and if there is an applicable exception, state the exception. In your application of the principle to the facts, discuss the main issue before any subsidiary issues. In your discussion, you may want to argue both sides. If so, argue one side first, then argue the other side.

Finally, after arguing both sides, you may want to come to a conclusion, particularly if the question has asked you to do so. In that case, you might respond to the question as if you were a judge. Keep your answer relevant to the question; we can tell you from first-hand experience that no instructor likes to read answers to unasked questions.

Bradene L. Moore

Kathleen Mercer Reed

CHAPTER 1

TODAY'S PROFESSIONAL PARALEGAL

CHAPTER OBJECTIVES

After completing this chapter, you will know:

- What a paralegal is and does.
- How and why the paralegal profession developed.
- The professional organizations that exist for paralegals and the benefits of membership in them.
- The education and training available to paralegals.
- The skills that are useful for a paralegal to have.
- Some important personal attributes of the professional paralegal.

Chapter Outline

I. INTRODUCTION
   A. The paralegal profession offers a wide variety of opportunities for personal and professional development.
   B. The paralegal profession is one of the fastest-growing occupations in the United States.

II. WHAT IS A PARALEGAL?
   A. The terms "paralegal" and "legal assistant" are interchangeable.
   B. A paralegal, or a legal assistant, is defined as a person sufficiently trained in law and legal procedures to assist attorneys in the delivery of legal services to the public.
   C. Legal assistants work under the supervision of attorneys, but not all of those who call themselves paralegals do.
   D. The ABA, NALA, NFPA, and AAfPE each have developed a definition of a paralegal, or legal assistant.
   E. All four definitions of a paralegal, or legal assistant, indicate that paralegals perform "substantive" legal work, meaning that paralegals, although they are not attorneys, often perform work that was traditionally undertaken only by attorneys.

III. WHAT DO PARALEGALS DO?
   A. Paralegals perform many of the tasks involved in legal representation that have traditionally been handled by attorneys.
   B. Today an increasing number of paralegals find work in nontraditional (non-law-office) settings.
   C. Today's paralegal performs many tasks using various types of legal software, electronic communications systems, and online databases.
   D. Typical paralegal tasks include:
      1. Drafting legal documents for attorney review.
      2. Calendaring and tracking important deadlines.
      3. Assisting attorneys in trial preparations and at trial.
      4. Interviewing clients and witnesses.
      5. Conducting legal investigations.
      6. Organizing and maintaining client files.
      7. Conducting legal research.
      8. Using computers and technology to do these tasks.

IV. HISTORY OF THE PARALEGAL PROFESSION
   A. Paralegal Associations and Professional Growth
      1. State and Local Paralegal Associations
         a. Practicing paralegals usually belong to a local and/or state paralegal association, as well as one of the national organizations.
         b. Many state bar associations allow paralegals to become associate members.
      2. National Federation of Paralegal Associations (NFPA)
         a. Founded in 1974, NFPA is actively involved in paralegal professional development.
      3. The National Association of Legal Assistants (NALA)
         a. Founded in 1975, NALA offers a certification program for paralegals.
      4. Other National Paralegal Associations
      5. Benefits of Professional Membership
         a. Opportunities to meet and network with others in the profession.
         b. Receipt of professional publications issued by the paralegal association.
         c. Participation in planning related to developing policies that regulate the paralegal profession.
         d. Continuation of training through organization-sponsored legal education seminars and workshops.
         e. Involvement in paralegal professional development.
         f. Access to special products and services offered by the association.

B. Economics and the Paralegal Profession
   1. Utilization of paralegals is an economic decision.
   2. By employing paralegals to do substantive legal work, lawyers can:
      a. Provide lower-cost legal services to their clients, because they can bill their clients at lower rates for paralegal work.
      b. Take on more clients and increase the firm's profits, because attorneys can concentrate on areas of legal work demanding their expertise.

V. PARALEGAL EDUCATION

A. Educational Options.
   1. Certificate Programs
      a. Paralegal certificates are obtained through programs of varying lengths—from three to eighteen months.
      b. A post-degree certificate program, for the student already holding a bachelor's degree, is usually offered through a college or university.
      c. Certificate programs are offered by private, for-profit business schools, trade schools, or colleges.
   2. Degree Programs
      a. Degree options include an associate's degree and a bachelor's degree.
      b. An associate's degree, specializing in legal assistant studies, is a two-year degree usually from a two-year community college and requires completion of approximately sixty semester hours.
      c. A bachelor's degree from a college or university requires the completion of about 120 semester hours of courses in legal assistant studies.
   3. Advanced Degree Programs
      a. Graduate degrees would advance your career opportunities.
      b. If you wish to earn a law degree, you must first obtain a bachelor's degree from a four-year college or university, and then attend law school for an additional three years.

B. Curriculum—A Blend of Substantive and Procedural Law
   1. The curriculum in paralegal programs emphasizes both **substantive** and **procedural law.**
   2. **Procedural law** specifies the methods or procedures that are employed to enforce **substantive law,** or the laws defining legal rights and obligations.

C. The ABA's Role in Paralegal Education
   1. Paralegal programs that meet the ABA's set of educational standards are usually referred to as **ABA-approved programs.**
   2. Paralegal programs are not required to obtain ABA approval.
   3. ABA approval is a voluntary process that gives extra credentials to those paralegal programs that successfully apply for it.

D. Certification
   1. NALA's Certification Program
   2. NFPA's Certification Program
   3. State Certification

E. Continuing Legal Education

VI. PARALEGAL SKILLS

A. *Organizational Skills*—Paralegals must be able to organize files, create procedures and checklists, and keep things running smoothly.

B. *Analytical Skills*—Paralegals need to be able to take complex theories and fact patterns and break them down into smaller, more easily understandable components.

C. *Computer Skills*—Computer experience and knowledge of computer technology, including online communications, database-management systems, and word processing, are essential for today's paralegal.

D. *Interpersonal Skills*—Communicating and interacting effectively with clients, witnesses, support staff, and attorneys is an important asset for paralegals.

E. *Communication Skills*—Paralegals must have excellent reading, analytical, speaking, listening, and writing skills to help win cases, clients, and promotions.

☞ STUDY TIP

Learning to Think Analytically

Developing the ability to think analytically—or "think like a lawyer"—requires effort. You must be able to decipher and understand legal concepts and then apply the facts of your particular case to them. As you will learn in Chapters 14, 15, and 16, an important aspect of legal research and writing involves analysis.

VII. PERSONAL ATTRIBUTES OF THE PROFESSIONAL PARALEGAL

A. *Responsibility and Reliability*—The responsible paralegal is reliable and is important to efficient teamwork in the law office.
B. *Commitment*—Paralegals must be committed to giving their best effort until the job is completed.
C. *Objectivity*—A paralegal must set aside personal emotions or biases, which interfere with the goal of serving the client's best interest.
D. *The Ability to Keep Confidences*—Paralegals share in the attorney's ethical and legal duty to keep all client information strictly confidential.
E. *Other Attributes*—Accuracy, efficiency, attentiveness to detail, discretion, diplomacy, and the ability to work under pressure are qualities of the professional paralegal.

VIII. THE FUTURE OF THE PROFESSION

A. The U.S. Department of Labor's Bureau of Labor Statistics predicts the paralegal profession will be one of the fastest-growing professions through the year 2005.
B. The paralegal profession continues to be a dynamic, changing, and growing field within the legal arena.

QUESTIONS FOR REVIEW

TRUE–FALSE QUESTIONS

____ 1. The paralegal profession has not yet been recognized as a profession by the American Bar Association.

____ 2. "Paralegal" and "legal assistant" are used interchangeably.

____ 3. The only organizations to which paralegals may belong are those related strictly to paralegals.

____ 4. Substantive law establishes the methods of enforcing rights.

____ 5. Procedural law includes laws that define, describe, regulate, and create legal rights.

____ 6. Voluntary certification involves recognition by a private professional group or state agency that an individual has met specified standards of proficiency.

____ 7. Certification as either a CLA or a CLAS is necessary to work as a paralegal.

____ 8. Paralegal training programs that meet a set of educational standards are usually referred to as ABA-approved programs.

____ 9. Organizational skills are of great service to a paralegal.

____ 10. Paralegals should have experience with word processing.

____ 11. The ability to communicate and interact effectively with people is not an important asset for a paralegal since the paralegal usually works independently.

____ 12. Body language is nonverbal communication that may illustrate an inappropriate response by a paralegal during a client interview.

____ 13. A paralegal who dislikes defending a firm's criminal defendant should give the assignments related to that representation low priority.

____ 14. Attributes of the professional paralegal include accuracy, efficiency, attentiveness to detail, discretion, diplomacy, and the ability to work under pressure.

____ 15. The paralegal profession has developed to a point where it probably will remain for the next several years.

FILL-IN QUESTIONS

There is/are ____________________ (one/several) paralegal educational option(s). The curriculum in paralegal programs emphasizes ____________________ (procedural/substantive) law. Membership in paralegal associations is important to a professional paralegal. Two national associations, National Association of Legal Assistants and National Federation of Paralegal Associations differ ____________________ (on the direction that the profession should take/on the educational standards necessary for certification). Membership in professional organizations provides ____________________ (no/many) opportunity/opportunities.

Paralegals may be asked to perform differing tasks including ____________________ (legal research/advising clients), ____________________ (setting fees/interviewing witnesses), and ____________________ (calendaring deadlines/representing a client in court). A plus for a paralegal is ____________________ (organizational/typing) skills.

MULTIPLE-CHOICE QUESTIONS

____ 1. The ABA's definition of a legal assistant includes:
- A. That a legal assistant may be qualified through education only
- B. That a legal assistant may work independently
- C. That a legal assistant may give advice
- D. That a legal assistant performs substantive legal work

____ 2. A law clerk is:
- A. A paralegal that has not yet graduated
- B. A law student
- C. A junior librarian
- D. A certified legal assistant specialist

____ 3. Member associations of the National Federation of Paralegal Associations are referred to as:
- A. Affiliates
- B. Law clerks
- C. Paralegals
- D. State bar associations

____ 4. The certificate awarded to a student who has a bachelor's degree and completes a certificate program is:
- A. A paralegal certificate
- B. An associate's degree
- C. A post-degree certificate
- D. A bachelor's degree

____ 5. A student who attends, after high school graduation, a certificate program offered by a private, for-profit business school, trade school, or college may receive:
- A. A paralegal certificate
- B. An associate's degree
- C. A post-degree certificate
- D. A bachelor's degree

____ 6. A student who graduates from a two-year community college after completion of general education courses and law courses will receive:
- A. A paralegal certificate
- B. An associate's degree
- C. A post-degree certificate
- D. A bachelor's degree

____ 7. A student who graduates after taking courses in general education as well as courses in a major area and a minor field will receive:
A. A paralegal certificate
B. An associate's degree
C. A post-degree certificate
D. A bachelor's degree

____ 8. The Certified Legal Assistant exam offered by NALA covers:
A. Communication skills
B. Ethics and human relations
C. Legal research and legal terminology
D. All of the above

____ 9. The areas covered by specialty exams offered by NALA to become certified as specialists include:
A. Bankruptcy
B. Civil litigation
C. Probate and estate planning
D. All of the above

____ 10. Analytical skills are necessary to a paralegal when engaging in tasks relating to:
A. Answering the telephone
B. Legal research and writing
C. Word processing assignments
D. Communicating with clients

____ 11. Communication skills that are important to a paralegal include:
A. Reading skills
B. Oral communication skills
C. Listening skills
D. All of the above

____ 12. Personal attributes of the professional paralegal include:
A. Responsible and reliable
B. Commitment
C. Objectivity
D. All of the above

____ 13. Which of the following is required of a paralegal:
A. Responsibility
B. Confidentiality
C. Reliability
D. All of the above

____ 14. The role of the paralegal will most likely expand, because:
A. The public is demanding access to more affordable legal services
B. More students are graduating with a bachelor's degree
C. Law clerks cannot meet the public demand
D. Attorneys need assistance

____ 15. Job opportunities for a paralegal include:
A. Corporations
B. Law firms
C. Governmental agencies
D. All of the above

Practice Questions

1. Your textbook discusses four different definitions of a legal assistant or paralegal that have been promulgated by four different organizations. Identify each organization and its definition.
2. List the reasons why membership in a paralegal association is important to a professional paralegal.

Questions for Critical Analysis

1. Sam Brown, a recent graduate with an associate's degree in legal assisting, has been asked by his new employer to prepare an answer to a complaint in negligence as well as a counterclaim for contributory negligence. The complaint must be filed that same day. Although Sam remembers preparing a complaint and vaguely recalls what negligence and contributory negligence are, he is concerned that he does not have sufficient time to properly prepare the answer. What should Sam do?

2. Samantha Stoane has worked for her employer, a sole practitioner, for ten years, and at his prompting, she has recently graduated from an ABA-approved program. Her employer promised her that upon graduation he would involve her more in his cases. However, her job responsibilities have not changed; the work she performs is clerical. What can Samantha do to try to change this?

Ethical Questions

1. Phillipa Rodriquez is a paralegal who previously worked for ten years as a secretary in a large law firm. She recently accepted a position in a medium-sized law firm and was assigned to work for Jerry Carter, a new attorney with the firm. Phillipa has been asked to work on a bankruptcy case with Jerry. She quickly recognizes Jerry's lack of knowledge in the bankruptcy area when he fails to ask the client for important tax documents. What should Phillipa do? Should she bring the matter to Jerry's attention? Should she discuss the issue with the firm's managing partner?
2. James Cook is a graduate of a paralegal program at the local university. He has been employed for the last five months at Braden, Reed & Moore, a large law firm. So far, James' assigned tasks have been updating the law library and making copies of cases for attorneys. His supervising attorney has been preparing the defense for a personal-injury trial. James knows a particular document needs to be prepared in the case, but the attorney is very busy. James feels confident he has the ability to draft the document. How should James handle this situation?

Technology and Today's Paralegal

On the Internet, browse through the materials found at the following Web sites. Each Web site has links to legal research sources, both state and federal, as well as to legal forms for documents drafted in many different areas of the law.

1. NFPA (*http://www.paralegals.org*). Notice the link to legal research. Click on that link, and browse through the site.
2. Katsuey's Legal Links (*http://www.netsmartinc.com/kat.htm*). This is a site specially designed for legal research. It has links to state and federal materials, as well as to legal forms for documents used in many areas of the law.

Answers

True-False Questions

1. F
2. T
3. F
4. F
5. F
6. T
7. F
8. T
9. T
10. T
11. F
12. T
13. F
14. T
15. F

Fill-In Questions

several; procedural; substantive; on the direction that the profession should take; many

legal research; interviewing witnesses; calendaring deadlines; organizational

Multiple-Choice Questions

1. D
2. B
3. A
4. C
5. A
6. B
7. D
8. D
9. D
10. B
11. D
12. D
13. B
14. A
15. D

Practice Questions

1. *American Bar Association's Definition:*

   A legal assistant or paralegal is a person, qualified by education, training, or work experience, who is employed or retained by a lawyer, law office, corporation, governmental agency or other entity and who performs specifically delegated substantive legal work for which a lawyer is responsible.

   National Association of Legal Assistants' Definition:

   Legal assistants, also known as paralegals, are a distinguishable group of persons who assist attorneys in the delivery of legal services. Through formal education, training, and experience, legal assistants have knowledge and expertise regarding the legal system and substantive and procedural law, which qualify them to do work of a legal nature under the supervision of an attorney.

National Federation of Paralegal Associations' Definition:

A paralegal/legal assistant is a person qualified through education, training, or work experience to perform substantive legal work that requires knowledge of legal concepts and that is customarily, but not exclusively, performed by a lawyer. This person may be retained or employed by a lawyer, law office, governmental agency, or other entity or may be authorized by administrative, statutory, or court authority to perform this work.

American Association for Paralegal Education's Definition:

Paralegals perform substantive and procedural legal work as authorized by law, which work, in the absence of the paralegal, would be performed by an attorney. Paralegals have knowledge of the law gained through education, or education and work experience, which qualifies them to perform legal work. Paralegals adhere to recognized ethical standards and rules of professional responsibility.

2. Reasons why membership in a paralegal association is important to a professional paralegal include:

    - To meet and network with other professional paralegals.
    - To receive publications issued by other associations.
    - To continue in paralegal education.
    - To participate in planning the future of the profession.
    - To reflect an involvement in the profession to prospective employers.

Questions for Critical Analysis

1. Sam could consider speaking with the assigning attorney, asking for further directions on this drafting assignment. Sam should indicate that he is confident he will be able to draft the pleading accurately and with less instruction the next time.
2. Samantha has an implicit ethical duty to do what she can to educate her employer about utilizing her expertise. Furthermore, her employer encouraged her to gain this expertise in an effort to involve her more in his case load. Finally, the ethical codes and guidelines regulating attorneys increasingly are urging attorneys to make effective use of paralegals in delivering legal services. Samantha should speak to her employer about these points.

Ethical Questions

1. Phillipa's immediate concerns should be for the welfare of the client. Without divulging Jerry's lack of knowledge in the bankruptcy area, Phillipa could contact the client and obtain the important tax documents. She could simply tell the client that those documents are needed to prepare the bankruptcy filing, without referring to Jerry's failure to request them. Then, Phillipa could bring the documents to Jerry's attention, telling him she knew he would be needing them for the bankruptcy filing. This would be a more subtle way of letting Jerry know he needed to educate himself in the bankruptcy area, while making sure the client's case was handled properly. However, if Jerry does not handle the bankruptcy tax problems properly, or if he continues to be deficient in the bankruptcy area, Phillipa should discuss the matter with the firm's managing partner.
2. As a legal professional, James assumes a duty to act in the client's best interest. Because reducing the cost of legal services to a client is obviously in the client's interest, James has an implicit ethical duty to educate his supervising attorney on how the attorney can best utilize James' expertise. Perhaps the attorney is unclear about the sort of work James could perform. James might provide the attorney with sample job descriptions from one of the national professional organizations (NALA or NFPA) or from his local paralegal organization.

    A more proactive approach might be to draft a legal document or do legal research that James knows the attorney needs. If James' daily schedule is quite full, this may require him doing the work on his own time. Once the attorney sees the level of professional work of which James is capable, he should be more willing to utilize James' expertise.

CHAPTER 2

CAREERS IN THE LEGAL COMMUNITY

CHAPTER OBJECTIVES

After completing this chapter, you should be able to:

- Identify the types of firms and organizations that hire paralegals.
- Describe some of the areas of law in which paralegals specialize.
- Understand what paralegals can expect to earn.
- Explain how paralegals are compensated for overtime work.
- Know how to prepare a career plan and how to pursue it.
- Discuss what is involved in a job search and how to go about it.

Chapter Outline

I. INTRODUCTION

II. WHERE PARALEGALS WORK

A. Law Firms

1. Traditionally, paralegals worked for law firms, and most paralegals continue to work in the law-firm environment.
2. Working for a Small Firm
   a. Small firms offer opportunities to gain experience in many different areas of the law, generally in a personal and informal environment. Salaries tend to be lower than in larger firms.
3. Working for a Large Firm
   a. Large law firms are usually more formal, with responsibilities more limited and well-defined.
   b. In a large firm, there are generally greater opportunities for career advancement, higher salaries, better benefits, more support staff for paralegals, more sophisticated computer technology, and greater access to research resources.

B. Corporations and Other Business Organizations

1. Increasingly, paralegals are finding employment in corporate legal departments.
2. Most major corporations have an in-house legal staff to handle corporate legal affairs.
3. Advantages in a corporate legal environment include regular hours and less stress than in law firms.

C. Government

1. A growing number of paralegals work for government agencies at the federal or state level.
2. Administrative Agencies.
   a. Most paralegals who work for the government work for administrative agencies, such as the Environmental Protection Agency or a state environmental resources department.
   b. Advantages to governmental work are regular working hours, good benefits, and less stress than in law firms.
   c. Salaries are on the average lower than in traditional law firms or in the private sector.
3. Legislative Offices
   a. Paralegals are sometimes hired as staff members by federal and state legislators to assist with legal research and writing.
4. Law Enforcement Offices and Courts
   a. Many paralegals find work with federal or state administrative court offices and with government law enforcement offices and institutions.

D. Legal Aid Offices

1. Paralegals who work in legal aid offices generally assume a wider range of responsibilities than in a more traditional setting. These paralegals find their jobs rewarding even though they often receive lower salaries than they would working in other areas of law.

E. Freelance Paralegals

1. **Freelance paralegals** own their own businesses, which allows them greater flexibility. They perform specified legal work for attorneys on a contract basis.
2. Freelance paralegals are *not* the same as ***independent paralegals.*** Independent paralegals do not work under the supervision of an attorney and sell their services directly to the public.

III. PARALEGAL SPECIALTIES

A. *Litigation Assistance*—Litigation paralegals specialize in assisting attorneys in the litigation process. They may work primarily on behalf of plaintiffs or defendants, performing work such as client interviews, drafting documents, preparing exhibits, and assisting at trial.

B. *Personal-Injury Law*—Personal-injury paralegals often work for law firms or for insurance companies in investigating claims. They perform work such as obtaining medical reports, employment data, witness statements, and police reports.

C. *Criminal Law*—Criminal law paralegals work for public prosecutors, public defenders, or criminal-defense attorneys. They may perform tasks such as drafting search or arrest warrants and assisting in posting bail.

D. *Corporate Law*—Corporate law paralegals work in a corporation's legal department or for a law firm specializing in corporate law. They draft articles of incorporation and corporate minutes and assist with corporate mergers.
E. *Bankruptcy Law*—Bankruptcy paralegals work for small and large law firms and for bankruptcy trustees. They may interview the debtor, review creditors' claims, and attend bankruptcy proceedings.
F. *Employment and Labor Law*—Paralegals in this area work for law firms, corporations and other business entities, or government agencies. They usually specialize in one area, such as workers' compensation, OSHA safety standards, or EEOC discrimination.
G. *Estate Planning and Probate Administration*—Estate and probate paralegals usually work for law firms but may also work for banks or the probate court. They perform work such as drafting wills, locating heirs, and assisting in the probate process.
H. *Intellectual-Property Law*—Patent, trademark, or copyright paralegals work mostly for large law firms or corporate legal departments. They perform work such as conducting research on prior patent or trademark protection, drafting contracts, and assisting in infringement litigation.
I. *Environmental Law*—Employers of environmental paralegals include administrative agencies, large law firms, and corporations. An environmental paralegal obtains permits from environmental agencies, prepares documents relating to hazardous waste, and assists in litigation.
J. *Real-Estate Law*—Real estate paralegals work for small and large law firms, corporations, banks, title companies, or real-estate agencies. They draft sale contracts, conduct title examinations, prepare deeds, and schedule and attend closings.
K. *Family Law*—Employers of family law paralegals include large and small law firms, state and local agencies, and the family court. They research state child custody laws, draft settlement agreements, prepare divorce documents, and assist in the divorce proceeding.
L. *Emerging Specialty Areas*—An increasing number of paralegals are finding work in specialty areas of the law, such as elder law or immigration law or as a legal nurse consultant (LNC).

IV. PARALEGAL COMPENSATION
- A. Compensation Surveys
  1. Salaries and wage rates for paralegal employees vary substantially.
  2. Factors affecting compensation include:
     - a. Geographical location.
     - b. Firm size.
     - c. Years of experience working as a paralegal.
     - d. Area of practice.
     - e. Type of employer (law firm, corporation, or government agency).
- B. Job Benefits
  1. Job benefits are an important component of compensation.
  2. Benefits include sick leave, paid holidays, and insurance coverage.
  3. When evaluating a job offer, consider the benefits you will receive and what these benefits are worth to you.
- C. Salaries versus Hourly Wages
  1. Most paralegals are salaried—that is, they are paid a specified amount per year, regardless of the number of hours worked.
  2. Other paralegals are paid an hourly wage rate for every hour worked.
  3. How paralegals are compensated for overtime work usually depends on whether they are salaried or hourly wage employees.
- D. Federal Law and Overtime Pay
  1. Overtime work of salaried employees may be compensated through year-end bonuses or in some other way, such as equivalent time off work.
  2. Hourly employees receive overtime wages for all hours worked exceeding forty hours per week.
  3. The Wage-Hour Law exempts "administrative," "executive," or "professional" employees from overtime pay.

4. There is a split of authority as to whether paralegals are "exempt" or "nonexempt."
5. As a result of the Page & Addison case, the issue of paralegal exempt status is decided on the basis of the specific facts of a given case.

V. PLANNING YOUR CAREER

A. Defining Your Long-Term Goals
   1. Long-term goals are those that may take several years or a lifetime to attain.
   2. Use personal reflection and self-assessment to define long-term career goals as clearly as possible.
   3. Recognize that at the outset of your career, you cannot know what opportunities might lie ahead.
   4. Recognize also that long-term goals change over time as you gain more experience and your life circumstances change.

B. Short-Term Goals and Job Realities
   1. Short-term goals are the steps that you take to realize your long-term goals.
   2. The realities of the job market may mean you may not find the "right" job or "perfect" employer at the outset of your career.
   3. Remember that you can gain valuable skills and experiences in *any* job environment. These skills and experience will help to achieve long-terms goals in the future.

VI. LOCATING POTENTIAL EMPLOYERS

A. Networking
   1. Career opportunities often go unpublished.
   2. Many paralegals learn of jobs through networking with other professionals.
   3. Students should begin networking while still in school.

B. Finding Available Jobs
   1. Classified ads, trade journals and similar publications, and online publications are sources that list paralegal job openings.

C. Identifying Possible Employers
   1. You should begin as a student to compile a list of law firms and organizations that offer the benefits, salary, opportunities for advancement, work environment, and legal specialty of your choice.
   2. The Yellow Pages is an excellent source of information for the names of attorneys, law firms, and other organizations that hire paralegals.
   3. Legal directories can be another useful source. They list attorneys and corporate legal departments, their locations and telephone numbers, and their areas of practice.

D. Job-Placement Services
   1. Most paralegal programs provide job-placement services to assist you in finding a job, preparing your resume, and making a list of prospective employers.
   2. Contact a local paralegal organization or the county or state bar association to locate other placement services. Many of those organizations have their own placement services, which offer placement free of cost.

VII. MARKETING YOUR SKILLS

A. The Application Process
   1. The Résumé
      a. Your résumé is a clear and concise summary of your employment and educational history.
      b. A résumé should include your name, address, telephone number, e-mail address, and fax number and should contain only information that is relevant to the job you are seeking.
      c. Do not include personal data in your résumé.
      d. Always carefully proofread your résumé before you send it out.
   2. The Cover Letter
      a. A carefully written cover letter should accompany your résumé.

3. List of Professional References
   a. You should provide a list of three to five professional references.
   b. Never list a reference unless you have permission to do so.
4. Your Professional Portfolio
   a. You should prepare a portfolio that contains samples of your legal writing, transcripts, and so on. Sample documents should not contain any identifying references to clients.

B. The Interview
1. Before the Interview
   a. Learn as much about the firm as possible.
   b. Questions should be anticipated and answers prepared in advance of the job interview.
2. At the Interview
   a. Interviewers use certain question formats, such as closed-ended questions, open-ended questions, hypothetical questions, and pressure questions, to elicit certain types of responses.
   b. Illegal questions need not be answered.
3. After the Interview
   a. After each interview, jot a few notes to refresh your memory in case you are called back for another interview.

C. The Follow-Up Letter
1. After the interview, send a follow-up letter to the interviewer.
2. The letter should thank the interviewer for her time.
3. The letter should also reaffirm the applicant's interest in the position.

D. Maintain Job-Hunting Files
1. Keep copies of job-search letters and any responses to them in your files.
2. Keep lists or notes on addresses, telephone numbers, dates of contact, and advantages or disadvantages of employment with various firms.
3. These files will provide you with an excellent resource for networking even after you have a permanent position.

E. Salary Negotiations
1. You should research the salaries of paralegals in similar job situations in your community before discussing salary with a prospective employer.
2. The best option in salary negotiations might be to state a salary range that is acceptable to you.
3. In addition to salary, remember benefits and other factors are important to you.

VIII. REEVALUATING YOUR CAREER

A. Career Paths
1. Career goals change over time, as do job opportunities.
2. Paralegals who want to advance in their careers normally have the options of:
   a. Being promoted or transferred to another department within the firm.
   b. Moving to another firm.
   c. Going back to school for additional education.

B. Creating Opportunities
1. Advancing in your career can be accomplished by educating your employer so that you can take on other responsibilities.
2. Suggest a plan to your employer that shows how you can provide more complex legal services if many of your existing responsibilities are delegated to a new paralegal employee.

C. Other Options
1. Apply for a position that has become available in a branch office of your firm.
2. Broaden your visibility both inside and outside the firm to make new contacts.
3. You can learn of new professional opportunities through active participation in paralegal professional organizations.

Questions for Review

True-False Questions

____ 1. Corporate environment paralegals generally are required to generate a specified number of "billable hours."

____ 2. Litigation refers to working a lawsuit through the judicial system.

____ 3. Litigation represents one area of specialization for a paralegal.

____ 4. Criminal acts are prohibited by federal statutes only.

____ 5. A civil case involves one party attempting to make the other party perform an act or pay for damages resulting from the failure to perform.

____ 6. Bankruptcy laws are provided by federal statutes.

____ 7. The two goals of bankruptcy law are (1) to protect a debtor by enabling a fresh start, and (2) to ensure creditors are treated fairly.

____ 8. Workers' compensation statutes are provided by federal statutes.

____ 9. Proving the genuineness of a will is referred to as probate.

____ 10. The establishment of a legal arrangement in which a property owner transfers legal title to another is referred to as a will.

____ 11. Real estate consists of land only.

____ 12. Family law is primarily governed by state statutes.

____ 13. When evaluating a job offer, a paralegal should consider salary and job benefits.

____ 14. Overtime wages, as established by federal law, are one and a half times the normal hourly rate for all hours worked beyond forty hours per month.

____ 15. Available jobs may be advertised in trade journals.

Fill-in Questions

Career planning first involves your ____________________ (specialization/career goals). Additionally, a paralegal will utilize ____________________ (investigative skills/open-ended questions) in looking for jobs. Pertinent information about law firms throughout the United States is contained in a directory called ____________________ (Martindale-Hubbel Law Directory/portfolio). Additionally, computerized legal services contain employer information, including ____________________ (networking/the Internet).

Professional application materials include a ____________________ (portfolio/trust). The résumé should be accompanied by a ____________________________ (cover letter/will). A paralegal should have ____________________ (three/family members as) references. References ____________________ (need not/must) have given their permission for the use of their names.

At the end of the year, a paralegal may receive a special payment or ____________________ (bonus/portfolio) recognizing the paralegal's devotion and high quality of work.

Multiple-Choice Questions

____ 1. A paralegal working for a small law firm has which of the following advantages:
A. The opportunity to gain experience in many different areas of law
B. More personal and less formal environment of the law office
C. Greater flexibility, in terms of working hours and employment procedures
D. All of the above

____ 2. A paralegal working for a large law firm has which of the following advantages:
A. Opportunities for promotions and career advancement
B. Higher salaries and better benefits packages
C. More support staff and sophisticated computer technology
D. All of the above

____ 3. Those who bring lawsuits are called:
A. Plaintiffs
B. Defendants
C. Specialists
D. Law clerks

____ 4. Those against whom lawsuits are brought are called:
A. Plaintiffs
B. Defendants
C. Specialists
D. Law clerks

____ 5. Civil law is concerned with:
A. Wrongs committed against the public as a whole
B. The formation, financing, merger and acquisition, and termination of corporations
C. The duties that exist between persons or between citizens and their governments
D. Obtaining relief from debts

____ 6. Criminal law is concerned with:
A. Wrongs committed against the public as a whole
B. The formation, financing, merger and acquisition, and termination of corporations
C. The duties that exist between persons or between citizens and their governments
D. Obtaining relief from debts

____ 7. Corporate law is concerned with:
A. Wrongs committed against the public as a whole
B. The formation, financing, merger and acquisition, and termination of corporations
C. The duties that exist between persons or between citizens and their governments
D. Obtaining relief from debts

____ 8. Bankruptcy law is concerned with:
A. Wrongs committed against the public as a whole
B. The formation, financing, merger and acquisition, and termination of corporations
C. The duties that exist between persons or between citizens and their governments
D. Obtaining relief from debts

____ 9. Estate planning involves:
A. Products that result from intellectual, creative processes
B. The owner's decision, before death, regarding transfer of property to others
C. Protection of the environment
D. Family matters

____ 10. Intellectual-property law involves:
A. Copyright law
B. Trademark law
C. Patent law
D. All of the above

____ 11. The process of making personal connections with others involved in the paralegal or legal profession is referred to as:
A. Litigation
B. Networking
C. Portfolio
D. Wills

____ 12. The résumé should list dates:
A. First
B. Last
C. In reverse chronological order
D. Only if relevant

____ 13. The résumé should include:
A. Personal data
B. Hypothetical questions
C. Education and experience
D. A photograph

____ 14. The portfolio should include:
A. Résumé
B. List of references
C. Sample legal documents with identifying references blackened out
D. All of the above

____ 15. After the interview, a paralegal:
A. Should send a follow-up letter
B. Should wait for a telephone call
C. Should discontinue the job search until notification is received
D. Should leave without saying "thank you"

Practice Questions

1. Which of the following are tasks that would be assigned to a family law paralegal:
   A. Interviewing a client to obtain information relating to a couple's assets and liabilities.
   B. Locating and interviewing witnesses.
   C. Drafting a will.
   D. Researching state laws governing child custody.
   E. Preparing articles of incorporation.
   F. Reviewing creditors' claims and verifying their validity.
   G. Drafting a settlement agreement.
   H. Assisting a client in financial planning.
   I. Locating heirs.
2. Which of the following are tasks that would be assigned to a bankruptcy paralegal:
   A. Interviewing the client to obtain information relating to income, debts, and assets.
   B. Locating and interviewing witnesses.
   C. Drafting a will.
   D. Researching state laws governing child custody.
   E. Preparing articles of incorporation.
   F. Reviewing creditors' claims and verifying their validity.
   G. Drafting a settlement agreement.
   H. Assisting a client in financial planning.
   I. Locating heirs.
3. Using the information in this chapter, prepare a cover letter for a paralegal position with a firm that practices bankruptcy law.

Questions for Critical Analysis

1. In assuming a paralegal job, what would be your strengths? Weaknesses?
2. Geographic location may determine the size of a law firm for which you could work. If you wanted to work for a large firm, would you consider relocating to another area in order to accept an offer? What considerations are important to you in evaluating the offer?

Ethical Questions

1. Sandra Day is a paralegal specializing in probate in a medium-sized law firm. Because Sandra is a very sensitive and kind individual, she spends a great deal of her time every day comforting the bereaved clients. As a result, she has not been preparing necessary forms in a timely fashion. What are Sandra's ethical obligations?
2. When applying for a job as a family-law paralegal, Phil Mallott indicated he had a specialty in family law. In truth, Phil's "specialty" consists of taking a family-law course in school. Phil got the job and now has been asked to draft all the documents relating to a client's divorce action. What should Phil do?

Technology and Today's Paralegal

Create a list of prospective employers in your area by accessing the following Internet sites: *www.nala.org*, *www.paralegalsclassfieds.com*, *www.lawjobs.com*, *www.paralegals.org*, *www.lawplacement.com*, *www.companylink.com*, *www.wld.com*, and *www.house.gov*, as well as any other Internet source.

Answers

True-False Questions

1. F
2. T
3. T
4. F
5. T
6. T
7. T
8. F
9. T
10. F
11. F
12. T
13. T
14. F
15. T

Fill-in Questions

career goals; investigative skills; Martindale-Hubbel Law Directory; Internet

portfolio; cover letter; three; must

bonus

Multiple-Choice Questions

1. A
2. D
3. A
4. B
5. C
6. A
7. B
8. D
9. B
10. D
11. B
12. C
13. C
14. D
15. A

Practice Questions

1. A, D, G, H
2. A, F

3. (Add the appropriate heading, including date, address, and salutation—see Exhibit 2.6, text page 57.)

   I am responding to your advertisement for a paralegal position with your firm.

   As you can see from the enclosed résumé, I recently graduated with an associate's degree from [school name]. My paralegal courses included debtor/creditor relations, constitutional law, civil procedures, and legal research and writing. I am anxious to pursue a career in the bankruptcy area, as I found that course to be one of the most interesting during my paralegal studies.

   I look forward to hearing from you.

   Sincerely,

   [Student name]

   Enclosures

Questions for Critical Analysis

1. A professional paralegal must be organized, articulate and confident. If you lack these traits, start working on them now.
2. Answers will vary.

Ethical Questions

1. Sandra has an ethical duty to make sure the clients' cases proceed as quickly as possible through the probate process. By not filing forms in a timely fashion, there are sure to be unnecessary delays. Those delays are costly and perhaps detrimental to the client. In addition, she may be subjecting her firm to a possible malpractice suit. Sandra must recognize she is a *legal* professional, not a counseling professional. She must learn to separate her emotions from the legal work for which she is responsible. Although she should still be caring and kind to bereaved clients, she should keep those activities to a minimum. She must concentrate on doing her job efficiently and responsibly, thus speeding up the probate process.
2. Phil has exaggerated his experience and misrepresented his qualifications. He has violated the professional responsibility to be honest and pay attention to detail, which also applies to the job-application process. Further, the firm's client may now suffer because of Phil's lack of knowledge in the family-law area. Phil's supervising attorney has been misled by Phil's "expertise" and may not give Phil's work the attention it should receive.

   Phil should immediately disclose to his supervising attorney the real extent of his training and expertise in the family law area. If Phil is still given this assignment, he has an obligation to educate himself where he is deficient and to make sure his supervising attorney carefully reviews all of his work.

CHAPTER 3

ETHICS AND PROFESSIONAL RESPONSIBILITY

CHAPTER OBJECTIVES

After completing this chapter, you should be able to:

- Describe why and how legal professionals are regulated.
- Identify some important ethical rules governing the conduct of attorneys.
- Understand how the rules governing attorneys affect paralegal practice.
- List the kinds of activities that paralegals are and are not legally permitted to perform.
- Explain some of the pros and cons of regulation, including the debate over paralegal licensing.

Chapter Outline

I. INTRODUCTION
   A. A Paralegal must know the ethical and legal responsibilities arising from the attorney-client relationship, why they exist, and how they affect the paralegal.
   B. The ethical duties imposed on attorneys by state law affect paralegals.
   C. Paralegals are indirectly regulated by attorney ethical codes and by state laws that prohibit nonlawyers from practicing law.

II. THE REGULATION OF ATTORNEYS
   A. Who Are the Regulators?
      1. Key participants in the regulation of attorneys are:
         a. Bar associations.
         b. State supreme courts.
         c. State legislatures.
         d. The United States Supreme Court.
   B. Licensing Requirements
      1. Licensing gives an attorney the right to practice law.
      2. Licensing is accomplished at the state level, and each state has different requirements.
      3. To obtain a license to practice law in a state, an attorney normally must:
         a. Receive a bachelor's degree from a college or university.
         b. Graduate from an accredited law school.
         c. Take and pass a state bar examination.
         d. Pass an extensive background inspection.
      4. By the 1930s, almost all states had enacted legislation on the unauthorized practice of law (UPL) prohibiting anyone but licensed attorneys from practicing law.
   C. Ethical Codes and Rules
      1. In addition to licensing requirements, the legal profession is regulated through ethical codes and rules adopted by each state.
      2. Today's state ethical codes are based, for the most part, on either the ABA Model Code of Professional Responsibility (1969) or the ABA Model Rules of Professional Conduct (1983).
         a. The Model Code of Professional Responsibility (or Model Code) consists of nine canons. Each canon is followed by "Ethical Considerations," which are not mandatory and "Disciplinary Rules," which are mandatory in character.
         b. The 1983 revision of the Model Code, called the Model Rules of Professional Conduct (or Model Rules), also spells out the ethical and professional duties governing attorneys and the practice of law.
   D. Sanctions for Violations
      1. Attorneys who violate their ethical duties may be subject to sanctions in the form of a:
         a. *Reprimand,* which is a formal "scolding."
         b. *Suspension,* that prohibits the attorney from practicing law for a specified period of time.
         c. *Disbarment,* which is a revocation of the attorney's license to practice law.
      2. Additionally, attorneys are subject to potential liability for malpractice or violation of criminal statutes.
      3. If a paralegal's breach of professional duty causes substantial harm to a client, the client may sue the attorney as well as the paralegal.

III. ATTORNEY ETHICS AND PARALEGAL PRACTICE
   A. The Duty of Competence
      1. How the Duty of Competence Can Be Breached
         a. Most breaches of competence are inadvertent and often have to do with missed deadlines.
         b. Use of a tickler system and good organization can make sure all deadlines are met on time.
         c. Other breaches, such as the inclusion of erroneous information in a document filed with the court, may expose the attorney and paralegal to liability for negligence.

2. Inadequate Supervision
   a. The Model Rules require attorneys to supervise the work of their nonlawyer assistants
   b. To ensure that your attorney is adequately supervising your work, improve communications between you and your attorney, and ask for feedback about your work.

B. Confidentiality of Information
   1. The rule of confidentiality is that all information relating to the representation of a client must be kept confidential unless the client consents to disclosure.
      a. Paralegals should regard all information about a client or a client's case as confidential.
   2. Exceptions to the Rule
      a. Client Consents to the Disclosure
         1) One exception to the rule of confidentiality is that an attorney may reveal confidential information if the client consents to the disclosure.
      b. Impliedly Authorized Disclosures
         1) Another exception is that an attorney may make disclosures that are impliedly authorized to carry out the representation.
      c. Client Intends a Harmful Act
         1) An exception to the rule of confidentiality occurs when a client reveals that she intends to commit a criminal act that may cause bodily harm or death to another.
      d. Defending Against a Client's Legal Action
         1) When a client files a malpractice lawsuit against an attorney, the attorney may disclose confidential information only to the extent that it is essential to defend against the lawsuit.
   3. Violations of the Confidentiality Rule
      a. Paralegals should take great care never to reveal the identity of a client when discussing a case. A better policy is to never discuss anything concerning your work.
      b. Conversations Overheard by Others
         1) Never discuss confidential information when you are in a common area.
      c. Electronic Communications and Confidentiality
         1) Special care should be taken when talking on the telephone, using a cellular or mobile phone, or sending a fax or an e-mail message to prevent disclosure of confidential information.
         2) Take care when sending e-mail messages that contain confidential information.
      d. Other Ways of Violating the Confidentiality Rule

C. Confidentiality and the Attorney-Client Privilege.
   1. What Kind of Information Is Privileged?
      a. State statutes and case law define what information falls under the **attorney-client privilege.**
      b. A certain part of the materials prepared by an attorney for a trial are protected under the **work product doctrine** and, as such, are privileged.
   2. When the Attorney-Client Privilege Arises
      a. The privilege and duty of confidentiality arises even though the attorney decides not to represent the client and even though the client is not charged any fee.
   3. Duration of the Privilege
      a. Outside of the exceptions named above, only the client may waive the attorney-client privilege.

D. Conflict of Interest
   1. Simultaneous Representation
      a. An attorney faces a conflict of interest if an attorney engages in an activity that adversely affects a client's interests.
      b. An attorney may represent two parties in a legal proceeding only if that representation will not adversely affect either party's interest and if both parties agree to such representation.
   2. Former Clients
      a. A lawyer who has formerly represented a client in a legal matter may not represent someone else in the same or a related matter in which that person's interests are adverse to the interests of the former client.

☞ STUDY TIP

What Paralegals Cannot (And Should Not) Do

Paralegals may not:

- Establish an attorney-client relationship.
- Set the fees to be charged for an attorney's services.
- Represent a client in court (with some statutory exceptions).
- Give legal advice or opinions.

b. Job Changes and Former Clients
   1) When a conflict of interest arises because of a lawyer's or paralegal's job change, an **ethical wall** is erected around the new employee to screen the employee from any information giving rise to the conflict of interest.

c. Walling-Off Procedures

3. Other Conflict-of-Interest Situations
   a. Other situations, such as receiving expensive gifts from a client, may create a conflict of interest.
4. Conflicts Checks
   a. Running a **conflicts check** is a standard procedure in any law office.

IV. THE INDIRECT REGULATION OF PARALEGALS

A. Paralegal Ethical Codes
   1. NFPA's Code of Ethics
   2. NALA's Code of Ethics
   3. Compliance with Paralegal Code of Ethics

B. Guidelines for the Utilization of Paralegals
   1. NALA's Model Standards and Guidelines
   2. The ABA's Model Guidelines
   3. State Guidelines

C. The Increasing Scope of Paralegal Responsibilities
   1. Today, paralegals can perform virtually any legal task as long as the work is supervised by an attorney and does not constitute the unauthorized practice of law (UPL).
   2. Other than tasks that only lawyers can legally perform, such as giving legal advice, paralegals may perform almost any type of legal work as long as the attorney authorizes the work and assumes responsibility for the paralegal's work product.

V. THE UNAUTHORIZED PRACTICE OF LAW

A. Giving Legal Opinions and Advice
   1. A paralegal may communicate an attorney's legal advice to a client, but the paralegal may not give legal advice.
   2. Paralegals are prohibited from giving any kind of advice—even simple, common-sense advice—because of the greater weight given to the advice of someone who has had legal training.

3. A paralegal should never advise a client or any other person on any matter if the advice may alter the legal position or legal rights of the one to whom the advice is given.

B. Representing Clients in Court
   1. Paralegals are allowed by statute to represent clients before some federal and state governmental agencies.
   2. Unless a statute or court rule provides otherwise, a paralegal is not allowed to appear in court on behalf of a client without the supervising attorney.

C. Disclosure of Paralegal Status
   1. Never assume that a client knows you are not an attorney. Always disclose your paralegal status to ensure that everyone with whom you communicate realizes that you are a paralegal and not an attorney.

D. Paralegals Freelancing for Attorneys
   1. In its landmark 1992 decision, the New Jersey Supreme Court stated that it could find no reason why freelance paralegals could not be just as adequately supervised by the attorneys for whom they worked as those paralegals working in attorneys' offices.
   2. Since 1992, other state courts and state bar associations have issued opinions holding that freelance paralegals who are adequately supervised by attorneys are not engaging in the UPL.

E. Independent Paralegals and the UPL
   1. Early Cases
      a. In 1978, the Florida Supreme Court held in *The Florida Bar v. Brumbaugh* that Brumbaugh, a paralegal, could (1) sell legal forms and other printed information regarding divorces and other legal procedures, (2) fill in the forms as long as the customer provided the information in writing, and (3) advertise her services.
      b. Another noteworthy case is *The Florida Bar v. Furman*, which was decided a year after *The Florida Bar v. Brumbaugh*. The *Furman* case received a great deal of publicity when Ms. Furman disobeyed later injunction and was sentenced to prison for contempt of court.
   2. An Ongoing Problem
      a. Other independent paralegals have been sued by bar associations and others for the UPL.
      b. Nolo Press, a well-known publisher of self-help legal books, has been attacked for the UPL, and as of early 1999, the Texas Supreme Court had not yet ruled on this matter.
      c. Any paralegal who wishes to work as an independent paralegal must thoroughly investigate the relevant state laws and court decisions on UPL before offering any services directly to the public.
      d. Independent paralegals must rigorously abide by the letter of the law as it relates to the UPL.

VI. SHOULD PARALEGALS BE LICENSED?

A. General versus Limited Licensing
   1. Several states—specifically New Jersey, Utah, Wisconsin, California, New York, Texas, and Minnesota—have considered implementing a **general licensing** program.
   2. General licensing would require all paralegals to meet certain educational requirements and other specific criteria.
   3. Over half the states are considering **limited licensing** for independent paralegals and legal technicians who wish to provide specified legal services directly to the public.

B. Direct Regulation—The Pros and Cons
   1. NFPA's Position
      a. NFPA endorses regulation of the paralegal profession on a state-by-state basis insofar as regulation expands the use of paralegals to deliver cost-efficient legal services.
      b. NFPA proposes a two-tiered system of licensing: general licensing and specialty licensing.

c. General licensing by a state board or agency would require all paralegals within the state to satisfy specific requirements as to education, experience, and continuing education; it would also subject practicing paralegals to disciplinary procedures by the licensing body.
d. Specialty licensing would require paralegals who wish to practice in a specialized area to demonstrate proficiency in that area through an examination.

2. NALA's Position
   a. NALA supports voluntary certification and believes that any type of licensing of the paralegal profession would be premature.
3. The AAfPE's Position
   a. AAfPE's predominant concern on this issue is that paralegals and paralegal educators have a voice in determining the educational and ethical requirements for licensing paralegals.

C. Other Considerations
   1. There are other groups, including lawyers, who are concerned about the issue of licensing the paralegal profession.

VII. A FINAL NOTE

A. As a professional paralegal, you will have an opportunity to voice your opinion on these important issues.
B. The most important thing to remember as a paralegal is to think and act in a professionally responsible way in your particular workplace.

QUESTIONS FOR REVIEW

TRUE-FALSE QUESTIONS

____ 1. Professional groups usually engage in a degree of self-regulation by establishing ethical or professional codes to regulate their conduct while serving the public.

____ 2. At the heart of the concept of a professional is service to others.

____ 3. Licensing of attorneys is accomplished at the federal level.

____ 4. Virtually all states have enacted legislation prohibiting the unauthorized practice of law.

____ 5. Failing to perform a duty is referred to as breaching.

____ 6. Keeping clients reasonably informed is only a courtesy.

____ 7. An attorney could compensate a paralegal for bringing business to the firm by offering a commission.

____ 8. It is unnecessary to bring to the supervising attorney's attention any statute, regulation, or court decision that supports the opponent's position.

____ 9. Attorneys supervise and bear responsibility for their assistants' actions.

____ 10. A professional who has failed to perform a legally recognized duty has committed malpractice.

____ 11. *Independent paralegal* or *legal technician* refers to a paralegal who practices independently, not under an attorney's supervision.

____ 12. Failing to cooperate with a court order is referred to as contempt of court.

____ 13. A paralegal may be subject to sanctions for breach of the ethical code.

____ 14. Paralegals are regulated indirectly.

Fill-in Questions

Duties of an attorney include ____________________ (diligence/communication), that is, keeping an accurate calendar. Another duty is that of communication, which includes keeping the client reasonably informed; reasonably informed ____________________ (is defined within/varies with) a case. A reasonable fee ____________________ (is/is not) dependent on more than one factor. A paralegal ____________________ (is/is not) required to keep client information confidential. Any delay in litigation proceedings ________________ (is acceptable/must serve some substantial purpose). A paralegal ____________________ (may/may not) be involved in handling client funds.

A ____________________ (general/limited) licensing program would require all paralegals to meet certain educational requirements and other specified criteria before being allowed to practice in their profession. A ____________________ (general/limited) licensing program would limit licensing requirements to those paralegals who wish to provide specified legal services directly to the public.

Multiple-choice Questions

____ 1. Regulators of the practice of law include:
   A. Bar associations
   B. State supreme courts
   C. State legislatures
   D. All of the above

____ 2. Generally, to be licensed, an attorney must:
   A. Have obtained a bachelor's degree and have graduated from an accredited law school
   B. Pass a state bar examination
   C. Pass an extensive personal background investigation
   D. All of the above

____ 3. Which of the following is false regarding the Model Code of Professional Responsibility:
   A. Ethical considerations are aspirational in character, suggesting ideal conduct
   B. It is identical in all states
   C. Disciplinary rules are mandatory in character, causing disciplinary action for violation of one of the rules
   D. It is referred to as the Model Code

____ 4. A formal scolding of the attorney for a violation of the rules governing professional conduct is referred to as a:
   A. Reprimand
   B. Disbarment
   C. Suspension
   D. Sanction

____ 5. Prohibiting an attorney from practicing law for a given period of time as a result of a violation of the rules governing professional conduct is referred to as a:
   A. Reprimand
   B. Disbarment
   C. Suspension
   D. Sanction

____ 6. Revocation of the attorney's license to practice law as a result of a violation of the rules governing professional conduct is referred to as a:
   A. Reprimand
   B. Disbarment
   C. Suspension
   D. Sanction

____ 7. Which of the following is true regarding freelance paralegals:
   A. They work for attorneys, and attorneys assume responsibility for the paralegals' work products
   B. They are the same as independent paralegals
   C. They are personally involved in a lawsuit
   D. They are self regulated

____ 8. According to the NALA Model Standards and Guidelines, which of the following may a paralegal perform:
   A. Establish attorney-client relationships
   B. Set legal fees

C. Give legal opinions or advice
D. A paralegal may not perform any of these functions

____ 9. A paralegal may:
A. Give his/her personal opinion to an individual about a legal position
B. Never advise an individual on any matter if the advice may alter the legal position
C. Give advice to friends and relatives
D. Represent a friend or relative in court

____ 10. A paralegal can perform virtually any legal task as long as:
A. The paralegal is licensed in that state
B. The paralegal carries malpractice insurance
C. The attorney authorizes the work and assumes responsibility for the work product
D. The paralegal is an independent paralegal

____ 11. Generally, the ethical responsibilities of paralegals include the duty to:
A. Disclose their status as paralegals at the outset of any professional relationship
B. Preserve the confidences and secrets of all clients
C. Follow the attorney's Model Code of Professional Responsibility
D. All of the above

____ 12. An exception to the duty of confidentiality is:
A. Client consent to disclosure
B. Third parties
C. Work product
D. All of the above

____ 13. If a client tells the paralegal that he intends a harmful act, the paralegal should:
A. Keep this information confidential
B. Not bill for the time spent talking to the client
C. Put this information in a work product document
D. Discuss the situation with the supervising attorney

____ 14. Conflict of interest situations include:
A. Gifts to an attorney conveyed through the client's will
B. Family members who represent adverse parties
C. Representing both a husband and a wife in a divorce action
D. All of the above

PRACTICE QUESTIONS

1. Moe Jarino is a client of the firm for which Sally, a paralegal, works. He filed a wrongful-death action against a drunk driver who killed his son, and the case is scheduled for trial next week. Sally received a telephone call from the opposing side, in the absence of her supervising attorney, offering to settle the case for $50,000; the complaint requests $1,000,000. When Sally's supervising attorney returned to the office, she informed him of the telephone call and the amount. The attorney said that the case was worth far more than that, and the offer should be refused. He then asked her if everything was ready for trial. Upon returning to her office, Sally became concerned that Moe may wish to settle, as he had commented to her several times that he did not want to go to trial and re-live his son's death. What obligation to Moe in these circumstances do Sally and her supervising attorney have?

2. Which of the following tasks may a paralegal legally perform:
A. Draft a motion for summary judgment at an attorney's request.
B. Prepare a warranty deed without an attorney's supervision.
C. Interview a witness to a slip-and-fall accident.
D. Investigate the facts of a slip-and-fall accident.
E. Give legal advice directly to an individual.

Questions for Critical Analysis

1. Assume that you were involved in an initial prospective-client interview with your supervising attorney. At its conclusion, the attorney told the individual that she would get back with him after reviewing the case to determine if the firm would accept the case. A few days later, the attorney asks you to call the individual and tell him that the firm would accept his case and that the charge would be $100 per hour for attorney time and $65 for paralegal time. Is this a telephone call that you should make? Why or why not? What should you consider doing?

2. Assume your supervising attorney, Dick, is representing a client, pro bono. He is pressed for time and knows that an answer must be filed today for the pro bono case. He is leaving for a deposition from which he will not return until next week and has asked that you prepare an answer, sign it, and file it with the court. When you suggest that this would not be ethical, Dick says that it really does not matter since this is a pro bono case. What might you respond?

Ethical Questions

1. Gary Shufert has worked as a paralegal for Jane Wilson for ten years. As a result of Gary's membership in a local service club, Gary has met numerous people in the community. On several occasions, Gary has referred some of those people to Jane for legal services. Several of those cases have been big winners for Jane. One day, Jane offers Gary a commission on his referrals. Is this an ethical violation? What should Gary do?

2. Debbie Spyer is a bankruptcy paralegal working for a large law firm. One day, when Debbie's supervising attorney is out of the office, a client calls and is referred to Debbie. The client has been having a great deal of financial difficulty and is contemplating filing bankruptcy. The client wants to know if he should sell several items of property in order to pay off one of his outstanding bills. What should Debbie do?

Technology and Today's Paralegal

Access NFPA's site for professional development at *http://www.paralegals.org/Development/home.htm* and read NFPA Informal Ethics and Disciplinary Opinions 96-1, which deals with the ethical implications concerning client confidentiality of paralegals communicating in cyberspace.

ANSWERS

True-False Questions

1. T
2. T
3. F
4. T
5. T
6. F
7. F
8. F
9. T
10. T
11. T
12. T
13. F
14. T

Fill-in Questions

diligence; varies with; is; is; must serve some substantial purpose; may
general; limited

Multiple-Choice Questions

1. D
2. D
3. B
4. A
5. C
6. B
7. A
8. D
9. B
10. C
11. D
13. A
14. D
15. D

Practice Questions

1. Model Rule 1.4 establishes the attorney's duty to keep the client reasonably informed. This obligation includes explaining the matter to the extent reasonably necessary to permit the client to make informed decisions regarding the representation. Even if Moe had not expressed his desire to obviate trial, he must be informed of the offer to settle. Sally may consider speaking with her supervising attorney to ensure his communication to Moe of the offer to settle. Alternatively, she may consider speaking with another attorney in the firm or discuss the matter, hypothetically, with a legal professional.
2. A. yes
   B. no
   C. yes
   D. yes
   E. no

Questions for Critical Analysis

1. Traditionally, establishing attorney-client relationships and setting legal fees have been regarded by the courts as activities that can only be undertaken by an attorney. A paralegal who has been asked to perform these tasks should decline. Although a paralegal may feel that the attorney has entrusted great responsibility upon the paralegal, remember that a paralegal has ethical obligations to consider. The paralegal should suggest that the attorney make the telephone call. Of course, the paralegal could also consider requesting that she begin working on the case. For example, she could offer to investigate the facts and the law necessary for drafting a complaint. The paralegal could also explain that she feels uncomfortable calling, because the client may ask questions she cannot answer. The paralegal may also say she does not feel comfortable calling, but she may offer to prepare a fee agreement.
2. An attorney has a duty to represent a client competently and diligently. This duty does not change if the case is pro bono. The same ethical considerations apply regardless of the amount (or lack) of a fee.

Ethical Questions

1. Yes, if Gary accepts such a commission, this is an ethical violation on the part of Gary and Jane. Lawyers are not allowed to split fees with nonlawyers, nor can they pay referral fees. Gary should bring this potential violation to Jane's attention, suggesting instead that Jane increase his salary or give him a bonus.
2. A paralegal should never advise a client on a matter if the advice may alter the client's legal position or legal rights. Here, the potential sale of the client's property may have serious implications on a later-filed bankruptcy. Debbie must inform the client that she cannot ethically give legal advice. Debbie should promptly refer the client's question to her supervising attorney.

CHAPTER 4

THE LEGAL WORKPLACE

CHAPTER OBJECTIVES

After completing this chapter, you should be able to:

- Describe how law firms are organized and managed.
- List some typical policies and procedures governing paralegal employment.
- Point out the importance of an efficient filing system in legal practice.
- Identify some typical filing procedures.
- Describe how clients are billed for legal services.
- Discuss how law-office culture and politics affect the paralegal's working environment.

Chapter Outline

I. INTRODUCTION

II. THE ORGANIZATIONAL STRUCTURE OF LAW FIRMS
   A. Sole Proprietorships
      1. A sole proprietorship is a business organization in which one individual owns the business.
      2. A sole proprietor is entitled to all the firm's profits.
      3. A sole proprietor bears the full personal responsibility for all of the firm's debts or obligations.
      4. When working for a sole practitioner, a paralegal will learn about different areas of the law as well as a variety of law-office procedures.
   B. Partnerships
      1. A partnership is a business organization in which two or more individuals—called partners—jointly own the business.
      2. Partners share jointly in the profits or losses of the firm.
      3. Partners are subject to personal liability for all of the firm's debts or other obligations.
      4. Partners may participate equally in managing the partnership, or they may designate a managing partner.
   C. Professional Corporations
      1. A professional corporation is an organization in which two or more individuals—called shareholders—own the business.
      2. The owner-shareholders of a professional corporation share the firm's profits or losses.
      3. Shareholders are not liable for the firm's debts or other obligations beyond the amount they invested in the corporation.

III. LAW-OFFICE MANAGEMENT AND PERSONNEL
   A. Law-Office Personnel.
      1. Upon first taking a job in a law firm, paralegals should learn the relative status of law-firm personnel.
      2. Particularly, paralegals should learn to whom they are accountable and who is accountable to them.

IV. EMPLOYMENT POLICIES
   A. Performance Evaluations
      1. Many law firms conduct periodic performance evaluations of their employees.
      2. Performance evaluations are designed specifically to allow both the law firm and paralegal to exchange their views about the paralegal's responsibilities and performance.
   B. Employment Termination
      1. Almost all policy manuals address the subject of employment termination.
   C. Employment Discrimination
      1. Traditionally, employers may hire and fire employees "at will" (i.e., for any reason or no reason at all).
      2. Under federal law (and many state statutes), employers may not fire employees for discriminatory reasons.

V. FILING PROCEDURES
   A. Client Files
      1. Opening a New Client File
         a. Filing procedures must maximize client confidentiality and ensure the safekeeping of documents and other evidence.
      2. Adding Subfiles
         a. Add subfiles as the file expands to ensure that documents will be easy to locate.
      3. File Use and Storage
         a. Proper file maintenance is crucial to a smoothly functioning law office. If a file is lost, the client may suffer irreparable harm.

4. Closing a File
   a. Although procedures for closing a file vary from firm to firm, original documents are typically returned to the client and extraneous materials are destroyed.
5. Destroying Old Files
   a. Old files are normally destroyed by shredding them to preserve their confidentiality.
   b. The date of the expiration of the statute of limitations in your state is an important factor in determining how long to retain a client's file.

B. Work-Product Files and Reference Materials
1. Many law firms keep copies of research projects, legal memoranda, and pleadings to refer to in future projects.
2. These work-product files prevent starting all over again when working on a claim similar to one dealt with in the past.

C. Forms Files
1. Every law firm keeps on hand various forms that it commonly uses.
2. When the attorney or paralegal works on a similar case in the future, the documents from the previous case are used as a model or guide.
3. Computerized forms simplify legal practice by allowing legal personnel to generate customized documents within minutes.

VI. FINANCIAL PROCEDURES

A. Fee Arrangements
1. Most law firms require each client to sign a retainer agreement.
2. Fixed Fees
   a. Fixed fees are paid for a specified legal service.
   b. Examples of fixed-fee procedures would be an incorporation or a simple divorce filing.
3. Hourly Fees
   a. Most clients pay hourly fees.
   b. These clients are billed monthly for the time spent by the attorneys or other legal personnel on the clients' cases or projects.
4. Contingency Fees
   a. Clients who are represented on a contingency-fee basis do not pay legal fees until the case or legal matter has been decided or completed.
   b. However, all costs incurred on behalf of clients are billed to the client monthly.
5. Alternative Fee Arrangements
   a. "Task-based billing" is charging a fixed fee for specific types of tasks that are involved in a client's matter.
   b. When "value billing" is used, the fees charged to the client may vary, depending upon the results of the representation.

B. Client Trust Accounts
1. A trust account is a bank account into which funds advanced to the firm, such as retainers, are deposited.
2. Funds held in a trust account may only be used for expenses relating to the costs of serving that client's needs.

C. The Prohibition Against Fee-Splitting
1. Rule 5.4 of the Model Rules prohibits lawyers or law firms from sharing legal fees with a nonlawyer.
2. Therefore, paralegals cannot become partners in a law partnership nor can they have a fee-sharing arrangement with an attorney.

D. Billing and Timekeeping Procedures
1. Documenting Time and Expenses
   a. Firms require attorneys and paralegals to fill out and submit time slips documenting time and expenses spent on a particular client's case.

2. Billable versus Nonbillable Hours
   a. Firms usually require attorneys and paralegals to generate a certain number of billable hours per year. This may subject legal personnel to significant stress and pressure.

E. Ethics and Client Billing Practices
   1. Double Billing
      a. Double billing occurs when a firm bills client for work that was done for a previous client.
   2. The American Bar Association's Response to Double Billing
      a. In 1993, the ABA stated that it is unethical to bill two clients for the same billable hours or legal work.

VII. COMMUNICATING WITH CLIENTS

A. Lawyers have a duty to keep their clients reasonably informed.
B. Copies of all letters sent to the client should be kept in the client's file, as well as a written record of every telephone call made to or received from the client.

VIII. LAW OFFICE CULTURE AND POLITICS

A. Law Firm Personality and Culture
   1. Each law office has its own personality, culture, and politics. These are shaped primarily by the attitudes of the firm's owners.
   2. Law-office culture and politics impact greatly on job satisfaction and comfort.
   3. Paralegals should make an effort to learn about the culture and politics of the law office as soon as possible after taking a job.

QUESTIONS FOR REVIEW

TRUE-FALSE QUESTIONS

____ 1. An employment policy manual is a written document that contains the policies and procedures of an office.

____ 2. Personal liability means that a business owner's personal assets may have to be used to pay business obligations.

____ 3. Shareholders share equally in a firm's profits and losses.

____ 4. A shareholder's personal liability includes personal assets, which may have to be used to pay business obligations.

____ 5. A legal administrator may delegate authority to an office manager and other supervisory employees.

____ 6. No statutes have been enacted that regulate employment relationships.

____ 7. A paralegal need not be concerned with confidentiality.

____ 8. Typically, documents in a subfile are filed in reverse chronological order, with the most recently dated document on top.

____ 9. A law firm may keep forms commonly used in a forms file.

____ 10. Procedures that can be fairly closely estimated by an attorney may be paid according to a fixed fee.

____ 11. Litigation attorneys representing plaintiffs in certain types of cases often charge on a contingency-fee basis; the fee is contingent on the case's outcome.

____ 12. An agreement indicating that the client is hiring the attorney or firm is referred to as a retainer agreement.

____ 13. An initial advance payment to the firm to cover part of the fee and costs is referred to as trust account.

____ 14. Funds advanced to a firm by its clients are deposited to a trust account.

____ 15. A paralegal should keep a personal time diary, or journal, in which it is noted how time is spent.

Fill-in Questions

Performance evaluations are designed for the ____________________ (employer/employer and employee) to exchange views on issues.

____________________ (Subfiles/Forms files) may be created for client documents that may be used as reference or evidence. An ____________________ (expense sheet/out card) is inserted in a file's place when a file is removed from storage. When a case is closed ____________________ (all/extra copies of) documents are typically destroyed.

Funds held in a trust account ____________________ (may/may not) be used for expenses relating to the costs of serving that client's needs.

____________________ (Time slips/expense slips) document the amount of time spent on a particular day on a particular task for a particular client. Court fees, telephone charges and copying expenses are entered on ____________________ (time slips/expense slips).

A law firm's financial success ____________________ (is/is not) dependent on the billable hours generated by its employees. ____________________ (Double billing/Conflict of interest) occurs when a firm bills a new client for work done for a previous client. The ABA has stated that if the attorney has agreed to bill solely on the basis of time spent, the benefit of the economies ____________________ (should/need not) be passed on to the client.

Multiple-choice Questions

____ 1. A business that is owned by one individual is referred to as a(n):
   A. Sole proprietorship
   B. Associate attorney
   C. Managing partner
   D. Partnership

____ 2. An attorney who is hired to assist with legal work and is paid a specific sum for the time expended but who does not have any ownership rights in a firm is referred to as a(n):
   A. Sole proprietorship
   B. Associate attorney
   C. Managing partner
   D. Partnership

____ 3. Two or more individuals who undertake to do business jointly form a(n):
   A. Sole proprietorship
   B. Corporation
   C. Professional corporation
   D. Partnership

____ 4. Managerial decisions may be made by a committee, one of whom is designated as a(n):
   A. Sole proprietor
   B. Associate attorney
   C. Managing partner
   D. Partnership

____ 5. A professional corporation is owned by:
   A. A sole proprietorship
   B. The associate attorneys
   C. Shareholders
   D. The support personnel

____ 6. The distinction between a professional corporation and a partnership is:
   A. Often more a legal formality than an operational reality
   B. Nonexistent
   C. Based on financial contributions
   D. Support personnel

____ 7. In larger firms, the individual who coordinates and oversees paralegal staffing and programs relating to educational and professional development is referred to as a(n):
A. Legal administrator
B. Office manager
C. Legal-assistant manager
D. Shareholder

____ 8. In larger firms, the individual who is hired to run the business end of the firm is referred to as a(n):
A. Legal administrator
B. Office manager
C. Legal-assistant manager
D. Shareholder

____ 9. Support personnel in a larger law firm may include:
A. Secretaries
B. Receptionists
C. Bookkeepers
D. All of the above

____ 10. The filing system of a law firm typically includes:
A. Client files
B. Forms files
C. Personnel files
D. All of the above

____ 11. Retention of a file depends on:
A. The nature of the client's legal matters
B. Governing statutes
C. Statute of limitations for legal malpractice
D. All of the above

____ 12. Time charged to a client is referred to as:
A. Billable hours
B. Nonbillable hours
C. Fixed fee
D. Retainer

____ 13. Nonbillable time includes:
A. Administrative work
B. Staff meetings
C. Performance reviews
D. All of the above

____ 14. Double billing refers to billing:
A. A client twice for the same work
B. More than one client for the same time
C. A third party for work performed on behalf of the client
D. An advocate for work performed on behalf of the client

PRACTICE QUESTIONS

1. Identify which of the following are most likely sole proprietorships, partnerships, or professional corporations:
   A. Able, Baker & Caldwell, P. C.
   B. John C. Able
   C. Baker & Caldwell
   D. Law Office of Lawrence A. Caldwell
   E. Able, Baker, Caldwell, Duran & Emmons

2. Identify the type of billing that is being used in each of the following examples:
   A. The client is charged $150 for preparation of a will.
   B. The client was involved in an automobile accident and is charged one-fourth of any amount recovered before trial.
   C. The client is billed $65 per hour for a paralegal's time, $95 per hour for an associate attorney's time, and $125 per hour for a partner's time.

QUESTIONS FOR CRITICAL ANALYSIS

1. If you are doing legal research for a project for a client that has retained your firm on a contingency fee, can you feel comfortable spending as much time as you want in order to complete that project?

ETHICAL QUESTIONS

1. Donna Sams, an attorney, receives a retainer from a client. She properly deposits it into the law firm's trust account. Donna had been expecting another client to pay their bill before the monthly rent payment was due. When it did not arrive, Donna borrowed money from the client trust account to pay the rent, fully intending to re-deposit the funds once the second client paid their bill. May Donna do this? Why or why not?
2. Billie Hernandez is a litigation paralegal working for a large law firm. Billie is under a great deal of pressure to meet the billable-hour requirement set for her by the firm's managing partner. Recently Billie spent two hours looking for a client's file that had been misplaced in the file room. Billie adds that time to her time slips for that client. What has Billie done that is ethically improper?

TECHNOLOGY AND TODAY'S PARALEGAL

E-mail is a valuable tool for attorneys and paralegals to communicate with clients, opposing counsel, and witnesses, but it can serve another useful purpose—networking with other legal professionals. Today there are a number of paralegal e-mail listserves that connect paralegals across the country with each other. Paralegals use them to ask each other for advice, research tips, and information.

NFPA has a number of paralegal listserves. It is not necessary to be a member of NFPA to join its student or education listserves. Access these listserves on the Internet at *http://www.paralegals.org/Forums/listsubscribe.htm.*

ANSWERS

True-False Questions

1. T
2. T
3. F
4. F
5. T
6. F
7. F
8. T
9. T
10. T
11. T
12. T
13. F
14. T
15. T

Fill-in Questions

employer and employee

subfiles; out card; extra copies of

may

time slips; expense slips

is; double billing; should

Multiple-Choice Questions

1. A
2. B
3. D
4. C
5. C
6. A
7. C
8. A
9. D
10. D
11. D
12. A
13. D
14. B

Practice Questions

1. A. Professional corporation
   B. Sole proprietorship
   C. Partnership
   D. Sole proprietorship
   E. Partnership
2. A. Fixed fee
   B. Contingency fee
   C. Hourly fee

Questions for Critical Analysis

1. Even though the client is not being charged for each hour spent on the project, and you may not be required to account for each hour spent, the supervising attorney should be consulted to determine if there is an hourly limit for the project. The attorney may determine that another individual may be able to complete the project in less time, freeing up your time for another project.

Ethical Questions

1. Donna may not use the money from the trust or escrow account, even if she intends to repay it. It is ethically improper for an attorney to "borrow" money from those funds, even for a seemingly innocent or reasonable purpose. Misuse of such accounts constitutes a breach of the firm's duty to the client. An attorney's personal use of these funds can lead to disciplinary action and possible disbarment, as well as criminal penalties.
2. Looking for a lost file, which the firm has mishandled, is not time legitimately added to a client's bill. This is a good example of "padding" the client's bill. This would be an ethical violation, which could result in attorney discipline and perhaps in Billie losing her job.

C H A P T E R 5

Sources of American Law

Chapter Objectives

After completing this chapter, you should be able to:

- Recognize the meaning and relative importance in the American legal system of constitutional law, statutory law, administrative law, and case law.
- Discuss how English law influenced the development of the American legal system.
- Describe what the common law tradition is and how it evolved.
- Distinguish between remedies at law and remedies in equity.
- List some of the terms that are commonly found in case law.
- Understand how national law and international law differ and why these bodies of law sometimes guide judicial decision making in American courts.

Chapter Outline

I. INTRODUCTION

II. WHAT IS LAW?
- A. Defining "Law"
  1. Law has been defined variously over the ages.
  2. Basically, law consists of a body of rules of conduct with legal force and effect, prescribed by the controlling authority of a society.
- B. Source(s) of Law
  1. In the United States, law comes from various sources:
     - a. Common law.
     - b. Constitutions.
     - c. Statutes.
     - d. Case law.
     - e. Administrative law.

III. CONSTITUTIONAL LAW
- A. The Federal Constitution
  1. The U.S. Constitution, as amended, is the supreme law of the land.
  2. A law in violation of the U.S. Constitution will be declared unconstitutional and will not be enforced.
  3. The U.S. Constitution sets forth the powers of the three branches of the federal government and the relationship between the three branches.
  4. Constitutional Rights
     - a. The first ten amendments to the U.S. Constitution are commonly known as the Bill of Rights.
  5. The Courts and Constitutional Law
- B. State Constitutions
  1. Each state also has a constitution that sets forth the general organization, powers, and limits of the state government.
  2. A state constitution is supreme within the states' respective borders, so long as it does not conflict with the U.S. Constitution.
- C. Constitutional Law and the Paralegal
  1. Paralegals often assist attorneys in handling cases that involve constitutional rights or provisions.
  2. A knowledge of constitutional law is beneficial, because the authority and underlying rationale for the substantive and procedural laws governing many areas of law are found in the Constitution.

IV. STATUTORY LAW
- A. Laws passed by the federal Congress and the various state legislatures are called **statutes.**
  1. An ordinance is a statute passed by a municipal or county government to govern matters not covered by federal or state law.
- B. The Expanding Scope of Statutory Law
  1. Legislative bodies and administrative agencies assume an increasing share of lawmaking.
- C. Statutory Law and the Paralegal
  1. A paralegal may often assist in cases involving violations of statutory law.
  2. A paralegal working on cases governed by statutory law needs to know how to both locate and interpret the relevant state or federal statutes.

V. ADMINISTRATIVE LAW
- A. Agency Creation and Function
  1. Administrative agencies are created by legislatures to administer and enforce legislation and to issue rules to implement the goals of specific legislation.
  2. Examples of federal administrative agencies are:
     - a. Environmental Protection Agency.
     - b. Occupational Safety and Health Administration.
     - c. Food and Drug Administration.

☞ STUDY TIP

Administering Environmental Laws

At the federal level, environmental law is inseparable from administrative law. The primary regulatory statutes are administered by agencies (among which the Environmental Protection Agency plays no small part). What that means is that the regulation of a business's conduct under environmental laws is subject to administrative law procedures and principles

B. Administrative Law and the Paralegal
   1. Paralegals frequently deal with administrative agencies.
   2. Paralegals may also work for administrative agencies, drafting new rules, mediating disputes, and numerous other tasks.

VI. CASE LAW AND THE COMMON LAW TRADITION
   A. Early English Courts of Law
      1. The body of law consisting of the decisions rendered by judges in cases that come before the courts is called case law.
      2. A major source of American law is the common law.
      3. Common law originated in medieval England with the creation of the king's court.
      4. A precedent is a court decision that furnishes an example of authority for deciding subsequent cases in which identical or similar facts are presented.
   B. The Doctrine of *Stare Decisis*
      1. The practice of deciding new cases with reference to former decisions, or precedents, is a cornerstone of the American judicial system.
      2. *Stare decisis* means "to stand on decided cases."
      3. Under this doctrine, judges are expected to abide by the law as established by previous court decisions.
      4. Departures from Precedent
         a. Occasionally a court will depart from precedent if the precedent is based on a clearly erroneous application of the law or if the political and cultural environment has changed so significantly that the precedent is no longer relevant.
      5. Cases of First Impression
         a. A case of first impression is one that presents a legal issue that has not yet been addressed by a court in a particular jurisdiction.
         b. In a case of first impression, the court may consider:
            1) Legal principles and policies underlying previous court decisions or existing statutes.
            2) Fairness.
            3) Social values and customs.
            4) Public policy.
            5) Data and concepts drawn from the social sciences.
   C. Remedies at Law versus Remedies in Equity
      1. Two parallel court systems emerged in medieval England:
         a. Courts of law.
         b. Courts of equity.
      2. Courts of law granted remedies at law, which consisted primarily of money damages.
      3. Courts of equity granted remedies in equity where remedies were sought by plaintiffs for whom money damages were not appropriate or adequate.

4. Equitable Principles and Maxims
   a. Equitable principles and maxims are propositions or general statements of rules of law that are frequently involved in equity jurisdiction.
   b. Laches is the equitable doctrine that bars a party's right to legal action if the party has neglected for an unreasonable length of time to act upon his or her rights.
5. Equitable Remedies
   a. Remedies in equity include:
      1) *Specific performance*—An order to perform the specific terms of the contract.
      2) *Rescission*—The cancellation of a contract so that the parties are returned to their precontractual status.
      3) *Injunction*—An order to refrain from engaging in certain conduct.
6. The Merging of Law and Equity
   a. Most states have adopted rules of procedure that combine courts of law and equity.
   b. Courts still distinguish between remedies at law and equitable remedies.

D. The Common Law Today
   1. Today, the common law governs all areas that are not covered by statutory law.

E. Statutory Law and the Common Law
   1. The body of statutory law has expanded greatly and continues to grow.
   2. To codify a statute means to arrange and organize it by topics.
   3. Even when legislation has been substituted for the common law, a court's interpretation and application of a statute may become precedent.

F. The Terminology of Case Law
   1. Case Titles
      a. The title of a case is sometimes referred to as the *style* of the case.
      b. The case title, or style, indicates the names of the parties to the lawsuit.
      c. The *legal citation* in the case title indicates in which reports or reporters the case can be found.
   2. The Parties
      a. The parties to the lawsuit are:
         1) *The plaintiff*—The person who initiates the lawsuit.
         2) *The defendant*—The person against whom the lawsuit is brought.
      b. Lawsuits frequently involve multiple parties.
   3. Judges and Justices
      a. All members of the United States Supreme Court are referred to as justices.
      b. Judges of appeals courts are sometimes also referred to as justices.
      c. Judges in the trial courts are referred to as judges.
   4. Decisions and Opinions
      a. The opinion contains:
         1) The court's reasons for its decision.
         2) The rules of law that apply.
         3) The judgment.
      b. There are four different types of opinions:
         1) *Unanimous opinion*—where all the judges or justices unanimously agree.
         2) *Majority opinion*—outlines the views of the majority of the judges or justices deciding the case.
         3) *Concurring opinion*—an additional opinion written by a judge or justice who feels strongly about making or emphasizing a point not made or emphasized in the unanimous or majority opinion.
         4) *Dissenting opinion*—written by a judge or justice who does not agree with the majority.

G. Common Law and the Paralegal
   1. A basic understanding of common law is needed to research and analyze case law.
   2. The concepts of *stare decisis,* legal remedies, and equitable remedies will become real and meaningful when applied to real-life situations faced by clients.

VII. NATIONAL AND INTERNATIONAL LAW

A. National Law
   1. National law consists of the laws of a particular nation.
   2. The legal systems of other countries are based on one of the following:
      a. *Common law system*—primarily used in Great Britain and the United States.
      b. *Civil law system*—a codified law system used in most of the other European, Latin American, African, and Asian countries.
   3. National law can be enforced by government authorities.

B. International Law
   1. International law is a body of written and unwritten laws observed by independent nations and governing the acts of individuals as well as governments.
   2. International law is enforced primarily for reasons of courtesy or expediency.
   3. No independent nation can be compelled to obey an international law.
   4. Nations voluntarily agree to be governed by international law to facilitate international trade and commerce.
   5. Treaties
      a. A treaty is an agreement between two or more nations that creates rights and duties binding on the parties to the treaty.
      b. The supreme power of each nation that is a party to the treaty must ratify it to give effect to a treaty.
   6. International Organizations and Conferences
      a. International organizations and conferences adopt resolutions, declarations, and other types of standards that often require a particular behavior of nations.

C. International Law and the Paralegal
   1. Both national and international law affect the outcome of cases brought in American courts.
   2. Because business and other activities are becoming increasingly global in scope, paralegals are more frequently dealing with national and international law matters.

☞ STUDY TIP

More than a Collection of Diplomatic Rules

It is clear that nations need to develop new forms of cooperation. In part, this is due to increased communication, population growth, pollution, and the threat of exhaustion of world resources. The need has also arisen as a consequence of the growing gap between economically developed and less developed countries. The changing political environment also plays a part.

The important point to keep in mind is that international law is not just a collection of diplomatic rules. The need for cooperation is inescapable. With this in mind, perhaps the most helpful perspective on the international legal framework is an awareness that international law has become an integral part of the domestic economic and social life of every nation.

QUESTIONS FOR REVIEW

TRUE-FALSE QUESTIONS

____ 1. Law consists of enforceable rules governing relationships among individuals and between individuals and their society.

____ 2. Precedent refers to deciding later cases with reference to former decisions involving a similar legal principle.

____ 3. A case of first impressions refers to a case in which there is a controlling state or federal law.

____ 4. Remedies in equity developed because the remedies at law were inadequate.

____ 5. Maxims are propositions or general statements of rules of law that courts often use in arriving at a decision.

____ 6. The citation indicates in which reporter a case can be found.

____ 7. The parties to the lawsuit are the plaintiff and defendant.

____ 8. The Bill of Rights, represented by the first ten amendments to the U.S. Constitution, are absolute rights, unrestricted in nature.

____ 9. Laws enacted by the federal Congress are called ordinances.

____ 10. Legislatures may delegate governing responsibilities to administrative agencies.

____ 11. The rules, orders, and decisions of administrative agencies is known as administrative law.

____ 12. In a civil law system, the primary source of law is a statutory code, and the doctrine of *stare decisis* does not apply.

____ 13. International law refers to a body of written and unwritten laws observed by independent nations and governing the acts of individuals as well as governments.

FILL-IN QUESTIONS

In the United States there are ____________________ (one/four) major sources of law. Judges attempt to decide ____________________ (similar/different) cases in a ____________________ (similar/different) way. These decisions serve as ____________________ (enabling legislation/precedents) for subsequent cases. However, if a court decides technology or society has changed, it may depart from ____________________ (precedent/judicial process).

Historically, plaintiffs had to specify whether the action was in equity or at law, as there existed ____________________ (one remedy for each/one remedy for a wrong). Today, the same court ____________________ (can/cannot) award both equitable and legal relief in the same case.

Equitable principles and maxims guide judges. One maxim, known as the equitable doctrine of laches, provides that once a statute of limitations has expired, a claim generally ____________________ (may be brought/is barred).

Statutory law has expanded greatly and has resulted in ____________________ (codification/analogizing), an arrangement in logical order. Many businesses and activities involve foreign parties or governments; a paralegal ____________________ (must/need not) be aware of international law.

Multiple-choice Questions

____ 1. Common law:
A. Is a body of general rules that prescribed social conduct
B. Applied throughout the entire English realm
C. Was an attempt to establish a uniform set of customs for the entire country
D. All of the above

____ 2. *Stare decisis* means:
A. Those that sleep on their rights
B. Similar legal principles
C. To stand on decided cases
D. To rescind an earlier agreement

____ 3. Remedies at law are represented by:
A. Economic considerations
B. Notions of justice and fair dealing
C. The Bill of Rights
D. Ordinances

____ 4. The time period for pursuing a particular claim against another party is now usually fixed by:
A. The Bill of Rights
B. Case law
C. A statute of limitations
D. A national law

____ 5. Equitable remedies include:
A. Economic considerations
B. Specific performance, rescission, and injunction
C. Money damages
D. Precedent

____ 6. Specific performance is:
A. An order to perform what was promised
B. Only available when the dispute before the court involves a contractual transaction
C. Available if the goods are unique
D. All of the above

____ 7. Rescission is:
A. The doctrine that encourages people to bring lawsuits while the evidence is still fresh
B. An action to undo a contract
C. An order directing the defendant to do or refrain from doing a particular act
D. An order to perform what was promised

____ 8. An injunction is:
A. The doctrine that encourages people to bring lawsuits while the evidence is still fresh
B. An action to undo a contract
C. An order directing the defendant to do or refrain from doing a particular act
D. An order to perform what was promised

____ 9. Case law is:
A. Statutory law
B. The Bill of Rights
C. Judge-made law
D. All of the above

____ 10. The opinion is:
A. The parties' own versions of the facts
B. The jury's verdict
C. Statutory law
D. The court's reasons for its decision, the rules of law that apply, and the judgment

____ 11. Statutory law:
A. Is judge-made law
B. Consists of legislative enactments
C. Is national law
D. Is common law

____ 12. Enabling legislation:
A. Creates an administrative agency, specifying the name, composition, and powers
B. Permits a state to regulate in an area in which the federal government regulates
C. Permits a municipality to pass a zoning ordinance
D. Implements case law

____ 13. National law is:
A. Statutes enacted by the federal legislature
B. The law of a particular nation
C. The rules of an administrative agency
D. Judge-made law

____ 14. An agreement between two or more nations that creates rights and duties binding on the parties is:
A. A citation
B. A law
C. An ordinance
D. A treaty

Practice Questions

1. Look at the Constitution in Appendix J of this text. Locate the language in the Bill of Rights that gives U.S. citizens the following rights and protections:
   A. Protection against being tried twice for the same crime.
   B. The right to an impartial jury.
   C. The right to trial by jury.
   D. Protection against excessive bail and fines.
   E. Protection against cruel and unusual punishment.
2. Identify the type of law (common law, constitutional law, statutory law, or administrative law) that applies in each of the following scenarios:
   A. Gene Jormane strongly disagrees with the U.S. government's decision to impose a trade embargo against a foreign country. She places an anti-embargo bumper sticker on her car. The municipality passes an ordinance that bans all such items.
   B. An official of the state department of Occupational Health and Safety learns that Widget Company has failed to keep the lunchroom free of waste. A complaint against the company for not properly disposing of this waste is issued.
   C. Mr. Sams was jogging through the park when a teenager on a skate board lost control and crashed into him. As a result, Mr. Sams broke his ankle and, according to doctors, will never be able to jog again. He sues the teenager for damages.
   D. Josephine Barnes is arrested and charged with the crime of robbery.

Questions for Critical Analysis

1. Administrative law has proliferated many areas and many administrative agencies have been established. Do you think this proliferation is necessary? Explain.
2. No statute or ordinance may be in violation of the U.S. Constitution. Is it necessary to have such an overriding document? Why or why not?

Ethical Questions

1. Paralegal Jennifer Creque has been asked to research an ethical question by her attorney. One of the firm's clients, another attorney, is planning to break away from the large law firm for which he now works and open his own firm. The client/attorney wants to know the ethical rule relating to notifying the clients of his old firm of his move. Jennifer does not realize that her state has recently adopted the ABA Rules of Professional Conduct. Instead, Jennifer does her research in the older ABA Code of Professional Responsibility. What consequences might Jennifer's supervising attorney face as a result of her oversight?
2. Jeremy Bates is a litigation legal assistant working for a large law firm. He has been asked to complete a legal research project for a client's workers' compensation case. Jeremy remembers that he worked on a very similar case several months ago. He pulls that file and uses the prior legal research memo to write the memo to his supervising attorney in this case. Because Jeremy did not verify that the earlier research is still "good law," he failed to find out that a new Supreme Court case has created a new precedent in the workers' compensation area. Has Jeremy violated any ethical rule?

Technology and Today's Paralegal

In your text, you learned that the U.S. Environmental Protection Agency coordinates and enforces federal environmental laws. There are several ways you could access the EPA on the Internet, but the most direct method would be to go to *http://www.epa.gov.* Other Internet addresses that would direct you to the EPA and other governmental agencies are FEDWORLD *(http://www.fedworld.gov/)* and GovBot, which indexes over 500,000 government sites *(http://business.gov/Search_Online.html).*

Go to *http://www.epa.gov.* This site lists over a dozen major statutes or laws that form the legal basis for the programs of the Environmental Protection Agency. Find the list of these laws and regulations, and then research further by clicking on the hyperlink that will take you to a more comprehensive list of laws (as of 1995) administered by the EPA.

Answers

True-False Questions

1. T
2. T
3. F
4. T
5. T
6. T
7. T
8. F
9. F
10. T
11. T
12. T
13. T

Fill-in Questions

four; similar; similar; precedents; precedent

one remedy for a wrong; can

is barred

codification; must

Multiple-Choice Questions

1. D
2. C
3. A
4. C
5. B
6. D
7. B
8. C
9. C
10. D
11. C
12. A
13. B
14. D

Practice Questions

1. A. Amendment V: " . . . nor shall any person be subject for the same offence to be twice put in jeopardy of life or limb"
   B. Amendment IV: ". . . in all criminal prosecutions, the accused shall enjoy the right to a speedy and public trial, by an impartial jury of the State"
   C. Amendment VII: "In Suits at common law, where the value in controversy exceed twenty dollars, the right of trial by jury shall be preserved"
   D. Amendment VIII: "Excessive bail shall not be required, nor excessive fines imposed"
   E. Amendment VIII: ". . . nor cruel and unusual punishments inflicted"

2. A. Constitutional law
   B. Administrative law
   C. Common law
   D. Statutory law

Questions for Critical Analysis

1. Yes, this proliferation is necessary, because our society has become so complex that the judicial system would be so inundated with litigation. As a result, many cases would not be decided until too late. The administrative agencies alleviate this backlog by providing much of the day-to-day enforcement of regulations.
2. Yes, it is necessary to have such an overriding document. The U.S. Constitution was intended to be an overriding document. All laws enacted by political subdivisions—including states, municipalities, and townships—are not to be in conflict. Thus, all citizens are assured certain rights that cannot be violated by a locality.

Ethical Questions

1. Paralegals share attorneys' ethical and legal obligation to render competent legal services to clients. The duty of competence requires, among other things, that attorneys and paralegals are aware of the law governing a client's legal matter.

   As a result of Jennifer's oversight, the attorney/client may well commit an ethical violation, which could result in his being suspended or disbarred. As the person ultimately responsible for Jennifer's work, her supervising attorney could well be sued by the client for negligence.
2. Jeremy's failure to update his research and, therefore, to find the newly created precedent, has led to serious consequences for the client. Jeremy has breached the ethical duty of competence owed to the client. This failure has exposed Jeremy's supervising attorney, as well as the entire law firm, to a negligence or malpractice lawsuit.

CHAPTER 6

THE COURT SYSTEM AND ALTERNATIVE DISPUTE RESOLUTION

CHAPTER OBJECTIVES

After completing this chapter, you should be able to:

- List the requirements that must be met before a lawsuit can be brought in a particular court by a particular party.
- Distinguish between the concepts of jurisdiction and venue.
- Identify the types of courts that make up a typical state court system.
- Describe the different functions of trial courts and appellate courts.
- Explain the organization of the federal court system.
- Recognize the relationship between state and federal jurisdiction.
- Discuss how cases reach the United States Supreme Court.
- Point out the various ways in which disputes can be resolved outside the court system.

Chapter Outline

I. INTRODUCTION

II. THE AMERICAN SYSTEM OF JUSTICE

A. Types of Jurisdiction
   1. Jurisdiction over Persons
      a. Generally, a court can exercise personal jurisdiction over residents of a certain geographical area.
      b. Personal jurisdiction is also known as *in personam* jurisdiction.
      c. Under a *long arm statute,* a court can exercise personal jurisdiction over a nonresident when the nonresident had sufficient contacts with the state.
   2. Jurisdiction over Property
      a. A court can exercise jurisdiction over property that is located within its boundaries.
      b. Jurisdiction over property is known as *in rem* jurisdiction.
   3. Jurisdiction over Subject Matter
      a. This is a limitation on the types of cases a court can hear.
      b. In both the state and federal systems, there are courts of general jurisdiction and limited jurisdiction.
         1) Courts of general jurisdiction can hear most types of disputes.
         2) Courts of limited jurisdiction are restricted in the types of actions they can decide.
      c. The subject-matter jurisdiction of a court is usually defined in the statute or constitution creating the court.
      d. In both state and federal courts, a court's subject-matter jurisdiction can be limited by:
         1) The subject of the lawsuit.
         2) The amount of money in controversy.
         3) Whether the case is a felony or a misdemeanor.
         4) Whether the proceeding is a trial or an appeal.
   4. Original and Appellate Jurisdiction
      a. Courts of original jurisdiction are courts in which the trial of a case begins.
      b. Any court having original jurisdiction is known as a trial court.
      c. Courts of appellate jurisdiction are reviewing courts.
      d. Appellate courts do not try cases anew but review the decisions of trial courts.

B. Jurisdiction of the Federal Courts
   1. Federal Questions
      a. When a lawsuit is based, at least in part, on some type of federal law, the case comes under the judicial power of the federal courts.
   2. Diversity Jurisdiction
      a. Federal courts can exercise jurisdiction over claims involving one of the following:
         1) A federal question, which arises from the U.S. Constitution, a federal treaty, or a federal law.
         2) Diversity of citizenship, which involves a controversy exceeding $75,000 *and* arises between citizens from different states, citizens from a foreign country and citizens of a state or of different states, or citizens of a state and citizens or subjects of a foreign country.
   3. Exclusive versus Concurrent Jurisdiction
      a. Exclusive jurisdiction exists when cases can be tried only in federal courts or only in state courts. Federal courts have exclusive jurisdiction in cases involving bankruptcy, federal crimes, patents, trademarks, copyrights, suits against the United States, and in some areas of admiralty law.
      b. Concurrent jurisdiction exists when both federal and state courts have the power to hear a case. States have exclusive jurisdiction in certain subject matters, such as divorce and adoptions.

C. Venue
   1. Venue is concerned with the most appropriate geographical location for a trial.
   2. The concept of venue reflects the policy that a court trying a suit should be in the geographic neighborhood in which the incident leading to the suit occurred or where the parties to the suit reside.

D. Standing to Sue
   1. Before a plaintiff can bring a lawsuit, she must have standing to sue.
   2. To have standing, a plaintiff must have a sufficient stake in a controversy to justify taking the issue before a court.
   3. The controversy must be a *justiciable controversy,* or a controversy that is actual and real, not hypothetical or academic.

E. Judicial Procedures
   1. Litigation in court must follow specifically designated procedural rules.
   2. Federal court procedures are set forth in the Federal Rules of Civil Procedure.
   3. State rules of procedure vary from state to state.
   4. Court procedural rules are different for civil cases than for criminal cases.

F. The American System of Justice and the Paralegal
   1. The paralegal's value to the legal team is directly related to his knowledge of the concepts affecting litigation procedures.
   2. Paralegals should be familiar with the concepts of jurisdiction, venue, and standing to sue.
   3. Paralegals should be familiar with the procedural rules of the specific court in which a case is filed.
   4. Paralegals need to have a basic understanding of the different types of courts that make up the American court system.

III. STATE COURT SYSTEMS

A. Trial Courts
   1. The structure of state court systems varies from state to state.
   2. A typical state court system may consist of several tiers.
   3. On the bottom tier are courts of limited jurisdiction.
   4. On the next tier are usually trial courts of general jurisdiction, such as county courts.
   5. Trial courts are courts of original jurisdiction; they are where lawsuits are initiated, trials are held, and evidence is presented.

B. Courts of Appeals
   1. Appellate courts are where trial courts' decisions can be appealed.
   2. Appellate courts are reviewing courts; they do not retry cases.
   3. The function of appellate courts is to review the trial courts' decisions in cases that are appealed.
   4. Intermediate Appellate Courts
      a. About three-fourths of the states have intermediate appellate courts.
      b. These courts do not retry cases; instead they review the record of the case on appeal and determine whether the trial court committed a prejudicial error of law.
   5. Highest State Courts
      a. The highest state appellate court is typically called the state supreme court, although there are exceptions.
      b. Cases can be appealed from state supreme courts to the United States Supreme Court only when issues of federal law are involved.

C. State Court Systems and the Paralegal
   1. Because each state has its own unique system of courts, paralegals must become familiar with the court system of their particular state.
   2. Paralegals must also become familiar with procedural requirements of special courts to assist attorneys in drafting legal documents to be filed in those courts.

IV. THE FEDERAL COURT SYSTEM

A. U.S. District Courts
   1. U.S. district courts are the trial courts of the federal court system.
   2. U.S. district courts are courts of general jurisdiction.
   3. There is a U.S. district court in every state.

B. U.S. Courts of Appeals
   1. Decisions from a district court can be appealed to the court of appeals of the circuit (geographical area) in which the district court is located.
   2. There are thirteen circuit courts of appeals.
   3. Decisions rendered by these circuit courts may be appealed to the United States Supreme Court.

C. The United States Supreme Court
   1. The United States Supreme Court is the highest court and consists of nine justices.
   2. The United States Supreme Court has original, or trial court, jurisdiction in a small number of situations—such as those affecting ambassadors. Otherwise the court has only appellate jurisdiction.
   3. How Cases Reach the Supreme Court
      a. There is no absolute right of appeal to the Supreme Court.
      b. If the Court decides to review a case, it will issue a writ of *certiorari.*
      c. A writ of *certiorari* is an order to a lower court requiring it to send to the Supreme Court the record of a case for review.
   4. Types of Cases Reviewed by the Supreme Court
      a. The Supreme Court generally reviews cases that raise important constitution questions, that conflict with other state or federal court decisions, or that issue and generate a decision to define the law on the matter.

D. The Federal Court System and the Paralegal
   1. Paralegals deal occasionally with the federal court system.
   2. Paralegals should know the specific requirements of the particular federal court in which a client's lawsuit is to be filed.

V. ALTERNATIVE DISPUTE RESOLUTION

A. Negotiation
   1. Negotiation is the simplest method of alternative dispute resolution (ADR).
   2. Negotiation may or may not involve a third party.

☞ STUDY TIP

Alternative to What?

In studying the material on ADR, you may find it helpful to consider what the alternative is. If there were no legal resolution structure—that is, no judicial system—most disputes would go unresolved or would be resolved by force. Thus, the judicial system is an alternative to self-help dispute resolution, or anarchy.

Judicial dispute resolution is the prototype for other dispute resolution devices. Because the American judicial system can operate less than perfectly, and because the number of cases filed and tried in American courts has increased, the other devices are receiving increased attention. Thus, when methods for alternative dispute resolution are discussed, the usual emphasis is on methods other than the judicial system.

3. The parties to the lawsuit simply try to work out their problems to avoid going to court.
4. A settlement agreement is an out-of-court resolution to a legal dispute, which is agreed to by the parties in writing.
5. Out-of-court settlement agreements are reached in the majority of lawsuits, usually before the trial begins.

B. Mediation
1. Mediation is a form of ADR in which the parties attempt to reach agreement with the help of a neutral third party.
2. A mediator or panel of mediators help the parties explore alternative possibilities for settling their differences as amicably as possible.
3. Usually a mediator charges a fee, which can be split between the parties.
4. The mediator proposes various solutions for the parties to consider.
5. Many state and federal courts now require that parties mediate their disputes before bringing the disputes before the court.
6. When mediation is required by the court, the court may appoint the mediator.
7. Because a mediator need not be a lawyer, this field is open to paralegals who acquire training and expertise in this area.

C. Arbitration
1. Arbitration is the most formal method of ADR.
2. In arbitration, a neutral third party renders a decision after the parties present their cases and evidence in a hearing.
3. In voluntary arbitration, the parties normally agree at the outset to be legally bound by the arbitrator's decision.
4. Arbitration Clauses and Statutes
   a. Increasingly, parties are including provisions in their contracts by which they agree to arbitrate any disputes that may arise under the contract.
   b. Arbitration clauses will likely be enforced under a federal or state arbitration statute.
5. The Arbitration Process
   a. The first step in the arbitration process is the submission agreement.
   b. The next step is the hearing.
   c. After each side has had an opportunity to present evidence and to argue its case, the arbitrator reaches a final decision, which is called an award.
6. The Role of the Courts in the Arbitration Process
   a. The role of the courts in the arbitration process is limited.
   b. However, courts may play an important role in the pre-arbitration and post-arbitration stages.
   c. An arbitrator's role may be set aside by the court if the award resulted from the arbitrator's misconduct or "bad faith."

D. Other ADR Forms
1. In binding mediation, a neutral mediator tries to facilitate agreement between the parties, but if no agreement is reached, the mediator issues a legally binding decision on the matter.
2. In mediation arbitration (med-arb), an arbitrator attempts first to help the parties reach an agreement. If no agreement is reached, then formal arbitration is undertaken, and the arbitrator issues a legally binding decision.
3. In early neutral case evaluation, the parties select a neutral third party to evaluate their respective positions. The evaluator then assesses the strengths and weaknesses of the parties' positions. This evaluation forms the basis of negotiations for a settlement.
4. In a mini-trial, each party's attorney briefly argues the party's case before representatives of each firm who have the authority to settle the dispute.

E. Court-Referred ADR
1. The majority of states either require or encourage parties to undergo mediation or arbitration prior to trial.
2. Several federal courts have instituted ADR programs.

3. In summary jury trials, the parties present their arguments and supporting evidence (other than witnesses), and the jury renders a verdict. However, the jury's verdict is not binding. It acts as a guide to the parties in reaching an agreement during the mandatory negotiations that immediately follow.

F. Providers of ADR Services
1. ADR services are provided by both government and private, for-profit organizations.
2. A major provider of ADR services is the American Arbitration Association (AAA), which can be accessed on the Internet at *www.adr.org.*
3. Hundreds of for-profit firms around the country also provide dispute-resolution services.
4. Many paralegals have found that becoming a mediator or arbitrator is an especially rewarding career option.

G. ADR and the Paralegal
1. State and federal courts are increasingly requiring litigants to undergo arbitration prior to bringing their suits before the courts.
2. Paralegals assist attorneys in work relating to the negotiation of out-of-court settlements.
3. Some paralegals are qualified mediators or arbitrators and directly assist the parties in reaching a mutually satisfactory agreement.

QUESTIONS FOR REVIEW

TRUE-FALSE QUESTIONS

____ 1. Before a court can hear a case, it must have jurisdiction over the person or property and over the subject matter.

____ 2. Probate courts handle only matters relating to the transfer of a person's assets and obligations on that person's death.

____ 3. Bankruptcy courts handle only bankruptcy proceedings, which are governed by federal bankruptcy law.

____ 4. Appellate courts usually have original jurisdictions.

____ 5. Federal court jurisdiction is limited to federal questions or diversity of citizenship in which the amount in controversy exceeds $75,000.

____ 6. Standing to sue refers to a party's stake in a matter, or a legally protected and tangible interest in the litigation.

____ 7. A justiciable controversy refers to a controversy that is hypothetical or academic.

____ 8. A writ of *certiorari* is an order issued by the appellate court to a lower court requiring the latter to send it the record of the case for review.

____ 9. The rule of four refers to the requirement that four of the nine United States Supreme Court Justices must approve of the issuance of a writ.

____ 10. A settlement agreement normally reflects the parties' agreement that the plaintiff will give up the right to continue the litigation, and the defendant will pay a designated, agreed-on sum of money.

____ 11. The role of a mediator is to help the parties view their dispute more objectively and to find common grounds for agreement.

____ 12. Disputes may be arbitrated because the contract includes an arbitration clause requiring submission to arbitration.

____ 13. The American Arbitration Association is a major provider of mediation services.

____ 14. The submission agreement typically identifies the parties, the nature of the dispute, the monetary amounts, the place of arbitration, and the powers that the arbitrator will exercise.

____ 15. Mini-trials are court sponsored.

FILL-IN QUESTIONS

Before filing a complaint, the court with the appropriate authority to hear the case, or ______________ (jurisdiction/venue) must be determined. If the complaint involves a divorce, the state court will most likely have ______________ (concurrent/exclusive) jurisdiction. The appropriate geographical area, or ______________ (jurisdiction/venue), must also be determined. The court in which the action will be tried is referred to as a court of ______________ (original/exclusive) jurisdiction. The next tier in the court structure is a court with ______________ (original/appellate) jurisdiction. If the issue is appealed to the United States Supreme Court, it ______________ (must/need not) hear that case.

______________ (ADR/Writ of *certiorari*) represent methods for resolving issues outside the courtroom. The parties may ______________ (negotiate/mediate) their disputes without the assistance of a third party. The most formal method is ______________ (mediation/arbitration), which involves a neutral third party who renders a decision. In fact, some courts ______________ (require/prohibit) these methods.

MULTIPLE-CHOICE QUESTIONS

____ 1. Personal jurisdiction over a nonresident may be obtained by:
A. An appellate court
B. A summary jury trial
C. A long arm statute
D. Arbitration

____ 2. Trial courts are courts in which:
A. Lawsuits begin
B. Evidence is presented
C. Trials take place
D. All of the above

____ 3. Appellate courts:
A. Act as reviewing courts
B. Hold trials
C. Receive evidence
D. All of the above

____ 4. A cause of action based on the U.S. Constitution, a treaty, or a federal law is referred to as:
A. Diversity of citizenship
B. Standing to sue
C. Federal question
D. Concurrent jurisdiction

____ 5. When both federal and state courts have the power to hear a case, the following exists:
A. Exclusive jurisdiction
B. Concurrent jurisdiction
C. Original jurisdiction
D. Appellate jurisdiction

____ 6. When a case can be tried only in federal courts or only in state courts, the following exists:
A. Exclusive jurisdiction
B. Concurrent jurisdiction
C. Original jurisdiction
D. Appellate jurisdiction

____ 7. Venue is concerned with:
A. The court's authority over nonresidents
B. The court's "power to speak the law"
C. The most appropriate location for a trial
D. A controversy that is real and substantial

____ 8. Alternative dispute resolution methods include:
A. Negotiation
B. Mediation
C. Arbitration
D. All of the above

____ 9. Negotiation is an alternative means of resolving disputes where:
A. The parties meet informally to see if a mutually satisfactory agreement can be reached
B. The parties reach agreement with the assistance of a third party
C. A third party hearing the dispute normally makes the decision for the parties
D. The parties present their arguments and evidence, and a jury renders a nonbinding verdict

____ 10. Mediation is an alternative means of resolving disputes where:
A. The parties meet informally to see if a mutually satisfactory agreement can be reached
B. The parties reach agreement with the assistance of a third party
C. A third party hearing the dispute normally makes the decision for the parties
D. The parties present their arguments and evidence, and a jury renders a nonbinding verdict.

____ 11. Arbitration is an alternative means of resolving disputes where
A. The parties meet informally to see if a mutually satisfactory agreement can be reached
B. The parties reach agreement with the assistance of a third party
C. A third party hearing the dispute normally makes the decision for the parties
D. The parties present their arguments and evidence, and a jury renders a nonbinding verdict

____ 12. The first step in the arbitration process is the:
A. Award
B. Settlement agreement
C. Submission agreement
D. Summary jury trial

____ 13. The final decision of an arbitrator is called:
A. An award
B. An alternative dispute resolution
C. Justiciable controversy
D. Summary jury trial

____ 14. Summary jury trial is an alternative means of resolving disputes where:
A. The parties meet informally to see if a mutually satisfactory agreement can be reached
B. The parties reach agreement with the assistance of a third party
C. A third party hearing the dispute normally makes the decision for the parties
D. The parties present their arguments and evidence, and a jury renders a nonbinding verdict

____ 15. ADR does all of the following except:
A. Relieves courts' burgeoning caseloads
B. Reduces the high costs associated with litigation
C. Permits paralegals to serve as arbitrators
D. ADR does all of the above

Practice Questions

1. Based on the information provided in this chapter, determine which court or courts—federal or state—could hear the following cases and on what jurisdictional grounds:
   A. A case in which a citizen claims the right of free speech has been prohibited
   B. A case in which a spouse seeks to increase child support
   C. A single person seeking to adopt a minor
   D. A lawsuit claiming that the defendant violated the federal kidnapping statute
2. Look at Exhibit 6-4. In which federal circuit are the following states located?
   A. Michigan
   B. New York
   C. California
   D. Colorado
   E. Hawaii

Ethical Questions

1. Betty Marker is a paralegal working on a civil lawsuit in state court. Her supervising attorney has asked her to draft a set of interrogatories (attorneys' written questions to the parties in a lawsuit). Betty knows there are limits on how many questions can be asked, so she refers to the Federal Rules of Civil Procedure to get that number. Has Betty done anything wrong?
2. Paul Wong, a paralegal, works for an attorney representing the plaintiff in a federal court lawsuit based on diversity-of-citizenship jurisdiction. The case involves a dispute exceeding $75,000. Paul has been working with the plaintiff on the answers to interrogatories submitted by the defendant. In doing so, Paul discovers that the plaintiff actually lives in the same state as the defendant. What should Paul do?

Technology and Today's Paralegal

Using the Web sites such as *www.courts.net* noted in your textbook in this chapter locate the Internet site for your state, and check the rules of civil procedure to find out whether any of the courts in your state allow any kind of electronic filing. If so, what are the requirements and procedures for the same?

If you are not achieving results with the Web sites listed in your text, the following sites might be useful:

http://www.llrx.com/columns/litigat.htm

http://www.law.du.edu/library/pubs/states.htm

If the courts in your state do not allow electronic filing, check with your state's Secretary of State. The general sequence for a state's Secretary of State database is: *http://www.sos.state(use postal abbreviation).us.* Another Internet address that might be useful is *http://www.faxxon.com.* Find out whether your state's Secretary of State allows any kind of electronic filings and, if so, what kind?

Answers

True-False Questions

1. T
2. T
3. T
4. F
5. T
6. T
7. F
8. F
9. T
10. T
11. T
12. T
13. T
14. T
15. F

Fill-in Questions

jurisdiction; exclusive; venue; original; appellate; need not
ADR; negotiate; arbitration; require

Multiple-Choice Questions

1. C
2. D
3. A
4. C
5. B
6. A
7. C
8. D
9. A
10. B
11. C
12. C
13. A
14. D
15. D

Practice Questions

1. A. U.S. District Court—federal question involving the U.S. Constitution
   B. State trial court
   C. State trial court
   D. U.S. District Court—federal question involving a federal statute
2. A. Sixth
   B. Second
   C. Ninth
   D. Tenth
   E. Ninth

Ethical Questions

1. Court structure and rules of court may vary significantly between federal and state courts and even from state court to state court. Paralegals must become familiar with the procedural requirements of specific courts in order to assist attorneys in drafting legal documents to be filed in those courts.

   Betty should have consulted the rules of procedure for her state court, not the federal court. By not doing so, she has breached the ethical duty of competence. The number of allowable interrogatories may well vary between the federal rules and those in Betty's state. If her error is not caught by her supervising attorney before the interrogatories are submitted, the other parties to the litigation could refuse to answer the interrogatories in whole or in part. This would most certainly delay the litigation process, perhaps causing harm to the client.

2. One way a federal court can exercise jurisdiction over a claim is where the amount in controversy exceeds $75,000 *and* the parties are citizens from different states. Paul has just discovered that diversity of citizenship does not exist here, and that jurisdiction is not proper in the federal court.

   Paul should immediately bring the matter to his supervising attorney's attention. In turn, the attorney should bring the matter to the federal court's attention. To not do so would be an ethical violation. The case will be dismissed for lack of jurisdiction. However, Paul's supervising attorney should be able to refile the case in state court.

CHAPTER 7

SUBSTANTIVE LAW I

CHAPTER OBJECTIVES

After completing this chapter, you should be able to:

- Name the kinds of torts and the purpose of tort law.
- Know the difference between a tort and a crime.
- Understand when the doctrine of strict liability is applied.
- List the elements of a valid contract.
- List the defenses to breach-of-contract actions.
- Discuss the law governing contracts for the sale of goods.
- Explain the difference between real property and personal property.
- Describe how one acquires, holds, and transfers ownership rights in property and the procedures involved in the sale of real estate.
- Understand the devices used in estate planning and the laws and procedures applicable when property is transferred on a person's death.

Chapter Outline

I. INTRODUCTION

II. TORTS

A. Intentional Torts
   1. In tort law, intent means that the actor intended the consequences of her act or knew with substantial certainty that certain consequences would result from the act.
   2. The law generally assumes that individuals intend the normal consequences of their actions.
   3. An assault is an intentional, unexcused act that causes another to reasonably fear immediate harmful or offensive contact.
   4. A battery is the completion of the fear-inducing act or any actual contact with another that is offensive to the other person.
   5. Defamation is the making of a false statement communicated to a third party that harms another's good reputation. Oral defamation constitutes the tort of slander; breaching it in writing or in any permanent form constitutes the tort of libel.
   6. Other examples of intentional torts include the following:
      a. Fraud.
      b. Intentional infliction of emotional distress.
      c. False imprisonment.
      d. Invasion of privacy.
      e. Trespass to land.

B. Negligence
   1. The Elements of Negligence
      a. The tort of negligence occurs when someone breaches a duty of care and that breach causes another person to suffer injury or harm.
      b. The Duty of Care and Its Breach
         1) The duty of care is measured generally under a reasonable person standard.
      c. The Injury Requirement
         1) If no injury or harm results from a given negligent action, there is nothing to compensate—and thus no tort.

☞ STUDY TIP

Mnemonic Devices and the Elements of Negligence

One method that students commonly employ to remember legal principles is the use of mnemonic devises. Mnemonic devices are aids to memory. A mnemonic devise may be a word, a formula, or a rhyme. As an aid to remembering the elements of a cause of action in negligence, for example, you might use "ABCD":

A A duty of care.

B Breach of the duty of care.

C Causation (the breach must cause an injury).

D Damage (injury or harm).

d. Causation
    1) To be compensated for an injury in a negligence action, the plaintiff must show that the injury was caused by the defendant's breach of duty of care.
    2) To decide whether the requirement for causation has been met, two questions must be addressed: (1) is there causation in fact, and (2) was the act the proximate cause of the injury?

2. Defenses to Negligence
    a. Defenses to negligence include:
        1) Assumption of the risk.
        2) Contributory negligence.
        3) Comparative negligence.
        4) The *last clear chance* doctrine.

C. Strict Liability
    1. Strict liability in tort law is liability imposed without regard to fault.
    2. Under the doctrine of strict liability, a party may be held liable even though he exercised reasonable care and was not at fault for the harm caused.
    3. Examples of strict liability torts include:
        a. Liability for dangerous animals.
        b. Product liability.

D. Tort Law and the Paralegal
    1. Many paralegals become extensively involved in tasks relating to tort lawsuits.
    2. Tasks typically performed in the tort law area are similar to those performed by litigation paralegals (described in Chapters 2, 10, and 11).

III. CONTRACTS

A. Contract Requirements
    1. Agreement
        a. A contract is an exchange of promises, either oral or in writing, that can be enforced in court.
        b. Further, a contract is an agreement formed by two or more parties who promise to perform or refrain from performing some act now or in the future.
        c. A contractual offer is a promise to do something in return for something of value.
        d. Acceptance occurs when the offeree indicates, by words or actions, that she agrees to the terms of the offer. Upon acceptance, a contract is formed.
    2. Consideration
        a. Consideration is normally defined as "something of value"—which may be money or the performance of certain actions that are not otherwise required.
    3. Contractual Capacity
        a. The third element required for the formation of a valid contract is contractual capacity, which exists when a person has the mental competence to enter into a contract.
    4. Legality
        a. A contract to do something that is prohibited by federal or state law is illegal and, as such, void at the outset (that is, no contract exists).

B. Defenses to Contract Enforceability
    1. A defense is a legally acceptable reason, raised by the defendant, as to why the court should not grant what the plaintiff is seeking.
    2. Types of defenses include the Statute of Frauds, genuine assent, unconscionability, or impossibility of performance.
    3. Each state has a Statute of Frauds.
    4. The Statute of Frauds requires certain types of contracts to be in writing in order to be enforceable.
    5. A party may also claim that a contract should not be enforced because he or she did not genuinely assent to its terms.
    6. Some contracts will not be enforced by the courts because they are contrary to public policy.
    7. An unconscionable contract will not be enforced.

8. An unconscionable contract is one so grossly one sided or unfair that it "shocks the conscience" of the court.
9. A contract that is objectively impossible to perform will not be enforced.
10. An example of a contract impossible to perform is one in which the subject matter is destroyed.

C. Sales Contracts and Warranties
   1. The Scope of Article 2
      a. Article 2 of the Uniform Commercial Code (UCC) deals with the sale of goods.
      b. The rules under Article 2 may vary depending on whether the buyer or seller is a merchant.
      c. A contract for the sale of goods is also subject to the common law requirements of agreement, consideration, contractual capacity, and legality.
      d. When the UCC speaks, its principles apply; when the UCC is silent on a particular matter, then the common law of contracts applies.
   2. Warranties under the UCC
      a. The UCC provides that the seller automatically warrants to a buyer that the seller has good title to the goods being sold.
      b. If the goods turn out to be stolen, for example, the seller will be liable to the buyer for the value of the goods.
      c. An express warranty is a promise made by a seller concerning the nature of the goods being sold.
      d. An express warranty can be either oral or written.
      e. Implied warranties also arise in sales transactions.
      f. The UCC provides for several types of implied warranties, such as:
         1) *Implied warranty of merchantability*—That is, the goods are "reasonably fit for the ordinary purposes for which such goods are used."
         2) *Implied warranty of fitness for a particular purpose*—When a buyer relies on the seller's skill or judgment in selecting suitable goods, they must be fit for the particular purpose for which they are sold.

D. Remedies for Breach of Contract
   1. A breach of contract is where one party fails to do what was promised in the contract.
   2. If one party breaches the contract, the other party can sue in court to obtain a remedy for the breach.
   3. Equitable remedies are normally granted only when a remedy at law is inadequate. These are:
      a. *Specific Performance*—The court orders the breaching party to perform the promised contractual obligation.
      b. *Rescission*—The contract is canceled, and the parties are returned to the positions they occupied prior to the transaction.
      c. *Restitution*—When a contract is rescinded or canceled, both parties return the goods, property, or money previously exchanged under the contract.
      d. *Reformation*—The court revises the contract to reflect the true intention of the parties.
   4. The buyer's remedies include:
      a. The right to reject nonconforming goods or improperly delivered goods.
      b. The right to buy the goods elsewhere and recover from the seller the extra cost of obtaining the substitute goods.
      c. The right to recover damages.
      d. In certain circumstances, the right to obtain specific performance of the sales contract.

E. Contract Law and the Paralegal
   1. As a legal professional, it is vital that the paralegal have some knowledge of contract law, because legal work frequently involves contracts.
   2. Paralegals also have a personal interest in contract law, because their individual employment agreements may be subject to that law.

3. Types of tasks a paralegal might perform in contract law include:
    a. Interviewing persons to obtain information about a contract.
    b. Reviewing contracts to make sure they contain the elements for a valid contract.
    c. Assisting in litigating a breach-of-contract claim.

IV. REAL PROPERTY

A. Ownership Rights in Property
  1. Fee Simple
     a. The most complete form of property ownership is the fee simple.
     b. An owner in fee simple is entitled to use, possess, or dispose of the real or personal property however he chooses during his lifetime.
     c. Upon the fee simple owner's death, the interests in the property descend to the owner's heirs.
  2. Concurrent Ownership
     a. One can also own property concurrently with others.
     b. Examples of this type of ownership include:
        1) *Joint Tenancy*—Two or more persons own undivided interests in property, and upon death, the deceased tenant's interest passes to the surviving joint tenant(s).
        2) *Tenancy in Common*—Two or more persons own undivided interests in the property, and upon death, the deceased tenant's interest passes to her heirs.
        3) *Tenancy by the entirety*—This co-ownership must be between husbands and wives and cannot be transferred within their lifetimes.
        4) *Community property*—In a few states, each spouse owns an undivided one-half interest in all property acquired during the marriage.
  3. Life Estates
     a. A life estate is held for the duration of the life of the holder, or in some situations, the life of someone other than the holder.
  4. Future Interests
     a. A future interest exists when an owner of real property conveys the property conditionally for a limited period of time.
     b. The original owner still retains an interest in the land, which may be transferred or passed to the owner's heirs on his death.

B. The Transfer and Sale of Real Property
  1. Contract Formation—Offer and Acceptance
     a. The common law contractual requirements of agreement, consideration, contractual capacity, and legality apply to real-estate contracts.
     b. The buyer normally tenders a sum of money, called earnest money, along with the offer.
     c. Once an offer is submitted, sellers have three options: they can accept the offer, reject it, or modify its terms.
  2. The Role of the Escrow Agent
     a. The sale of real property normally involves three parties: the buyer, the seller, and the escrow agent.
     b. The escrow agent holds the deed until the buyer pays the seller for the property at the closing.
     c. The escrow agent also holds any money paid by the buyer, including the earnest money, until the sale is completed.
  3. Financing
     a. Commonly, buyers of real property finance the purchase by obtaining a mortgage loan from a bank, a mortgage company, or some other party.
  4. Inspection of the Premises
     a. Buyers may have the premises inspected to see if there are major electrical or plumbing problems, structural defects, termite or insect infestation, or other problems.

5. Title Examination and Insurance
   a. A title examination involves carefully checking the records at the county recording office to make sure that the seller is actually the owner of the property described in the purchase offer and to determine whether claims on the property exist that were not disclosed by the seller.
   b. The history of past ownership and transfers of property are normally already summarized in a document called an abstract.
   c. Title examinations are not foolproof, and buyers of real property generally purchase title insurance to protect their interests in the event that some defect in the title was not discovered during the examination.
6. The Closing
   a. The closing is coordinated by the escrow agent.
   b. At the closing, the buyer signs the mortgage note, title insurance is obtained, the seller receives the proceeds of the sale, and the deed to the property is delivered to the buyer.
   c. A deed is the instrument of conveyance of real property.
   d. Closing costs consist of fees for services, including those performed by the lender, escrow agent, and title company.

C. Leases
1. Ownership rights in property can also be transferred by leasing.
2. Leasing is temporarily renting property to another.

D. Property Law and the Paralegal
1. Paralegals frequently undertake tasks requiring some understanding of real-property law.
2. Types of tasks a paralegal might perform include:
   a. Interviewing and assisting clients.
   b. Drafting documents necessary to the sale of property.
   c. Conducting title examinations.
   d. Handling (in some states) or assisting at closing.

V. WILLS, TRUSTS, AND ESTATES

A. Wills
1. Laws Governing Wills
   a. To probate a will means to establish its validity and carry the administration of the estate through a process supervised by a probate court.
2. Requirements for a Valid Will
   a. Most states uphold the following basic requirements for executing a will:
      1) A testator must have testamentary capacity.
      2) Generally, a will must be in writing.
      3) A will must be signed by the testator, generally at the end of the document.
      4) A will must be witnessed.
      5) In some states, a will must be published.
3. The Probate Process
   a. For small estates, most state statutes provide for the distribution of assets without a formal probate proceeding.
   b. A majority of states also provide for family settlement agreements.
   c. For larger estates, formal probate proceedings are normally undertaken, and the probate court supervises every aspect of the settlement of the decedent's estate.

B. Trusts
1. Living Trusts
   a. A living trust is a trust executed by a grantor during her lifetime.
   b. Living trusts may be revocable or irrevocable.
   c. In an irrevocable living trust, the grantor permanently gives up control over the property; in a revocable living trust, the grantor retains control over the trust property during his lifetime.
2. Testamentary Trusts
   a. A testamentary trust is a trust created by a will to come into existence on the settlor's death.
   b. If a will establishes that the testamentary trust is invalid, then the trust will also be invalid.

3. Special Types of Trusts
   a. A trust designed for the benefit of a segment of the public or the public in general is a charitable trust.
   b. In a spendthrift trust, the beneficiary is permitted to draw only a certain portion of the total amount to which she is entitled at any one time.
   c. A *Totten,* or tentative, trust is a special type of trust created when one person deposits money in his own name as a trustee for another.

C. Other Estate-Planning Devices
   1. Because the probate process can be long and involved, some persons arrange to have property transferred in ways other than by will and outside the probate process.

D. Estate Administration
   1. Estate administration is the process of collecting a decedent's assets, settling her debts, and distributing all remaining assets.
   2. Once the assets have been distributed, an accounting is rendered to the court, the estate is closed, and the personal representative is relieved of any further responsibility or liability for the estate.

E. Wills, Trusts, and Estates and the Paralegal
   1. Paralegals are often involved in legal work relating to wills, trusts, other estate-planning devices, and estate administration.
   2. Types of tasks a paralegal might perform include:
      a. Interviewing clients.
      b. Drafting a will for a client.
      c. Creating the necessary documents to establish a trust.
      d. Monitoring a trust fund's investments.
      e. Locating beneficiaries named in a will or the next of kin of a person who died intestate.
      f. Filing a will with the probate court.
      g. Researching laws governing estate and inheritance taxes.
      h. Researching state laws governing wills and probate procedures.

QUESTIONS FOR REVIEW

TRUE-FALSE QUESTIONS

____ 1. A promise is a declaration that something either will or will not happen in the future.

____ 2. A contract that will be enforced by a court is referred to as a valid contract.

____ 3. The offeror is the person to whom the offer is made and the offeree is the person making the offer.

____ 4. Acceptance of an offer can occur at any time.

____ 5. Consideration for a contract is always money.

____ 6. Anyone, regardless of age or mental capacity, can form a valid contract.

____ 7. Defamation is a legally acceptable reason, raised by a defendant in a lawsuit, why the court should not grant what the plaintiff is seeking.

____ 8. A contract that does not meet the Statute of Frauds is generally not enforceable.

____ 9. Defenses to a breach of contract include fraud, unconscionability, and impossibility of performance.

____ 10. The Uniform Commercial Code deals with the sale of real estate or services.

____ 11. A tort action is a civil action; a criminal action is prosecuted by a government entity.

____ 12. Punitive damages are available in a criminal action.

____ 13. Oral defamation is slander; written or permanent defamation is libel.

____ 14. Conveyance of real property is accomplished by a deed.

____ 15. One who dies after having made a valid will is said to have died testate.

____ 16. An executor is a personal representative appointed by the court for a decedent who dies without a will.

____ 17. It is not necessary for most wills to be witnessed.

Fill-in Questions

A person who takes advantage of another in inducing the individual to enter into a contract, shocking the conscience of the court, is said to have created a(n) ________________________ (fraudulent/unconscionable) contract.

Under the UCC, when sellers promise that they have good title to the goods, they provide a(n) ________________ (warranty of title/express warranty). Additionally, when sellers promise that the goods are reasonably fit for the ordinary purpose for which such goods are used, they provide a ______________ (warranty of merchantability/warranty of fitness for a particular purpose).

Legal liability of sellers to buyers for injuries resulting from defects in the goods is known as ______________ (strict liability/product liability).

If the actor neither intends to bring about the consequences of his act nor believes that the consequences will occur, the actor may have been ______________ (negligent/strictly liable). In negligence, the duty of care that one individual has to another is measured under the standard of ______________ (reasonable person/contractual capacity). All negligent actions may not result in compensation as legal causation, or ______________ (strict/proximate) cause, must exist.

Liability for injury without regard to intent or reasonableness is referred to as ______________ (product/strict) liability.

Co-ownership of real estate permitting ownership rights to pass, upon death, to the heirs is referred to as ________________ (tenancy in common/joint tenancy). Contrarily, the passing of the decedent's interest to the surviving tenant is referred to as ________________ (tenancy in common/joint tenancy).

Multiple-choice Questions

____ 1. Which of the following is false regarding a contract:
   A. It is an exchange of promises
   B. It can be enforced in court
   C. Two or more parties promise to perform or refrain from performing some act now or in the future
   D. All of the above

____ 2. Failure to perform that which was promised in the contract is referred to as a(n):
   A. Battery
   B. Breach
   C. Deed
   D. Acceptance

____ 3. The requirements for a valid contract include:
   A. Agreement
   B. Consideration
   C. Contractual capacity
   D. All of the above

____ 4. The agreement requirement of a contract refers to:
   A. When the offeree indicates that she agrees to the terms of the offer
   B. One party's offer to form a contract
   C. A promise to do something in return for something of value
   D. One party's offer to form a contract and the other party's acceptance of that offer

____ 5. The offer requirement of a contract refers to:
A. When the offeree indicates that he agrees to the terms of the offer
B. One party's offer to form a contract
C. A promise to do something in return for something of value
D. One party's offer to form a contract and the other party's acceptance of that offer

____ 6. The acceptance requirement of a contract refers to:
A. When the offeree indicates that she agrees to the terms of the offer
B. One party's offer to form a contract
C. A promise to do something in return for something of value
D. One party's offer to form a contract and the other party's acceptance of that offer

____ 7. A minor who changes his mind regarding a contract may cancel the contract or:
A. Disaffirm
B. Void
C. Breach
D. Deed

____ 8. Statute of Frauds specifies that in order for certain types of contracts to be enforceable, they must be:
A. In writing
B. Made by individuals who have contractual capacity
C. By agreement
D. Voidable

____ 9. Returning goods, property, or money previously conveyed is referred to as:
A. Restitution
B. Reformation
C. Strict liability
D. Intentional tort

____ 10. Revising a contract to reflect the true intention of the parties is referred to as:
A. Restitution
B. Reformation
C. Strict liability
D. Intentional tort

____ 11. An intentional tort refers to the:
A. Actor's intent to harm
B. Actor's intent to commit the act
C. Reprehensible nature of the act against society
D. Wrongdoer's liability

____ 12. An intentional, unexcused act that causes another to reasonably fear immediate harmful or offensive contact is a(n):
A. Assault
B. Battery
C. Defamation
D. Invasion of privacy

____ 13. An offensive contact with another is a(n):
A. Assault
B. Battery
C. Defamation
D. Invasion of privacy

____ 14. Harming another's good reputation by making false statements is:
A. Assault
B. Battery
C. Defamation
D. Invasion of privacy

____ 15. The buyer of real property finances the purchase by obtaining a loan called a(n):
A. Lease
B. Fee simple
C. Mortgage
D. Deed

____ 16. A contractual agreement under which a property owner agrees to rent property to another for a specified period of time is referred to as a(n):
A. Lease
B. Mortgage
C. Deed
D. Warranty

____ 17. In an irrevocable trust:
A. The grantor retains control over the trust property during his or her lifetime
B. The grantor permanently gives up control over the property
C. The management of one's investments is given to an outside person over whom the beneficiary has no control
D. None of the above

Practice Questions

1. Using the information on intentional torts and negligence presented in this chapter, identify the following torts:
   A. Harry is picking up his child from the day care center. His son is waiting on the sidewalk, and Harry accidentally leaves his car out of gear when he walks around the front of the car to open the door for his son. While Harry is out of the car, it begins to roll backward as a result of a slight incline and hits the bumper of the car parked behind him.
   B. Tom is assisting the school soccer coach in coaching his son's team. The team loses the first game, and the school coach yells at Tom and makes his hands into two fists, approaching Tom as he yells.
   C. Assume the facts in "b" above, except that the coach actually hits Tom.
2. Using the material on ownership rights in property presented in this chapter, identify the types of ownership rights described in the following statements.
   A. Sally and Dick, husband and wife, jointly own a summer home. They have rights of survivorship.
   B. Sally and Dick, good friends, jointly own a summer home. On each of their deaths, the interest is conveyed in their wills.
   C. Sally owns her house, and she can do anything with it.

Questions for Critical Analysis

1. Litigation of medical malpractice actions, a form of negligence, has resulted in huge jury awards to injured plaintiffs. Do you think there should be some monitoring of the amounts available to plaintiffs?
2. Ownership in fee simple does not provide the owner with absolute rights. That is, zoning laws may prohibit certain usages and, of course, the government has the power of eminent domain. Do you think these limitations are too restrictive, or is there a societal purpose served by these limitations?

Ethical Questions

1. Lynn Rodriguez is a litigation paralegal. Her law firm is representing the plaintiff in a personal-injury lawsuit. Lynn's supervising attorney has requested that she send a settlement letter to the defendant's attorney by a certain date. However, Lynn fails to send the letter. Lynn's supervising attorney is under the impression that Lynn has sent the letter. Subsequently, the client is harmed as a result and brings suit against the attorney. Is the attorney liable? Is Lynn?
2. Brenda Brown is a real-estate paralegal working on a closing. In preparing the deed, Brenda accidentally inserts the word "North" in place of "South" throughout the property description. Brenda fails to proofread the deed, and the mistake was not noticed until sometime after the closing. As a result, much time and effort was required to correct the mistake. What effect may Brenda's mistake have on her attorney?

TECHNOLOGY AND TODAY'S PARALEGAL

Your text notes several sites on the Internet where you can find sources for contract forms. Log onto the Internet, and type the address for the search engine "HotBot": *http://www.hotbot.com.* Now perform a search for legal forms. Notice the variety of sites that your search retrieves and the variety of forms that are available. These are merely the results of one search with one search engine.

A word of caution, however. Anyone can put anything on the Internet. Before you adopt one of the forms you find online, make sure the source is reliable, and revise the form to fit your client's needs.

ANSWERS

True-False Questions

1. T
2. T
3. F
4. F
5. F
6. F
7. F
8. T
9. T
10. F
11. T
12. F
13. T
14. T
15. T
16. F
17. F

Fill-in Questions

unconscionable

warranty of title; warranty of merchantability

product liability

negligent; reasonable person; proximate

strict

tenancy in common; joint tenancy

Multiple-Choice Questions

1. D
2. B
3. D
4. D
5. C
6. A
7. A
8. A
9. A
10. B
11. B
12. A
13. B
14. C
15. C
16. A
17. B

Practice Questions

1. A. negligence
   B. assault
   C. battery
2. A. joint tenancy
   B. tenancy in common
   C. fee simple

Questions for Critical Analysis

1. Concern for the cost of health care resulting from possible malpractice actions has affected the health care costs. However, a necessary element of a plaintiff's case is to prove damages; an award must be based on the facts.
2. Zoning restrictions are an attempt to keep certain areas for certain purposes. That is, if an area is residential, residents would most likely not favor a factory next door with added congestion, noise, and other environmental factors not conducive to family living. Eminent domain is the government's right to property for public use; the government must justify that the public at large will benefit by the taking of private property.

Ethical Questions

1. The attorney, as the person responsible for the paralegal's work, will bear the legal consequences of the paralegal's negligent action. It will not matter that the attorney delegated the task to Lynn or that the attorney believed Lynn had sent the letter. Although the attorney is ultimately liable to the client, it is possible that the attorney could bring a negligence suit against Lynn to recover any damages paid to the client.
2. When handling paperwork relating to real-estate transactions, the paralegal must make absolutely sure that the documents are accurate. Brenda failed to proofread the deed, resulting in harm to the client. She has exposed her attorney to a possible malpractice action by the client for breach of the standard of care.

CHAPTER 8

SUBSTANTIVE LAW II

CHAPTER OBJECTIVES

After completing this chapter, you should be able to:

- Discuss what agency relationships are and why they are established.
- Describe how agency law affects business operations and relationships.
- Name the most common forms of business organizations
- Identify how these business organizations are created and operated.
- Explain how the profits, losses, risks, and liabilities are distributed in different types of business organizations.
- Identify what constitutes intellectual property and the basic forms it takes.

Chapter Outline

I. INTRODUCTION

II. AGENCY LAW

- A. Fiduciary Duties
    1. An agency relationship is a fiduciary relationship.
    2. A fiduciary relationship is one that involves trust and gives rise to certain duties.
    3. The principal has a duty to the agent to:
        - a. Cooperate.
        - b. Provide safe working conditions.
        - c. Reimburse for work performed and expenses incurred.
    4. The agent has a duty to the principal to:
        - a. Perform work competently.
        - b. Obey and be loyal.
        - c. Notify of knowledge or events significant to the agency.
        - d. Render an accounting of how the principal's funds were used.
- B. Agency Relationships and Third Parties
    1. The principal is bound by an agent's authorized actions and contracts with third parties.
    2. Under the doctrine of *respondeat superior,* the principal may be liable for the agent's torts committed within the scope of the agency.
- C. Agency Law and the Paralegal
    1. Knowledge of agency law is important for paralegals, because they will be directly involved in an agency relationship with their attorney.
    2. Paralegals also deal with agents in their work.

III. FORMS OF BUSINESS ORGANIZATION

- A. Sole Proprietorships
    1. Formation of a Sole Proprietorship
        - a. A sole proprietorship is easier and less costly to start than any other kind of business.
        - b. In a sole proprietorship, there are no partners.
        - c. This is the simplest form of business to create.

☞ STUDY TIP

Agents Are Everywhere

No area of the law is more pervasive than the law of agency. The law of agency affects virtually everyone everyday. Agency can involve any power conferred by one person on another to do something for the first. In other words, an agency exists when one person acts for another.

You may find it helpful to remember how common agency relationships are. Agency law applies in the areas of travel and insurance, for instance. Other agencies are banks involved in the check collection process; corporate shareholders; and gas stations, car dealers, and other franchisors and franchisees.

2. Advantages of Sole Proprietorships
   a. The sole proprietor is entitled to all the profits made by the firm.
   b. The sole proprietor is free to make any decision she wishes concerning the business.
   c. A sole proprietor is allowed to establish tax-exempt retirement accounts designed for self-employed persons.
3. Disadvantages of Sole Proprietorships
   a. The sole proprietor, as the firm's sole owner, is personally liable for any losses, debts, and obligations incurred by the business enterprise.
   b. If the sole proprietor wishes to expand the business, it may be difficult to obtain capital.
4. Taxation and Sole Proprietorships
   a. A sole proprietor must pay income taxes on business profits, but those profits are reported on the sole proprietor's personal tax return and are taxed as personal income.
5. Termination of the Sole Proprietorship
   a. In a sole proprietorship, the owner is the business. When the owner dies, so does the business.
   b. If the business is transferred or sold to someone else, a new proprietorship is created.

B. Partnerships
1. Partnership Formation
   a. A partnership is created when two or more persons, orally or in writing, agree to undertake business jointly for a profit.
2. Rights and Duties of Partners
   a. Each partner is the agent of the other partners and assumes certain rights and fiduciary duties.
   b. A partnership is based on a voluntary contract between two or more competent persons who agree to place some or all of their money or other assets, labor, and skill in a business, with the understanding that the profits and losses will be proportionately shared.
   c. The rights of the partners are often written into a partnership agreement.
3. Liability of Partners
   a. Traditionally, a partnership cannot be sued or initiate a lawsuit in its own name.
   b. In some states, only the individual partners—not the partnership—can be sued.
   c. Under the theory of **joint liability,** partners may be held personally liable not only for their own actions and those of the partnership as an entity but also for the actions of other partners.
   d. Partners may also be subject to **joint and several liability,** which allows a plaintiff to sue and seek judgment against any one—or all—of the jointly liable defendants.
4. Taxation of Partnerships
   a. The partnership itself does not pay federal income taxes.
   b. Partners declare their shares of the partnership's profits on their personal income tax returns and pay taxes accordingly.
5. Partnership Termination
   a. The partnership agreement may specify the duration of the partnership by indicating that the partnership will end on a certain date or on the occurrence of a certain event.
   b. If the agreement does not specify the duration of the partnership, the partners are free to withdraw at any time without incurring liability to the remaining partners.
   c. Partnership termination is a two-step process. Dissolution is the first step, and the second step is the winding up of partnership affairs.
6. Limited Partnerships
   a. The general partners manage the business operations and assume personal responsibility for the firm's obligations.
   b. The limited partners are, for the most part, investors only.
   c. Limited partners do not participate in management.
   d. Limited partners' liability for business obligations is limited to the amount of their investment in the enterprise.

C. Corporations
   1. A corporation is a separate legal entity, formed with the state's permission through a state-issued charter.
   2. The majority of state statutes are guided by the Revised Model Business Corporation Act (RMBCA).
   3. Corporate Formation
      a. The first step in forming a corporation consists of preliminary organizational and promotional undertakings.
      b. Promoters take the preliminary steps in organizing a corporation by making contracts to purchase corporate shares (stock) on behalf of the future corporation.
      c. A prospectus describes the corporation and its operations so that those who wish to purchase stock and invest in the corporation have the basis for making an informed decision.
      d. The second step in forming a corporation is the process of incorporation.
      e. Articles of incorporation include basic information about the corporation and serve as a primary source of authority for its future organization and business functions.
      f. The articles are incorporation are filed with the appropriate state office and become public record.
      g. After the articles of incorporation have been filed, the secretary of state issues a certificate of incorporation representing the state's authorization for the corporation to conduct business.
   4. Classifications of Corporations
      a. A corporation is classified depending on its purpose, ownership characteristics, and location.
      b. A private corporation is one that is privately owned.
      c. A public corporation is formed by the government for a political or governmental purpose.
      d. A public corporation is not the same as a publicly held corporation.
      e. Corporations may be classified as "for profit" or "not-for-profit" (nonprofit).
      f. Corporations held by a small group of shareholders are called close, or closely held, corporations. Close corporations cannot sell their shares on public securities markets and usually place restrictions on the transfer of corporate shares.
      g. Lawyers, physicians, accountants, architects, engineers, and other professionals frequently incorporate as professional corporations.
   5. Directors and Officers
      a. The articles of incorporation name the initial board of directors, which is appointed by the incorporators. Thereafter, the board of directors is elected by a majority vote of the shareholders.
      b. The directors' rights include the right to participate in board meetings and the right to inspect the corporate books and records.
      c. The directors' responsibilities include declaring and paying dividends, appointing and removing officers, and making significant policy decisions.
      d. The board of directors appoints the following corporate officers: the president, vice president, secretary, treasurer, chief financial officer, and chief executive officer.
      e. Corporate officers are employees and agents of the corporation.
   6. Shareholders
      a. Any person who purchases a share in the corporation becomes an owner of the corporation.
      b. Shareholders do not manage the daily affairs of the corporation, nor are they liable for corporate debts or other obligations beyond the amount of their investments.
   7. Corporate Taxation
      a. A corporation pays income taxes on corporate profits.
      b. When the profits are distributed to the shareholders as dividends, the shareholders pay personal income taxes on the income they receive.
      c. S corporation shareholders declare their proportionate shares of the corporation's net income on their personal tax returns and pay taxes on that income accordingly.

8. Corporate Merger and Consolidation
   a. A merger is a process through which one corporation acquires all the assets and liabilities of another corporation.
   b. In a consolidation, both existing corporate entities disappear, and a completely new corporation is formed.
   c. Generally, in order to accomplish a merger or a consolidation, the following requirements must be met:
      1) The board of directors and shareholders of each corporation involved must approve the merger or consolidation.
      2) Once the merger or consolidation is approved, articles of merger or articles of consolidation must be filed with the state, usually with the secretary of state.
      3) When state formalities have been satisfied, the state issues a certificate of merger to the surviving corporation or a certificate of consolidation to the newly consolidated corporation.
   d. An acquisition occurs when one corporation acquires or purchases all or almost all of the assets of another company.
9. Corporate Termination
   a. Corporate termination involves two steps. First, the dissolution extinguishes the legal existence of the corporation. Second, the liquidation involves the winding up of the corporation's business affairs.

D. Limited Liability Companies and Partnerships
1. Limited Liability Companies
   a. A limited liability company (LLC) is a hybrid form of business enterprise that combines the pass-through tax benefits of S corporations and partnerships with limited liability of limited partners and corporate shareholders.

☞ STUDY TIP

The Law of Corporations

Sources for the law concerning corporations include state and federal statutes and common law. For instance, each state has its own set of statutes relating to corporations. Many of these laws are based on the Revised Model Business Corporation Act (RMBCA). Federal law relating to corporate issues includes statutes governing the issue and sale of stock. Relevant common law includes cases setting out broad principles for interpreting these laws.

The simplest way of viewing a corporation is to think of it as an artificial entity independent of its owners (shareholders). It can do business in its own name just as a "real" person can.

Another way to view a corporation is as a contract. The contract may be seen as existing among the shareholders, or between the shareholders and the corporation, or between the corporation and the state.

   b. An LLC has several advantages:
      1) It does not pay taxes as an entity.
      2) The liability of its members is limited to the amount of their investments.
      3) LLC members are allowed to participate fully in management activities.
      4) Corporations and partnerships, as well as foreign investors, can be LLC members.
      5) There is no limit on the number of members of the LLC.
      6) LLC members can decide themselves how to operate various aspects of the business through a simple operating agreement.
   c. The major disadvantage has been the lack of uniformity among state statutes with respect to LLCs.
2. Limited Liability Partnerships
   a. The difference between a limited liability partnership (LLP) and an LLC is that the LLP is designed more for professionals who normally do business as partners in a partnership.
   b. The major advantage of an LLP is that it allows a partnership to continue as a pass-through entity for tax purposes but limits the personal liability of the partners for partnership tort liability.
   c. Although LLP statutes vary from state to state, generally state statutes limit in some way the liability of partners.
3. Family Limited Liability Partnerships
   a. A family limited liability partnership (FLLP) is an LLP in which the majority of the partners are related to one another.
4. Limited Liability Limited Partnerships
   a. A limited liability limited partnership (LLLP) is a type of limited partnership, except that the liability of a general partner in an LLLP is the same as the liability of a limited partner.

E. Business Organizations and the Paralegals
1. Paralegals must understand business organizations, because they often work on behalf of clients who run their businesses as sole proprietors, partnerships, or corporations.
2. The following list is only a sample of the types of work paralegals may perform in this area of the law:
   a. Researching state laws governing partnerships, corporations, and limited liability organizations.
   b. Assisting in litigation relating to a corporate employer or client.
   c. Drafting documents such as partnership agreements; a corporate prospectus; stock-option agreements; articles of merger or consolidation; or applications for licenses, certificates, or permits.
   d. Maintaining corporate stock-transfer records on the sale or purchase of stocks.
   e. Reserving corporate names for an incorporator.
   f. Scheduling directors' and shareholders' meetings.
   g. Maintaining corporate records, including minutes of directors' and shareholders' meetings.
   h. Assisting in the dissolution of a partnership or corporation.

IV. INTELLECTUAL PROPERTY

A. Forms of Intellectual Property
1. A patent is a grant from the federal government that allows an inventor to have the exclusive right to make, use, and sell her invention for a period of up to twenty years following the date of filing the application for a patent.

2. A trademark is a distinctive mark or motto that a manufacturer stamps, prints, or otherwise affixes to the goods it produces so that those goods can be distinguished from the goods of other manufacturers and merchants.
3. A copyright gives the creator of a literary or artistic production the right to the exclusive use of that work for a specified period of time.
4. Some business processes and information that are not patented, copyrighted, or trademarked are nevertheless protected under the law as trade secrets.

B. Intellectual Property and the Paralegal
1. An increasing number of paralegals are working in the corporate environment with patents, trademarks, or copyrights.
2. Tasks a paralegal might perform in the area of intellectual-property law are:
   a. Interviewing a client to obtain information regarding intellectual property to be registered.
   b. Researching applications for patents and trademarks.
   c. Drafting application documents and contracts.
   d. Reviewing marketing data and sales statements.
   e. Assisting in infringement litigation.

QUESTIONS FOR REVIEW

TRUE-FALSE QUESTIONS

____ 1. An agency relationship includes an agent and a principal.

____ 2. The relationship between a principal and an independent contractor may not involve an agency relationship.

____ 3. In an agency relationship, only the agent has duties.

____ 4. The agent has the duty to act solely for the benefit of the principal.

____ 5. An agent can act on behalf of a principal but cannot bind a principal in a contract with a third party.

____ 6. The product of one's mind includes a form of intangible personal property referred to as intellectual property.

____ 7. An agency relationship can only be terminated through mutual agreement.

____ 8. A Keogh plan is a retirement program designed for self-employed persons by which such persons can shelter a certain percentage of their income from taxation.

____ 9. In their relationship to one another, partners are bound by the fiduciary ties that bind an agent and principal under agency law.

____ 10. Partners may have joint liability or joint and individual liability.

____ 11. A partnership pays federal income taxes.

____ 12. The formal disbanding of a partnership is referred to as consolidation.

____ 13. General partners are simply investors; limited partners manage the business.

____ 14. The process of incorporation is initiated by the articles of incorporation.

Fill-in Questions

If a principal or agent dies or becomes mentally incompetent, generally, the agency ____________________ (continues/is terminated). Partnership termination is a two-set process; the first step is ____________________ (dissolution/winding up), and the second is ____________________ (dissolution/winding up).

A corporation can acquire all assets and liabilities of another corporation through a ____________________ (merger/consolidation). If both existing corporate entities disappear and a new corporation is formed, it is called a ____________________ (merger/consolidation).

Funds borrowed from investors through corporate financing are represented by ____________________ (bonds/stocks). Ownership interest is represented by ____________________ (bonds/stocks).

The grant to an inventor to have the exclusive right to make, use, and sell an invention is called a ____________________ (trademark/patent). A distinctive mark placed on goods permitting them to be distinguishable from other manufacturers' goods is called a ____________________ (trademark/copyright). The right giving the creator of a work the exclusive use of that work for a given period of time is called a ____________________ (trademark/copyright).

Multiple-Choice Questions

____ 1. The party who agrees to represent or act for another party is called a(n):
A. Agent
B. Principal
C. Employee
D. Independent contractor

____ 2. The party who is represented in an agency relationship is called a(n):
A. Agent
B. Principal
C. Employee
D. Independent contractor

____ 3. An individual whose physical conduct is controlled by, or subject to the control of, the employer is called a(n):
A. Agent
B. Principal
C. Employee
D. Independent contractor

____ 4. A person who contracts with another to do something for that party but who is not controlled by, nor subject to the control of, the other party in respect to the physical performance is called a(n):
A. Agent
B. Principal
C. Employee
D. Independent contractor

____ 5. Which of the following is false regarding a fiduciary:
A. It refers to a person who has a duty created by his/her undertaking to act primarily for another's benefit in matters connected with the undertaking
B. It refers to a relationship involving trust and confidence or duties
C. All of the above are true

____ 6. The principal's duties to the agent include which of the following:
   A. Duty to cooperate with the agent
   B. Duty to provide safe working conditions for the agent
   C. Duty to reimburse the agent for expenses
   D. All of the above

____ 7. The agent's duties to the principal include which of the following:
   A. Duty to perform tasks competently
   B. Duty to obey and be loyal to the principal
   C. Duty to notify the principal of knowledge or events significant to the agency
   D. All of the above

____ 8. Vicarious liability refers to:
   A. Personal liability
   B. Liability without regard to personal fault
   C. Corporate liability
   D. Limited liability

____ 9. Partners have the right:
   A. To hold an ownership interest in the firm and to receive a share of the profits
   B. To inspect partnership books and records
   C. To an accounting of partnership assets and profits
   D. All of the above

____ 10. The owners of the business are called:
   A. Shares
   B. Shareholders
   C. Directors
   D. Officers

____ 11. The persons elected to direct corporate affairs are called:
   A. Shares
   B. Shareholders
   C. Directors
   D. Officers

____ 12. The person hired to manage the day-to-day operations of a corporation are called:
   A. Shares
   B. Shareholders
   C. Directors
   D. Officers

____ 13. The document that describes the corporation and its operations permitting investors to make an informed decision is called a(n):
   A. Article of incorporation
   B. Prospectus
   C. Certificate of incorporation
   D. Corporate charter

____ 14. The state's authorization for a corporation to conduct business is represented by a(n):
   A. Article of incorporation
   B. Prospectus
   C. Certification of incorporation
   D. Corporate by-laws

____ 15. Payments to shareholders representing their share of corporate profits are called:
   A. Dividends
   B. Bonds
   C. Security
   D. Bona fide occupational qualification

Practice Questions

1. Determine whether each of the business firms described below is a sole proprietorship, a partnership, or a corporation:
   A. Larry and Lars own a business together. Each contributed 50 percent needed to begin conducting business. Each receive 50 percent of the profit or experience 50 percent of any losses. Each makes management decisions.
   B. Attorney Lewis practices law by himself.
   C. The Banana Company is a business that filed articles of incorporation. It provides limited liability for its owners.

Questions for Critical Analysis

1. Assume that you become privy to information about a foreseeable increase in some particular corporation's stock and that you hint to your mother about this information. Have you compromised your position?

Ethical Questions

1. Rupert Howard works for a general practice attorney, Sam Malone. Sam's client, Sue Smith, has asked Sam to liquidate some of the property she inherited from her mother. Sam asks Rupert to find a buyer for Sue's Cadillac convertible. Rupert finds an interested buyer and negotiates a purchase price of $8,000. When the time comes to sign over the car title, Sue balks. She is not happy with the amount of the sale. Is Sue bound by this purchase contract?
2. Dora Menendez works as a paralegal for an attorney representing several large corporations. During a client conference, Dora discovers that the corporation is making plans to build a manufacturing facility on 40 acres of farm land. The corporation has not yet acquired the property but plans to pay up to one million dollars for its acquisition. Dora lives near this farmland and knows the farmer who owns this property. She also knows that the farmer is experiencing financial difficulties. That evening Dora offers the farmer $20,000 for the property, and he accepts. Has Dora acted unethically or improperly?

Technology and Today's Paralegal

To learn more about current developments in intellectual-property law and some of the legal issues it raises, access the following Internet sites:

Copyright Basics from Uncle Sam—*http://lcweb.loc.gov/copyright/circs/circ1.html*

Manual of Patent Examining Procedure (6th Ed., Revision 3, revised 7/98)—*http://www.uspto.gov/web/offices/pac/mpep/index.html*

Trademark Acceptable Identification of Goods and Services—*http://www.uspto.gov/web/offices/tac/doc/gsmanual/manual.html*

Trademark Manual of Examining Procedure (2nd Ed., Revision 1.1, revised 8/97)—*http://www.uspto.gov/web/offices/tac/tmep/index.html*

Trademark Trial and Appeal Board Manual of Procedure (1st Ed., revised 7/95)—*http://ftp.uspto.gov/pub/tbmp*

ANSWERS

True-False Questions

1. T
2. F
3. F
4. F
5. F
6. T
7. F
8. T
9. T
10. T
11. F
12. F
13. F
14. T

Fill-in Questions

is terminated; dissolution; winding up

merger; consolidation

bonds; stocks

patent; trademark; copyright

Multiple-Choice Questions

1. A
2. B
3. C
4. D
5. D
6. D
7. D
8. B
9. D
10. B
11. C
12. D
13. B
14. C
15. A

Practice Questions

1. A. partnership
   B. sole proprietorship
   C. corporation

Questions for Critical Analysis

1. Initially, information received as a result of your employment relationship (through clients, for example) is confidential information and may not be communicated to third parties. Additionally, the communication constitutes insider trading, for which you may be liable. State and federal laws impose penalties for dissemination of such information.

Ethical Questions

1. Sue is most probably bound by this contract. Sam and Sue have an agency relationship. Rupert is Sam's agent and Sue's subagent. Sue has delegated the authority to sell the car to Sam. As a subagent, Rupert was delegated that authority through Sam and can bind Sue by his acts. As an agent and subagent, Rupert should have used utmost care in those relationships. If he negotiated a price on the automobile that was far below its value, he failed to exercise that care.
2. Dora has acted both unethically and improperly. As a paralegal, Dora has an ethical duty to act in the best interest of the client. Clearly, purchasing the property from the farmer so that she can, in turn, sell the property at a profit to the corporation is not in the client's best interest. Dora has also acted improperly in an agency relationship. An agent owes the principal the duty of loyalty. An agent also must notify the principal of knowledge or events significant to the agency. Dora has violated both of these agency duties.

C H A P T E R 9

ADMINISTRATIVE LAW AND GOVERNMENT REGULATION

CHAPTER OBJECTIVES

After completing this chapter, you should be able to:

- Discuss the purpose, types, powers, and essential functions of administrative agencies.
- Identify how administrative agencies establish and enforce rules.
- Understand how the government protects consumers against unfair business practices and harmful products.
- Describe the major laws regulating environmental pollution.
- Understand how the government regulates employer–employee relationships.

CHAPTER OUTLINE

I. INTRODUCTION

II. ADMINISTRATIVE LAW
- A. Types of Administrative Agencies
  - 1. Executive Agencies
    - a. Executive agencies include the cabinet departments of the executive branch and the subagencies within those departments.
    - b. Executive agencies are subject to the authority of the president, who has the power to appoint or remove federal officers.
  - 2. Independent Regulatory Agencies
    - a. Independent regulatory agencies are outside the major executive departments and are more independent of presidential control.
    - b. The officers of independent regulatory agencies serve for fixed terms and cannot be removed without just cause.
- B. Agency Powers
  - 1. Administrative agencies are created by Congress and handle executive, legislative, and judicial functions normally associated with the three branches of government.
  - 2. Enabling Legislation
    - a. When Congress wants to create an administrative agency, it passes enabling legislation.
    - b. Enabling acts are important research resources for paralegals.
    - c. Enabling acts create "rules and regulations for the purpose of carrying out the Act" and grant powers to the agency created to conduct investigations of business practices, among other things.
  - 3. Agency Power and the Constitution
    - a. Agency powers are unusual because they exercise powers that are normally divided among the three branches of government.
    - b. The enabling legislation's grant of power to an agency incorporates the functions associated with the legislature (rulemaking), the executive branch (law enforcement), and court adjudication (formal resolution of disputes).
    - c. Administrative agencies make legislative rules that are legally binding.
    - d. The constitutional authority for Congress' delegating powers to administrative agencies is implied in Article I, Section 8, of the U.S. Constitution.
    - e. Article I, Section 8, is known as the delegation doctrine.
- C. Administrative Process
  - 1. Administrative process is how the functions of rulemaking, enforcement, and adjudication—the three main functions of an administrative agency—are carried out.
  - 2. The Administrative Procedure Act (APA) of 1946 imposes detailed procedural requirements that all federal agencies must follow.
  - 3. Rulemaking
    - a. A major function of an administrative agency is rulemaking.
    - b. When a federal agency decides to create a new rule, it publishes a notice of the proposed rulemaking proceedings in the *Federal Register,* a daily publication of the executive branch.
    - c. A "comment period" follows during which interested parties have the opportunity to express their views on the proposed rule.
    - d. After comments have been received and reviewed, the agency drafts the final rule and publishes it in the *Federal Register.*
    - e. Later, the rule is compiled in the *Code of Federal Regulations.*
  - 4. Enforcement—Investigation
    - a. Administrative agencies conduct investigations of regulated entities to monitor compliance with agency rules.
    - b. Normally a business will comply with an agency request to inspect the facilities or business records, but in some instances, the firm may refuse to comply with the request. In those situations, the agency may resort to using a subpoena or search warrant.

5. Enforcement—Adjudication
   a. Once an investigation is over, the agency may begin an administrative action against an individual or organization.
   b. The majority of such actions are resolved through negotiated settlements without the need for formal adjudication.
   c. If a settlement cannot be reached, the agency may issue a formal complaint against the offending party and adjudicate the dispute, which would be heard by an administrative law judge (ALJ).
   d. The ALJ has the power to administer oaths, take testimony, rule on questions of evidence, and make determinations of fact.
   e. Hearing procedures vary widely from agency to agency.
   f. After the hearing, the ALJ renders a decision, which may be appealed to the commission or board that governs the agency.
6. Usually, a reviewing court defers to an agency's findings of fact, and the scope of judicial review is limited.
7. When reviewing an administrative agency decision, the court considers the following:
   a. Whether the agency exceeded its authority under the enabling legislation.
   b. Whether the agency properly interpreted the applicable agency law.
   c. Whether the agency acted in accordance with the procedural requirements of the applicable agency law.
   d. Whether the agency's actions were arbitrary, capricious, or an abuse of discretion.
   e. Whether any conclusions drawn by the agency were not supported by substantial evidence.

D. State Administrative Agencies
   1. Administrative agencies exist at all levels of American government—federal, state, and local.
   2. Not all States publish agency regulations in a compiled form like the federal government, which makes it difficult to research the regulations for that state.
   3. A state agency is created as a parallel to a federal agency to provide similar services on a more localized basis.
   4. Not all federal agencies have parallel state agencies (for example, The U.S. Postal Service, The Federal Bureau of Investigation, and the Nuclear Regulatory Commission).
   5. If a conflict of law arises between a federal and state agency, the supremacy clause of Article VI of the U.S. Constitution governs.
   6. Under the supremacy clause, the federal agency's decisions or rules take priority over those of the state agency.

☞ STUDY TIP

Remember Judicial Review

Constitutional law is concerned primarily with the exercise of judicial review. The emphasis is on the way that courts in general and the United States Supreme Court in particular interpret provisions of the U.S. Constitution. *State decisis* does not have as much impact in constitutional law as in other areas of the law. In this area, courts are not reluctant to overrule statutes, regulations, precedential case law, or other law.

Constitutional law is an unsettled and constantly changing area. In general, the law in this area is not always certain. Differences in the law are due in part to different judges or justices interpreting the law differently and in part to changing circumstances. Overall, there is reasonableness to the law. That is, some laws or legal decisions may seem irrational, but on the whole and over time there is a common sense to the law.

☞ STUDY TIP

In the News

You can better understand administrative law by paying attention to current affairs and by tracking their effects on the law. For instance, watch for news articles about current business-related problems being dealt with by agencies.

E. Paralegal Practice Before Administrative Agencies
   1. Some agencies permit qualified paralegals to represent and advise clients during administrative proceedings under Section 555 of the Administrative Procedure Act.
   2. A client must ordinarily sign a form authorizing the paralegal to act as the client's agent.
   3. The paralegal must meet agency requirements for nonlawyer representation.

F. Administrative Law and the Paralegal
   1. The functions of administrative agencies permeate almost every area of legal practice.
   2. No matter where you work, you should anticipate that sooner or later you will be interacting with a government agency.

III. CONSUMER LAW

A. Deceptive Advertising
   1. Over the past thirty years, consumers have received more protection against deceptive advertising, which has come more from statutes and government agency rules than from the common law.
   2. At the federal level, the most important agency regulating advertising is the Federal Trade Commission (FTC), enacted by the Federal Trade Commission Act of 1914.
   3. The test for whether an advertisement is deceptive is *whether a reasonable consumer would be deceived by it.*
   4. If the FTC succeeds in proving that an ad was deceptive, it usually issues a cease-and-desist order requiring that the challenged advertising be stopped. It might also impose a sanction known as "counteradvertising," which requires the offending company to supply new advertising to inform the public about the earlier misinformation.

B. Labeling and Packaging Laws
   1. Many federal and state laws now require manufacturers and sellers to provide labels giving consumers accurate information or warnings about products or their possible misuse.
   2. The Fair Packaging and Labeling Act of 1966 requires, among other things, that consumer goods have labels that identify the product, the manufacturer, the packer or distributor and its place of business, the net quantity of the contents, and the quantity of each serving if the number of servings is stated.
   3. The federal Food and Drug Administration (FDA) has guidelines to standardize the nutritional information on packaged foods.

C. Sales Transactions
   1. Article 2 of the Uniform Commercial Code (UCC), which has been adopted by virtually all states, governs the purchase and sale of goods in the marketplace.
   2. Product-liability laws also protect consumers by allowing them to sue manufacturers and sellers for compensation when they are harmed or injured by faulty products.
   3. Federal and state statutes, such as the Federal Trade Commission, also protect consumers who purchase specific types of goods and services.

D. Consumer Health and Safety
   1. The Pure Food and Drug Act passed in 1906 by Congress was the first step toward protecting consumers against adulterated and misbranded food and drug products.
   2. The Federal Food, Drug, and Cosmetic Act of 1938 was passed by Congress to strengthen the 1906 legislation.
   3. In 1906, Congress passed the Meat Inspection Act, the first of a series of laws that established inspection requirements for all meat and poultry sold for human consumption.
   4. Congress has enacted a number of statutes in an attempt to protect individuals from harmful products such as cigarette smoking.
   5. Statutes such as the Flammable Fabrics Act of 1953 or the Consumer Product Safety Act of 1972 are categorized as product-safety acts meant to protect consumers by carefully regulating the distribution of hazardous or defective products.

E. Consumer Credit Protection
   1. One of the most significant statutes regulating credit and the credit-card industry is the Truth-In-Lending Act (TILA), the name commonly given to Title 1 of the Consumer Credit Protection Act passed by Congress in 1974.
   2. The Truth-In-Lending Act
      a. The TILA requires sellers and lenders to disclose credit and loan terms so that individuals can more effectively shop around for the best financing arrangements.
      b. The TILA applies to any transaction involving an installment sales contract by which payments are to be made in more than four installments.
      c. In 1974, Congress enacted the Equal Credit Opportunity Act (ECOA), which prohibits the denial of credit solely on the basis of race, religion, national origin, color, gender, marital status, or age.
      d. The TILA also contains provisions for credit cards.
   3. Fair Credit Reporting
      a. The Fair Credit Reporting Act (FCRA) was passed by Congress in 1970. This act covers all credit bureaus, investigative reporting companies, detective and collection agencies, and computerized information-reporting companies.
   4. Fair Debt-Collection Practices
      a. The Fair Debt-Collection Practices Act was passed by Congress in 1977 to curb what were perceived as abuses by collection agencies.
   5. Garnishment Proceedings
      a. Garnishment is a remedy available to creditors when consumers fail to pay their debts.
      b. Garnishment occurs when a creditor, after complying with the procedures set out by state law, legally seizes a portion of the debtor's property (such as wages) in the possession of a third party (such as an employer).
      c. State laws governing garnishment vary state by state.
      d. To protect consumers, federal and state laws limit the amount of income that can be taken from a debtor's weekly take-home pay.

F. Consumer Law and the Paralegal
   1. In the area of consumer law, paralegals may be asked to perform the following types of tasks:
      a. Investigate a client's complaint alleging deceptive advertising.
      b. Assist in work relating to a business client who has been charged with violating the Federal Trade Commission rules governing deceptive trade practices.
      c. Develop acceptable standards for a food producer to ensure compliance with labeling laws.
      d. Investigate a client's use of hazardous products to ensure compliance with Consumer Product Safety Commission standards.
      e. Draft a letter to a credit-reporting agency to rectify an error on a client's credit report.
      f. Assist a client in collecting a debt through garnishment proceedings.
      g. Maintain and keep current the law firm's consumer law library.

IV. ENVIRONMENTAL LAW
   A. Common Law Actions
      1. Common law remedies against environmental pollution originated centuries ago in England, and injured individuals today rely on the common law to obtain damages and injunctions against business polluters.
      2. Toxic torts (actions against toxic polluters) is a developing area of tort law.
   B. Federal Regulation of the Environment
      1. Environmental Regulatory Agencies
         a. The Environmental Protection Agency (EPA) was created in 1970 to coordinate federal environmental responsibilities.
         b. Other federal agencies (such as the Department of the Interior, Department of Defense, Department of Labor, Food and Drug Administration, and the Nuclear Regulatory Commission) together with all other agencies of government must take environmental factors into consideration when making significant decisions.
      2. Environmental Impact Statements
         a. The National Environmental Policy Act (NEPA) of 1969 requires that an environmental impact statement must be prepared for every major federal action that significantly affects the quality of the environment.
   C. Air Pollution
      1. The federal Clean Air Act was passed by Congress in 1963, and various amendments to the act strengthened the government's authority to regulate the quality of air.
      2. The 1990 amendments to the Clean Air Act require manufacturers to cut new automobiles' emissions of nitrogen oxide by 35 percent. By 1998, all new cars had to meet these standards, and another set emission controls may be ordered after 2000.
      3. The Clean Air Act authorizes the EPA to establish air-quality standards for stationary sources, such as manufacturing plants, electric utilities, and other nonmoving sources of pollution.
      4. The EPA can assess civil penalties up to $25,000 per day.
      5. The EPA is authorized to obtain a penalty equal to the violator's economic benefits from noncompliance.
   D. Water Pollution
      1. Navigable Waters
         a. Navigable waters include coastal waters, freshwater wetlands, and lakes and streams used by interstate travelers and industry.
         b. In 1948, Congress passed the Federal Water Pollution Control Act (FWPCA), but its regulations and enforcement proved to be inadequate.
         c. In 1972, amendments to the FWPCA, known as the Clean Water Act, were enacted to make waters safe for swimming, to protect fish and wildlife, and to eliminate the discharge of pollutants into the water.
         d. Under the Clean Water Act, violators are subject to a variety of civil and criminal penalties.
      2. Drinking Water
         a. The Safe Drinking Water Act of 1974 requires the EPA to set maximum levels for pollutants in the public water systems.
      3. Ocean Dumping
         a. The Marine Protection, Research, and Sanctuaries Act of 1972, known as the Ocean Dumping Act and amended in 1983, prohibits the ocean dumping of certain materials, including chemical and high-level radioactive waste.
      4. Oil Pollution
         a. In response to the supertanker *Exxon Valdez* oil-spill disaster in 1989, Congress passed the Oil Pollution Act of 1990.

  b. Under this act, damage to natural resources, private property, and the local economy, including the increased cost of providing public services, is compensable.

E. Toxic Chemicals
  1. Pesticides and Herbicides
    a. Under the Federal Insecticide, Fungicide, and Rodenticide Act of 1947, pesticides and herbicides must be registered before they can be sold, used only for approved applications, and used in limited quantities when applied to food crops.
  2. Toxic Substances
    a. The Toxic Substances Control Act of 1976 regulates chemicals and chemical compounds that are known to be toxic.
  3. Hazardous Wastes
    a. When not properly disposed of, some industrial, agricultural, and household wastes present a substantial danger to human health and the environment.
    b. Resource Conservation and Recovery Act
    c. Superfund
F. State and Local Regulation
G. Environmental Law and the Paralegal
  1. Paralegals working in the environmental law area might perform one or more of the following tasks:
    a. Obtain permits from federal, state, and local environmental agencies.
    b. Draft and file documents necessary to include another polluting company as a defendant in an action brought by a government agency.
    c. Monitor the *Federal Register* on a routine basis to determine if new environmental regulations have been proposed by the EPA.
    d. Research a particular regulation to determine whether a client's planned action has violated a rule, whether a permit is required, and so on.
    e. Prepare for and attend hearings before environmental agencies.
    f. Assist in negotiations.
    g. Coordinate a corporation employer's environmental programs and policies and monitor corporate activities.

V. EMPLOYMENT RELATIONSHIPS

A. Employment At Will
  1. The employment-at-will doctrine stated that an employment relationship could be terminated at any time either by the employee or the employer for any reason or no reason at all.
B. Labor Laws
  1. National Labor Relations Act
    a. The National Labor Relations Act (NLRA) was passed in 1935 to protect the workers' efforts to organize into unions and to promote collective bargaining as a peaceful method of dispute resolution.
  2. Fair Labor Standards Act
    a. The Fair Labor Standards Act (FLSA) of 1938 prohibited the oppression and exploitation of children by regulating the employment of minors.
    b. The FLSA established guidelines regulating overtime pay and minimum hourly wages.
    c. Certain employees (including administrative and professional employees) are exempt from the FLSA's provisions.
C. Family and Medical Leave
  1. The Family and Medical Leave Act (FMLA) of 1993 was passed by Congress to protect employees who need time off work for family or medical reasons.
  2. Remedies for violation of the FMLA include (a) damages for unpaid wages or salary, lost benefits, denied compensation, and actual monetary losses; (b) job reinstatement; and (c) promotion.

D. State Workers' Compensation Laws
   1. Workers' compensation laws establish an administrative procedure for compensating workers who are injured on the job.
   2. Generally, the employee's right to recover benefits is based wholly on the existence of an employment relationship and the fact that the injury was accidental and occurred on the job or in the course of employment, regardless of fault.
   3. An employee's acceptance of workers' compensation benefits bars the employee from suing for injuries caused by the employer's negligence.
   4. However, an employee can sue an employer who *intentionally* injures the worker.

E. Employment Discrimination
   1. Title VII of the Civil Rights Act of 1964
      a. This law was enacted to protect certain groups from discriminatory practices of business owners, educational, institutions, employers, and other groups.
      b. Title VII prohibits employers from discriminating against employees or potential employees on the basis of race, color, national origin, religion, or gender.
   2. The Application of Title VII
      a. The courts have also extended Title VII protection to those who are subject to sexual harassment in the workplace.
      b. *Quid pro quo harassment* occurs when a superior doles out some kind of award in exchange for sexual favors.
      c. *Hostile-environment harassment* occurs when an employee is subjected to offensive sexual comments, jokes, or physical contact in the workplace that makes it difficult or impossible for the employee to perform a job satisfactorily.
   3. The Equal Employment Opportunity Commission
      a. The Equal Employment Opportunity Commission (EEOC) is a federal agency that administers and enforces Title VII, the laws prohibiting employment discrimination based on disability or age, as well as other federal antidiscrimination laws.
      b. Employers' Liability under Title VII
   4. Discrimination Based on Age
      a. The Age Discrimination in Employment Act of 1967 prohibits employers from discriminating against workers between the ages of forty and seventy on the basis of their age.
   5. Discrimination Based on Disability
      a. Under the Americans with Disabilities Act (ADA), an employer is not permitted to discriminate against a person with a disability if reasonable accommodations can be provided to assist the worker in satisfactorily performing the job.

F. Employment Relationships and the Paralegal
   1. Here are a few tasks that paralegals commonly undertake in the area of labor and employment law:
      a. Drafting employment contracts or policy manuals
      b. Assisting with contract negotiations between labor and management.
      c. Preparing for arbitration proceedings or attending administrative hearings.
      d. Preparing notices about a firm's employment policies or important changes in the employment laws or preparing reports and furnishing documentation in response to an EEOC investigation.
      e. Gathering factual information to counter or support a claim of employment discrimination.

QUESTIONS FOR REVIEW

TRUE-FALSE QUESTIONS

____ 1. Administrative agencies may exercise only those powers delegated to them by Congress in enabling legislation.

____ 2. The significant difference between the two types of agencies lies in the accountability of the regulators—the extent to which the agency is subject to the president's authority.

____ 3. Officers of independent regulatory agencies are subject to appointment and removal by the president.

____ 4. Administrative agencies combine functions associated with the executive, legislative, and judicial branches.

____ 5. The Administrative Procedure Act sets forth procedural requirements that both state and federal administrative agencies must follow.

____ 6. The court's formal resolution of disputes is referred to as rulemaking.

____ 7. Administrative agencies cannot make legislative rules that are as legally binding as laws passed by Congress.

____ 8. Administrative agencies constitute the bureaucracy and are sometimes referred to as the "four branches" of the American government.

____ 9. The most common rulemaking procedure involves notice of the proposed rulemaking proceedings, comment period, and the final rule.

____ 10. If a dispute cannot be settled, the case is then heard before an administrative law judge in a trial-like setting.

____ 11. A significant difference between a trial and an administrative agency hearing is that generally more information may be introduced at a trial.

____ 12. Absent an appeal, the ALJ's decision becomes the final order of the agency.

____ 13. Administrative agencies exist only on the federal level.

____ 14. A paralegal may never represent a client before state and federal agencies unless accompanied by an attorney.

____ 15. A paralegal could save valuable time by creating an agency contacts notebook to use as a quick reference guide in locating names and other pertinent information about administrative agencies.

____ 16. The test for whether an advertisement is deceptive is whether a reasonable consumer would be deceived by the ad.

____ 17. The Fair Packaging and Labeling Act established standards for foods, specified safe levels of potentially dangerous food additives, and created classifications of foods and food advertising.

____ 18. Garnishment occurs when a creditor, after complying with state law, legally seizes a portion of a debtor's property (e.g., wages) in the possession of a third party, such as an employer.

____ 19. All states permit garnishment of wages.

____ 20. Because of changing laws and the Federal Insecticide, Fungicide, and Rodenticide Act, it is no longer necessary to register herbicides or pesticides before they can be sold.

____ 21. According to the employment-at-will doctrine, an employment relationship can be terminated at any time either by the employee or the employer for any reason or no reason at all.

____ 22. The Family and Medical Leave Act enables any employee to take an unlimited amount of time off of work for any important reason.

____ 23. If an injury occurs while an employee is commuting to or from work, it is covered by workers' compensation.

____ 24. Title VII of the Civil Rights Act has been interpreted to prohibit both intentional and unintentional discrimination.

____ 25. An employer is not permitted to discriminate against any person with a disability if reasonable accommodations can be made to assist that employee in satisfactorily performing his or her job.

Fill-in Questions

_________________ (Administrative agencies/administrative law judges) are charged with administering and implementing legislation. Paralegals _________________ (often/rarely) deal with these. Paralegals _________________ (may/cannot) work for these.

There are two types of agencies. An example of an executive agency would be the _________________ (Occupational Safety and Health Administration/Federal Trade Commission). An example of an independent regulatory agency would be the _________________ (Occupational Safety and Health Administration/ Federal Trade Commission). Officers of independent agencies _________________ (cannot be removed/can be removed with just cause). Checks and balances on administrative agencies include the president's ability to _________________ (veto/implement) enabling legislation. Congress also exercises authority by establishing _________________ (time and monetary limits/notice-and-comment rulemaking) of the programs.

The agency may, during an investigation, compel a witness to hand over documents through issuance of a _________________ (initial order/subpoena duces tecum). During an investigation, an agency may conduct a search for evidence; the Fourth Amendment protection against unreasonable searches and seizures _________________ (does/does not) apply to the administrative process.

Multiple-Choice Questions

____ 1. Enabling legislation creates an agency and:
- A Specifies the name
- B. Specifies the purpose and function
- C. Specifies the powers
- D. All of the above

____ 2. Executive agencies include:
- A. The cabinet departments of the executive branch
- B. The departments outside the executive branch
- C. Congressional committees
- D. All of the above

____ 3. Independent regulatory agencies include:
- A. The cabinet departments of the executive branch
- B. The departments outside the executive branch
- C. Congressional committees
- D. All of the above

____ 4. Courts have interpreted the U.S. Constitution to permit Congress to establish administrative agencies through what is known as:
- A. Rulemaking
- B. The supremacy clause
- C. The delegation doctrine
- D. Enabling legislation

____ 5. Administrative process involves:
- A. The administration of law by administrative agencies
- B. The administration of law by the courts
- C. The creation of an agency
- D. The formulation of new regulations

____ 6. Judicial process involves:
- A. The administration of law by administrative agencies
- B. The administration of law by the courts
- C. The creation of an agency
- D. The formulation of new regulations

____ 7. Rulemaking involves:
A. The administration of law by administrative agencies
B. The administration of law by the courts
C. The creation of an agency
D. The formulation of new regulations

____ 8. A final rule is published in the:
A. Agency contacts notebook
B. *Federal Register*
C. Initial order
D. Final order

____ 9. An agency may investigate:
A. By on-site inspections
B. Through issuance of a subpoena
C. Through issuance of a search warrant
D. All of the above

____ 10. Following an administrative hearing, the ALJ renders:
A. An adjudication
B. A rulemaking
C. An initial order
D. A final order

____ 11. A party may request that an agency decision be reviewed by the:
A. Commission or board that heads the agency
B. Administrative law judge
C. Independent regulatory agency
D. Executive agency

____ 12. A party challenging an agency decision must meet which of the following requirements before a court will review the case:
A. The case must be one that is reviewable
B. The party must have standing to sue the agency
C. The party must have exhausted all available administrative remedies
D. All of the above

____ 13. The priority of federal law over state law, in the event of a conflicting state law, is based on:
A. The supremacy clause
B. Enabling legislation
C. Judicial process
D. The delegation doctrine

____ 14. Administrative agencies exist at the:
A. Federal level
B. Federal and state levels
C. Federal, state and local levels
D. Executive branch

____ 15 Which act requires that consumer goods have labels that identify the product, the manufacturer, the packer or distributor and its place of business:
A. The Federal Trade Commission
B. The Fair Packaging and Labeling Act
C. The Uniform Commercial Code
D. None of the above

____ 16. Which Act prohibits the denial of credit solely on the basis of religion, race, color, gender, national origin, marital status, or age:
A. The Truth-in-Lending Act
B. The Equal Credit Opportunity Act
C. The Consumer Protection Act
D. The Fair Credit Reporting Act

____ 17. The National Environmental Policy Act requires that a(n) ____________________ must be prepared for every major federal action that significantly affects the environment.
A. "Reasonable Certainty of No Harm" Affidavit
B. Application for registration with the FCC
C. Environmental Impact Statement
D. Recycling Study

____ 18. The ____________________ was passed by Congress in response to increasing concern of the effects of hazardous waste materials on the environment and requires all producers of hazardous waste materials to label and package properly any hazardous waste to be transported.
A. Environmental Protection Act
B. Toxic Substances Control Act
C. Federal Insecticide, Fungicide, and Rodenticide Act
D. Resource Conservation and Recovery Act

____ 19. The Fair Labor Standards Act established guidelines for:
A. Regulating the employment of minors
B. Regulating overtime pay and minimum hourly wages
C. Employing children under the age of sixteen
D. (a) and (b) only
E. (a), (b), and (c)

Practice Questions

1. Assume the facts given in this chapter's Practice Question and Assignment 4, except that the inspector has requested invoices relating to purchase dates of various food items used in the restaurant business. Must the client allow the inspector to review these invoices?

Questions for Critical Analysis

1. Do you think that it is appropriate for hearsay to be admissible at an administrative agency hearing when such evidence is inadmissible in a court trial? Explain.
2. Do you think the requirements for judicial review are appropriate? Explain.

Ethical Questions

1. LeRoy Howell is an experienced paralegal working in the area of unemployment compensation. Although LeRoy's state authorizes paralegals to represent clients before the agency, the administrative law judge (ALJ) is obviously biased against him. After a dozen or so hostile and intimidating remarks, LeRoy loses his patience. He makes an angry response to the ALJ during the hearing. What has LeRoy done wrong?
2. Mary Lou is a legal assistant attempting to assist a client in obtaining food stamps. After getting the run around for two weeks straight, Mary Lou informs the administrator of the local office of what she thinks of the frustrating and inefficient food-stamp system. Has Mary Lou served the interests of her client?

Technology and Today's Paralegal

The Better Business Bureau has long been a source of consumer protection. You can locate the Better Business Bureau on the Internet by using any search engine and searching for "Better Business Bureau"—be sure to add the quotation marks. You might want to check out this site for *The Daily Diffs:* http://www.dailydiffs.com/dop000qk.htm. It also has links to the Federal Trade Commission, U.S. Consumer Gateway, the National Consumer's League, and other consumer safety alerts.

Answers

True-False Questions

1. T
2. T
3. F
4. T
5. F
6. F
7. F
8. T
9. T
10. T
11. F
12. T
13. F
14. F
15. T
16. T
17. F
18. T
19. F
20. F
21. T
22. F
23. F
24. T
25. T

Fill-in Questions

administrative agencies; often; may

Occupational Safety and Health Administration; Federal Trade Commission; can be removed with just cause; veto; time and monetary limits

subpoena duces tecum; does

Multiple-Choice Questions

1. D
2. A
3. B
4. C
5. A
6. B
7. D
8. B
9. D
10. C
11. A
12. D
13. A
14. C
16. B
17. B
18. C
19. D
20. E

Practice Questions

1. A subpoena duces tecum compels an individual or organization to hand over specified books, papers, records or documents. Administrative agencies may use this type of subpoena in obtaining needed documents. If the client has not been served with this type of subpoena, the business is not obligated to permit the inspector's review of the invoices.

Questions for Critical Analysis

1. It may be difficult to obtain certain types of evidence directly on point to prove a violation of an administrative regulation. Suppose that toxic waste has been dumped by a company in violation of an administrative regulation. The chief operating officers may not wish to admit responsibility. The individual who was directed to dump the waste may not wish to admit to these actions because of personal liability or loss of employment. Second-hand information then may be the only source for obtaining information. Furthermore, the appellate procedure permits review of evidence admitted at the administrative hearing and reversal of erroneous decisions.
2. The first requirement, that the action be reviewable, is met by the act's creation of a presumption. The second requirement, that the party has standing to sue, is a requirement for most litigation in the court system; this requirement is not unique to the judicial process. The third requirement, that the party has exhausted all possible administrative remedies, provides for the administrative agency with expertise in solving a violation to be addressed prior to judicial review. The agency will be able to address the problem more effectively and quicker; thus, this requirement is not unduly burdensome to the party. Finally, that there be an actual controversy is a requirement for most litigation in the court system.

Ethical Questions

1. As an advocate, LeRoy is governed by Rule 3.5 of the Model Rules of Professional Conduct. This rule requires LeRoy to "protect the record for subsequent review and preserve professional integrity by patient firmness." LeRoy was at the hearing to serve the client's interest. His sharp words will only worsen his client's chances for a favorable decision. Since his remarks were on the record, they may also affect the outcome if the decision is appealed.
2. As an advocate of the client's interests, Mary Lou should have set her personal feelings aside. She should have concentrated solely on the client's needs, rather than venting her personal frustrations. Her remarks may have interfered with enlisting the agency's cooperation in obtaining the urgently needed food stamps. As such, Mary Lou has not properly served the interests of her client.

CHAPTER 10

CIVIL LITIGATION—BEFORE THE TRIAL

CHAPTER OBJECTIVES

After completing this chapter, you should be able to:

- Identify the basic steps in the civil litigation process.
- Describe some of the tasks that paralegals may perform during each step of the pretrial phase.
- Define what a litigation file is, what it contains, and how it is organized, maintained, and reviewed.
- Discuss how a lawsuit is started and what documents are filed during the pleadings stage of the civil litigation process.
- Define a motion.
- Understand how certain pretrial motions, if granted by the court, will end the litigation before the trial begins.
- Explain what discovery is.
- Describe the kind of information that attorneys and their paralegals may obtain from parties to the lawsuit and from witnesses when preparing for trial.

CHAPTER OUTLINE

I. INTRODUCTION

II. CIVIL LITIGATION—A BIRD'S EYE VIEW
- A. Pretrial Settlements
  1. In most cases, the parties reach a settlement before the case goes to trial.
  2. Since lawsuits are costly in terms of time and money, it is usually in the interest of both parties to settle the case out of court.
  3. To be prepared for trial, both the attorney and paralegal must assume that the case *will* go to trial while, at the same time, attempting to reach a settlement.
- B. Procedural Requirements
  1. The procedural rules of the court in which the lawsuit is brought must be followed.
  2. All federal civil trials are governed by the Federal Rules of Civil Procedure (FRCP).
  3. Each state has its own rules of civil procedure. In many states these are similar to the FRCP.
  4. Additionally, many courts have their own local rules of procedures that supplement the federal or state rules.
- C. A Hypothetical Lawsuit

III. THE PRELIMINARIES
- A. The Initial Client Interview
  1. Only an attorney can accept a case, set a fee, and give legal advice. Therefore, the initial client interview should be conducted by the attorney.
  2. Because the paralegal will be working with the attorney on the case, the paralegal should attend the initial client interview.
  3. During the initial client interview, the attorney will:
     - a. Explain the fee structure to the client.
     - b. Have the client sign a retainer agreement.
     - c. Have the client sign release forms for obtaining relevant medical, employment, and other information relating to the claim.
     - d. Ask the paralegal to schedule follow-up interviews to obtain more details from the client.
- B. Preliminary Investigation
  1. The attorney and paralegal may undertake this investigation together.
  2. At this point in the pretrial process, the paralegal may engage in extensive investigation.
- C. Creating the Litigation File
  1. All documents and records pertaining to the lawsuit are kept in the litigation file.
  2. Check the specific procedures for organizing and maintaining litigation files in your law firm or department.
  3. Subfiles are set up as the case progresses. They may include the following:
     - a. Pleadings.
     - b. Discovery.
     - c. Research.
     - d. Bills.
     - e. Notes.
     - f. Other documents and information relating to the litigation.
  4. The litigation file is a comprehensive record of the case. The file is important so others in the firm can quickly acquaint themselves with the progress of the case.

IV. THE PLEADINGS
- A. Drafting the Complaint
  1. The complaint is a document that contains the following:
     - a. A caption.
     - b. Jurisdictional allegations.
     - c. General allegations (the body of the complaint).

   d. A prayer for relief.
   e. Signature.
   f. A demand for jury trial.
2. The Caption
   a. The caption identifies the court in which the action is being filed, the names of the parties, and the designation of the document as the "Complaint" and contains the case number and the name of the judge handling the case.
3. Jurisdictional Allegations
   a. Each complaint must have an allegation that the court in which the case has been filed has jurisdiction to hear the case.
4. General Allegations (the Body of the Complaint)
   a. An allegation is a party's statement, claim, or assertion that sets forth the issue that the party expects to prove.
   b. A party must not exaggerate the facts or make false statements.
   c. When drafting the complaint, a party should use clear language and favor simple and direct statements over more complex sentences.
   d. The paralegal should check all relevant court rules.
5. Prayer for Relief
   a. The prayer for relief asks that judgment be entered for the party submitting the pleading or document and appropriate relief be granted.
6. Signature
   a. In federal practice, the signature following the prayer for relief certifies that the attorney has read the pleading or document and that the facts alleged true to the best of her knowledge.
7. Demand for Jury Trial
   a. In most states and federal courts, one of the parties must request a jury or the right is presumed to be waived.
   b. The decision to exercise a right to a jury trial usually depends on what legal theory the party is using and which judge is assigned to the trial.

B. Filing the Complaint
1. Normally, the lawsuit is initiated by the filing of a complaint with the clerk of the appropriate court (state or federal).
2. The complaint must be filed within the period of time allowed by law for bringing legal actions. This fixed period is known as the statute of limitations.
3. Normally, no action can be brought after the time allowed under the statute of limitations has expired.

C. Service of Process
1. The defendant is notified of a lawsuit by the delivery of the complaint and a summons. This is known as service of process.
2. The Summons
   a. The summons does the following:
      1) Identifies the parties to the lawsuit.
      2) Identifies the court in which the case will be heard.
      3) Directs the defendant to respond to the complaint within a specified time period.
3. Serving the Complaint and Summons
   a. Under FRCP 4(c)(2), service of process in federal court cases may be effected "by any person who is not a party and who is at least 18 years of age."
   b. Many state courts require that the complaint and summons be served by a public officer, such as a sheriff.
   c. A "return-of-service" form is signed by the process server and submitted to the court to prove that a defendant received a summons.

4. Serving Corporate Defendants
    a. The summons and complaint must be served on the *registered agent* of the corporation.
5. Finding the Defendant
    a. Paralegals sometimes have to investigate and attempt to locate a defendant so that process can be served.

D. Notice and Waiver of Service—FRCP 4(d)
1. Revised FRCP 4 applies in federal court cases, and allows for a simpler and less costly alternative to service of process.
2. Under this rule, the plaintiff's attorney is permitted to notify the defendant of the lawsuit by first-class mail or other reliable means.
3. Enclosed with the notice of the lawsuit is a form that the defendant can sign to waive the requirement of service of process.
4. If the defendant does not sign and return the form, then the plaintiff's attorney must have the defendant served with the complaint and summons.

E. The Defendant's Response
1. On receiving the complaint (and summons, if process is served), the defendant has several options.
2. The defendant may do any one of the following:
    a. Submit an answer, denying any wrongdoing or asserting an affirmative defense. The answer must respond to each allegation in the plaintiff's complaint.
    b. Submit a counterclaim with the answer, asserting a claim against the plaintiff for injuries that the defendant suffered from the same incident.
    c. Submit a cross-claim with the answer, alleging that another party named as a defendant in the suit should bear some or all of the liability for the plaintiff's injury. (A cross-claim can also be filed by one plaintiff against another plaintiff.)
    d. Alternatively or simultaneously, the defendant might make a motion to dismiss the case.
    e. If the defendant fails to respond to the plaintiff's complaint within the proper time period, the court will enter a default judgment.
    f. If a default judgment is entered against the defendant, the case is over and the defendant has lost the case.
3. The Answer
    a. The answer begins with a caption and ends with an attorney's signature, which may be followed by an affidavit signed by the defendant and a demand for jury trial.
    b. Answer and Affirmative Defenses
        1) An affirmative defense is a response to a plaintiff's claim that does not deny the plaintiff's facts but attacks the plaintiff's legal right to bring an action.
        2) Contributory negligence is a theory in tort law under which a complaining party's own negligence, if it contributed to or caused the injuries complained of, is an absolute bar to recovery.
    c. Answer and Counterclaim
        1) A counterclaim is like a reverse lawsuit in which the defendant asserts a claim against the plaintiff for injuries that the defendant suffered from the same incident.
4. Motion to Dismiss
    a. A motion is a procedural request submitted to the court by an attorney on behalf of his client.
    b. A motion to dismiss requests the court to dismiss the case for reasons provided in the motion.
    c. In a motion to dismiss, the defendant usually admits the facts as alleged by the plaintiff but asserts that the plaintiff's claim fails to state a cause of action or that there are other grounds on which a suit should be dismissed.

F. Amending the Pleadings
1. Subject to procedural rules, both the complaint and the answer may be amended.
2. Amending is appropriate as the case evolves and as more evidence is discovered.

V. PRETRIAL MOTIONS

A. Motion for Judgment on the Pleadings

1. This is a pretrial motion that may be filed by either party after all pleadings and amendments have been filed, when it appears from the pleadings that the plaintiff has failed to state a cause of action.
2. The motion may be granted if it can be shown that only questions of law need to be decided and no facts are in dispute.

B. Motion for Summary Judgment

1. This motion may be filed by either party during or after the discovery stage of litigation.
2. This motion asks for judgment to be entered without a trial being held.
3. In determining whether to grant the motion, the judge can consider evidence apart from the pleadings—such as evidence contained in affidavits, depositions, and interrogatories.
4. This motion will not be granted if any facts are in dispute.

VI. TRADITIONAL DISCOVERY TOOLS

A. Interrogatories

1. Interrogatories are written questions, that must be answered, in writing, by the parties of the lawsuit who must also sign the answers under oath.
2. Drafting Interrogatories
   a. Before drafting the questions the paralegal should always check the court rules in which an action is filed to find out whether that court limits the number of interrogatories that can be used and to review any other court rule that might affect how interrogatories should be drafted.
3. Answering Interrogatories
   a. Parties are required to respond to interrogatory requests within a certain time period.
   b. Answers must be in writing and under oath.

B. Depositions

1. At the deposition, oral questions are directed to witnesses, or to parties by attorneys and are answered under oath.
2. Drafting Deposition Questions
   a. Although paralegals may attend depositions, they do not ask questions of the deponent.
   b. Deposition questions are often drafted by the paralegal.
3. Preparing the Client for a Deposition
   a. The deposed party and her attorney will want to prepare for the deposition by formulating mock answers to anticipated questions.
   b. This kind of preparation does not mean that the lawyer or paralegal tell the deponent what to say. Instead, the lawyer or paralegal offers suggestions as to how the answers to certain questions should be phrased.
   c. A deponent's answers should always be truthful.
4. The Role of the Deponent's Attorney
   a. The deponent's attorney has a limited role at the deposition.
   b. The deponent's attorney may make objections when the opposing attorney asks questions that may appear to be irrelevant to the case or ask for privileged information.
   c. The deponent's attorney may also caution his client or witness to avoid speculation or limit his responses to a question.
5. The Deposition Transcript
   a. A court reporter usually records the deposition and creates an official deposition transcript.
   b. The transcript may be used by either party to prove a particular point or impeach the credibility of a witness or party.
6. Summarizing and Indexing the Deposition Transcript
   a. Usually, a paralegal will summarize the deposition transcript.
   b. Often, the paralegal provides an index to the transcript as well as a summary.
   c. Together, the summary and index allow anyone involved in the case to locate information quickly.

C. Other Discovery Requests
   1. The attorney for either side may also submit any or all of the following:
      a. A request for production of documents in the possession of the other party or opposing counsel (or a third party).
      b. A request for admission (of the truth of certain statements) by the opposing party.
      c. A request for examination (to establish the truth of claimed injuries or health status).

VII. **REVISED DISCOVERY PROCEDURES UNDER FRCP 26**

A. Initial Disclosures
   1. Each party to a lawsuit has a duty to disclose to the other party specified types of information prior to the discovery stage of litigation.
   2. Information disclosed by all parties must even include information that might be dangerous to the producing party.
   3. A party need not disclose priviledged information.
   4. A party is not excused from disclosing relevant information simply because the party has not yet completed an investigation into the case or because the other party has not yet disclosed the required information.

B. Discovery Plan
   1. The attorneys must work out a discovery plan at the initial meeting and submit a report describing the plan to the court within ten days of the meeting.

C. Subsequent Disclosures
   1. Attorneys must automatically disclose relevant information. All subsequent disclosures must be made in writing, signed by the attorneys, and filed with the court.
   2. Any time an attorney learns about supplemental information relating to witnesses, documents, and other relevant information, that information must be disclosed to the other party.
   3. Expert Witnesses
      a. Each party must disclose to the other party the names of any expert witnesses who may be called to testify during trial.
   4. Other Pretrial Disclosures
      a. Under the court rules, each party must also disclose to the other party any relevant information about witnesses who will testify at trial or any exhibits that may be used.

QUESTIONS FOR REVIEW

TRUE-FALSE QUESTIONS

____ 1. The various stages of the civil litigation process are specified by statute.

____ 2. The complaint contains statements regarding the plaintiff's claims against defendant, the court's jurisdiction, and the remedy sought.

____ 3. A paralegal should call the court before filing the complaint in order to obtain the file/docket number to be inserted in the caption of the complaint.

____ 4. A compulsory counterclaim arises from a transaction separate than the one forming the basis for the original lawsuit.

____ 5. A defendant may never bring a third party into the litigation.

____ 6. An allegation is an assertion that sets forth the issue that the party expects to prove at trial.

____ 7. The complaint may contain only facts known to be true.

____ 8. A complaint may never be amended.

____ 9. Service of process refers to a plaintiff's filing of the complaint with the court.

____ 10. The process server must complete a return-of-service form evidencing delivery of the summons and complaint to the defendant.

____ 11. A motion for summary judgment permits the court to consider affidavits and deposition transcripts—evidence outside the pleadings.

____ 12. Depositions are written questions that can only be served on parties.

____ 13. In federal court cases, it is necessary that attorneys cooperate and disclose certain relevant information.

____ 14. An out-of-court resolution of a dispute is referred to as a settlement.

____ 15. Once the trial begins, a paralegal can feel comfortable informing the client of the probable outcome.

Fill-in Questions

The ____________________ (complaint/summons) initiates a lawsuit. After service of process, the defendant must file ____________________ (an answer/a reply) or a ____________________ (motion to dismiss/motion for judgment on the pleadings), or a ____________________ (summary judgment/default judgment) may be entered against the defendant. The plaintiff and the defendant then become the ____________________ (parties/deponents).

Once the pleadings have been filed, the court will consult with the attorneys often through a ____________________ (scheduling conference/deposition). The parties begin obtaining information from each other, which is known as ____________________ (negotiations/discovery).

In order to learn the possible testimony to be given by a witness who is expected to testify in the lawsuit, a party may serve ____________________ (interrogatories/a notice of deposition) upon that witness. If it appears, during or after completion of discovery, that no material facts are disputed, a party may file a ____________________ (motion for default judgment/motion for summary judgment). The court's decision on the matter is through the issuance of a ____________________ (summons/judgment).

Multiple-Choice Questions

____ 1. The allowable period of time within which a legal action may be filed is referred to as:
A. Affirmative defense
B. Statute of limitations
C. Summons
D. Prayer for relief

____ 2. A litigation file should contain:
A. Research
B. Investigation results
C. Documents and exhibits
D. All of the above

____ 3. A plaintiff's response to a defendant's counterclaim is called a(n):
A. Answer
B. Interrogatory
C. Affirmative defense
D. Reply

____ 4. An answer is filed in response to which of the following:
A. Complaint
B. Cross-claim
C. Third-party complaint
D. All of the above

____ 5. A complaint contains all of the following except:
A. Caption
B. Jurisdictional and general allegations
C. Affirmative defenses
D. Prayer for relief

____ 6. The body of the complaint contains:
A. The money damages sought
B. The factual events that gave rise to the claim
C. The certification that the attorney has read the complaint
D. The jury demand

____ 7. Service of a summons and complaint upon a corporate defendant is effected by:
A. Serving the secretary of state
B. Serving the majority shareholder
C. Serving the headquarters
D. Serving the registered agent

____ 8. In answering a plaintiff's complaint, the defendant may:
A. Deny allegations
B. Assert a counterclaim
C. Assert affirmative defenses
D. All of the above

____ 9. An affidavit is:
A. A sworn statement
B. A defendant's assertion of a claim against the plaintiff
C. A set of written questions
D. The list of cases entered on a court's calendar

____ 10. A defendant that believes the complaint was improperly served should file a:
A. Motion to strike
B. Motion to make more definite and certain
C. Motion for judgment on the pleadings
D. Motion to dismiss

____ 11. Discovery serves all of the following purposes except:
A. Obtaining privileged information
B. Preserving evidence
C. Eliminating surprises at trial
D. Leading to an out-of-court settlement

____ 12. A memorandum of law:
A. Reduces the damages by a percentage representing the plaintiff's negligence
B. Is a stenographic recording of a deposition
C. Presents the legal basis for a motion
D. Contains communications that need not be presented in court

____ 13. Which of the following is false regarding interrogatories:
A. Generally, the number is limited by court rules
B. They are written questions served on parties and witnesses
C. They are to be answered within a specified period
D. They are answered under oath

____ 14. Persons asked to testify at trial are called:
A. Parties
B. Deponents
C. Process servers
D. Witnesses

____ 15. Which of the following is false regarding jury trials:
A. A trial can be held with or without a jury
B. The Seventh Amendment to the U.S. Constitution guarantees the right to a jury trial in federal courts in all "suits at common law" when the amount in controversy exceeds $20
C. Most states have constitutional guarantees similar to that in the U.S. Constitution
D. Absent a request to the contrary, a jury trial is presumed

Practice Questions

1. Assume the facts given in this chapter's Practice Question and Assignment 1 and that your firm has been asked to represent David Namisch. David believes Sandra could have avoided the accident if she had been more cautious and that her injuries would have been minimized if she had been wearing her seat belt. Draft affirmative defenses to be included within David's answer.

2. Assume the facts given in this chapter's Practice Question and Assignment 4 and that the interrogatories were served on Sandra Nelson six weeks ago. To date, you have received no response. Prepare an appropriate motion.

Questions for Critical Analysis

1. Julie Callas, a citizen of Kentucky, was walking near a busy street near Memphis, Tennessee, when a large crate flew off a passing truck and caused her to suffer serious injuries. The trucking company's headquarters are in Michigan. Julie filed a complaint requesting $300,000 in damages. Assume that your firm represents the trucking company. As a result of your investigation into the incident, it appears the crates were loaded by employees of a different firm and that, specifically, one of the employees was intoxicated at the time of the loading. Additionally, it appears that the cables used to secure the crates were of a poor quality. What pleading might your firm consider filing?

Ethical Questions

1. Pamela Beach, a paralegal, works for a law firm specializing in defending clients against large product-liability claims. She is currently assigned to a food-poisoning case filed in federal district court against their client, Good Food, Inc. Through discovery, Pamela's attorney and their client have disclosed all of the information they have relating to witnesses, documents, and all other relevant information. After discovery has been completed, and two days before trial, Pamela comes across a previously undiscovered document at Good Food, Inc.'s offices. The document is a confidential internal memorandum from the company's president. The memorandum makes it clear that Good Food, Inc. was aware of a problem in the food-preparation system at issue in the current lawsuit. Pamela knows that producing the document to the other side will mean her law firm will lose Good Food, Inc.'s case. What should Pamela do? What are the law firm's ethical obligations in this situation?
2. Bill Parkinson works as a paralegal for a sole practitioner, Mark Jones. Mark is a struggling new attorney with much promise. However, Mark is in court so much that it is up to Bill to handle most of the incoming phone calls. One day Bill receives a phone call from a woman who has what sounds to Bill like a great case for Mark. The woman's son was badly injured on a local department store's escalator. The store manager has admitted to the woman that the escalator had been in disrepair for some time, but no signs had been posted or precautions taken to prevent injury. In seeking an attorney, the woman got Mark's name and phone number from the advertising section of the phone book. She wants to know if Mark will take the case and how much he will charge. Bill knows that Mark would jump at the chance to take on this case and that Mark had always indicated he would take a big case on a one-third contingency basis. Bill can tell that if he makes the woman wait until Mark returns from court, she will probably call the next telephone book advertising listing, and Mark will lose her as a client. What should Bill do? How can he help the woman without violating professional ethical standards?
3. Sally Boltz, a paralegal, has been assigned to conduct a follow-up interview with client, Ben Brown, to obtain more facts on his medical-malpractice claim. During the course of the interview, Ben asks Sally, based upon her experience, if she thinks he has a good chance to win his case. How should Sally respond? Does your answer change if Sally knows Ben's case looks very good? Very bad?

Technology and Today's Paralegal

There are many litigation support groups on the Internet that are willing to assist you and your firm with a variety of tasks, including summarizing depositions.

To find these support groups, search for "deposition summaries" using a search engine. We recommend *lawcrawler.com* for this particular search. One in particular, D-M Information Systems, offers deposition summaries that are created by specially trained attorneys, law students, paralegals, and professional writers who are adept at recognizing the substantive text in the deposition transcripts and prepare a concise, but complete, summary.

Other support groups you might wish to investigate are:

http://www2.lovvorn.com/lovvorn/legal/deposition.html

http://www.summation.com/Articles/Compsforlaws/index.html

Answers

True-False Questions

1. F
2. T
3. F
4. F
5. F
6. T
7. F
8. F
9. F
10. T
11. T
12. F
13. T
14. T
15. F

Fill-in Questions

complaint; an answer; motion to dismiss; default judgment; parties

scheduling conference; discovery

a notice of deposition; motion for summary judgment; judgment

Multiple-Choice Questions

1. B
2. D
3. D
4. D
5. C
6. B
7. D
8. D
9. A
10. D
11. A
12. C
13. B
14. D
15. D

Practice Questions

1. Although denying that the Plaintiff is entitled to the relief prayed for in the Plaintiff's Complaint, Defendant further states that the Plaintiff is barred from recovery hereunder by reason of the following:
   (1) That the Plaintiff's injuries were proximately caused by her own contributory negligence and want of due care under the circumstances prevailing at the time of the accident.
   (2) That the Plaintiff failed to exercise that standard of care that a reasonably prudent person would have exercised under the same or similar conditions for her own safety and that her own negligence, contributory negligence, and/or comparative negligence caused or was a contributing factor to the incident out of which the Plaintiff's cause of action arose.
   (3) That the Defendant reserves the right, by an appropriate Motion, to move the Court to amend the Defendant's Answer to the Plaintiff's Complaint, to allege other New Matters and Affirmative Defenses as may be revealed by discovery yet to be had and completed in this case.

2.

[Caption—Court Title and Cause]

MOTION TO COMPEL DISCOVERY

The Plaintiff, Sandra Nelson, by her attorney, moves the court as follows:

1. On ____________________, Plaintiff served on the Defendant in this cause, ten (10) interrogatories in writing pursuant to Rule ____________________, which interrogatories are attached hereto.
2. Defendant failed to answer the interrogatories under oath as required by Rule ____________.
3. Plaintiff requests that this court enter an order directing and requiring Defendant to answer all of said interrogatories under oath.

WHEREFORE, Plaintiff moves that this court enter an order directing and requiring Defendant to answer all of said interrogatories under oath, and for an order awarding Plaintiff the reasonable expenses, including attorney's fees incurred in this motion and for such other and further relief as Plaintiff is entitled.

Respectfully submitted,

____

Attorney for Plaintiff

Questions for Critical Analysis

1. It appears that third parties may be responsible for the injuries Julie sustained. A third-party complaint could, therefore, be filed against the loading employees and the cable manufacturer. The complaint would assert that the loading employees and the cable manufacturer should be liable for Julie's injures because the crates were misloaded and the cable was defective.

Ethical Questions

1. Pamela should immediately disclose the existence of the document to her supervising attorney. Since this case is in federal court, FRCP 26 applies to discovery procedures. The law firm has a ongoing duty to disclose relevant information to the other side. The internal memorandum must be disclosed even though it will jeopardize Good Food, Inc.'s chance of winning the case.
2. Only an attorney can accept a case or set a fee. However, to keep from losing the client, Bill should identify himself as a paralegal. He should explain that only a highly trained attorney, such as Mark, can properly evaluate her case. Then Bill should immediately schedule her for an appointment with Mark—preferably for that same day or evening.
3. Evaluating the success of a case is giving legal advice. Paralegals are not ethically permitted to give legal advice. This does not change if the case appears to be a good or a bad one or if Sally believes she knows the answer based upon her experience. Sally should explain this to Ben and call her attorney into the meeting to answer Ben's question. If the attorney is not available, Sally should tell Ben she will ask the attorney to contact him with an answer as soon as possible.

CHAPTER 11

TRIAL PROCEDURES

CHAPTER OBJECTIVES

After completing this chapter, you should be able to:

- Describe how attorneys prepare for trial.
- Explain the ways in which paralegals assist in trial preparation.
- Discuss how jurors are selected.
- Identify the role of attorneys and their legal assistants in the jury-selection process.
- List the various phases of a trial.
- Indicate the kinds of trial-related tasks that paralegals often perform.
- State the options available to the losing party after the verdict is in.
- Understand how a case is appealed to a higher court for review.

Chapter Outline

I. INTRODUCTION

II. PREPARING FOR TRIAL
  A. Contacting and Preparing Witnesses
    1. Typically, litigation paralegals are responsible for ensuring that witnesses are available and in court on the day of the trial.
    2. Expert witnesses, who have specialized knowledge in a particular field, may be required.
    3. Contacting Witnesses and Issuing Subpoenas
      a. Paralegals often assist in contacting and issuing subpoenas to witnesses to secure their attendance at trial.
      b. The paralegal should comply with the court's requirements regarding witness fees and subpoenas.
    4. Preparing Witnesses for Trial
      a. The paralegal may be asked to prepare witnesses for trial by asking them questions and role playing.
      b. The attorney will advise the witness on trial procedures, when and how the witness will testify, and so on.
  B. Exhibits and Displays
    1. Attorneys for both sides and their paralegals gather and organize all evidence, documents, and other materials relating to the case.
    2. From this information, paralegals are frequently asked to prepare exhibits or displays that will be presented at trial.
    3. Exhibits and displays may include blow-ups, diagrams, artists' renderings, and video tapes.
  C. The Trial Notebook
    1. Many paralegals assume responsibility for preparing the trial notebook for the attorney.
    2. The trial notebook should contain copies of the pleadings, discovery, deposition transcripts and summaries, pretrial motions, a list of exhibits, a witness list, relevant legal research, and any other document or information that will be used during trial.
    3. The paralegal should consult with the attorney to see how she wishes the trial notebook to be categorized.
    4. The documents in the trial notebook should be copies instead of the originals.

III. PRETRIAL CONFERENCE
  A. Prior to trial, the attorneys for both sides usually meet with the trial judge in a pretrial conference.
  B. At the pretrial conference, the attorneys and judge decide whether a settlement is possible.
  C. If a settlement is not possible, the attorneys and judge decide how the trial will be conducted and what types of evidence will be admissible.
  D. A motion *in limine* (to limit evidence) may be made by one or both of the attorneys at the pretrial conference.

IV. JURY SELECTION
  A. *Voir Dire*
    1. The jury-selection process is called *voir dire.*
    2. During *voir dire,* attorneys for both sides question jurors to determine if bias exists or whether, for other reasons, certain jurors should be excluded from the jury.
  B. Challenges during *Voir Dire*
    1. Types of Challenges
      a. A challenge for cause is exercised when a particular prospective juror is biased for some reason.
      b. No reason need be given for excluding a juror based on a peremptory challenge. However, such challenges cannot be discriminatory.

2. Alternate Jurors
   a. The court seats alternate jurors who will also hear the entire trial and will take the place of any jurors who have been dismissed for whatever reason.
   b. Unless they replace jurors, alternate jurors do not participate in jury deliberations at the end of the trial.

V. THE TRIAL

A. Opening Statements
   1. The trial begins with opening statements, during which both attorneys give a brief version of the facts of the case and the evidence supporting their views that will be used at trial.

B. The Plaintiff's Case
   1. Direct Examination
      a. After opening statements, the plaintiff's attorney presents evidence supporting the plaintiff's claim, including the testimony of witnesses.
      b. An attorney's questioning of the witnesses called to testify on behalf of the attorney's client is referred to as direct examination.
      c. Leading questions are questions that suggest or lead to a desired answer. They may distort the testimony by discouraging witnesses from telling their stories in their own words.
   2. Cross-examination
      a. Cross-examination is the questioning of an opposing witness during the trial.
      b. During cross-examination, the opposing attorney is primarily concerned with reducing the witness's credibility.
      c. The opposing attorney must confine her questions to matters that were or could have been brought up during direct examination and matters that relate to the witness's credibility.
   3. Redirect and Recross
      a. Redirect examination is the questioning of a witness following the adverse party's cross-examination.
      b. Recross-examination is the questioning of an opposing witness following the adverse party's redirect examination.

C. Motion for a Directed Verdict (Motion for Judgment as a Matter of Law)
   1. After the plaintiff's attorney has presented his client's case and both attorneys have examined the witnesses, the defendant's attorney may make a motion for a directed verdict.
   2. A directed verdict is also called a motion for judgment as a matter of law.
   3. The motion asserts that the plaintiff has not offered enough evidence to support the validity of the plaintiff's claim against the defendant.
   4. If the judge grants the motion, the case will be dismissed.

D. The Defendant's Case
   1. After the plaintiff's attorney has presented her case, the defendant's attorney presents evidence and testimony to refute the plaintiff's claims.
   2. Any witnesses called to the stand by the defendant's attorney will be subject to direct examination by that attorney, cross-examination by the plaintiff's attorney, redirect examination by the defendant's attorney, and recross-examination by the plaintiff's attorney.

E. Closing Arguments
   1. After the defendant's attorney has finished her presentation, both attorneys give their closing arguments.
   2. Each attorney summarizes the major points made during the trial and attempts to show how the evidence presented favors a verdict in his or her client's favor.
   3. Closing arguments are made before the jury charge.

F. Jury Instructions
   1. Following the attorneys' closing arguments, the judge instructs the jurors.
   2. The judge instructs the jurors in a charge, which is a document that includes statements of the applicable laws and a review of the facts as they were presented during the trial.

☞ STUDY TIP

Results

In reading and studying civil litigation and trial procedures (in this chapter and in Chapter 10), you may find it helpful to keep in mind that a case can generally have only one of the following three results:

1. The plaintiff proves her side of the case and wins.
2. The plaintiff fails to prove her side of the case and loses.
3. The defendant proves his side of the case, and the plaintiff loses.

- 3. The jury must not disregard the judge's instructions as to what the applicable law is and how it should be applied to the facts of the case as interpreted by the jury.
- 4. After the jury instructions, the jury then begins its deliberations.

G. The Verdict
- 1. When the jury has reached a decision, it issues a verdict in favor of one party or another.

VI. POSTTRIAL MOTIONS AND PROCEDURES

A. Posttrial Motions
- 1. After the verdict is pronounced and the trial concluded, the losing party's attorney may make one or both of the following posttrial motions:
  - a. Motion for judgment notwithstanding the verdict.
    - 1) This motion is also called a motion for judgment as a matter of law in federal courts.
    - 2) This motion alleges that the judge should enter a judgment in favor of the losing party in spite of the verdict actually reached.
    - 3) The basis for this motion is that the verdict was not substantiated by the evidence or was otherwise erroneous.
  - b. Motion for a new trial.
    - 1) This motion asserts that the trial was so flawed that a new trial should be held.
    - 2) The basis for this motion is judge or juror misconduct or other pervasive errors in the first trial.

B. Appealing the Verdict
- 1. An appeal seeks a higher court's review of a lower court's decision for the purpose of correcting or changing the lower court's judgment or decision.
- 2. Notice of Appeal
  - a. When an appeal involves a federal district court decision, the appellant must file a notice of appeal with the district court that rendered the judgment.
  - b. The district court then notifies the appellee, and the clerk forwards a transcript of the trial court proceedings with any related documents or exhibits to the appellate court. These materials constitute the record on appeal.

3. The Appellate Brief and Oral Arguments
   a. When a case is appealed, both parties submit written briefs that present their position and arguments.
   b. Once the court has reviewed all briefs on appeal, it may set aside time for the attorneys to argue their positions before a panel of judges.
4. The Appellate Court's Options
   a. After reviewing the record and reading the parties' briefs, judges have several options as to how to decide the appeal.
   b. The judge or panel of judges may decide to affirm, reverse, remand, or revise the trial court's decision.
   c. A state appellate court's decision may be appealed to the state supreme court.
   d. A federal appellate court's decision could be appealed to the United States Supreme Court.

VII. ENFORCING THE JUDGMENT

A. Even though the plaintiff wins a lawsuit for damages, it may be difficult to enforce the judgment against the defendant, particularly if the defendant has few assets.

B. If the defendant does not personally have the amount of money available to pay the judgment, the plaintiff's attorney must request that the court issue a writ of execution.

C. A writ of execution directs the sheriff to seize and sell a particular asset of the defendant in order to pay the judgment to the plaintiff.

D. A judgment creditor is one who is legally entitled, by a court's judgment, to collect the amount of the judgment from a debtor.

QUESTIONS FOR REVIEW

TRUE-FALSE QUESTIONS

____ 1. Friendly witnesses, those favorable to your client's position, need not be served with a subpoena.

____ 2. Attorneys should never discuss a witness's testimony with the witness before trial, because it might look like the attorney told the witness what to say.

____ 3. Preparation of a trial notebook should begin at the outset of the lawsuit.

____ 4. The question-and-answer session with each prospective juror is known as *voir dire*.

____ 5. Challenges for cause are exercised without giving any reason for excluding a particular juror.

____ 6. The number of peremptory challenges is unlimited.

____ 7. Hostile witnesses are uncooperative witnesses or those who are testifying on behalf of the other party.

____ 8. Cross-examination questions may be of any matter relative to the issues.

____ 9. Once the plaintiff has presented the case, the plaintiff is never permitted to offer additional evidence.

____ 10. In federal courts, posttrial motions may be filed anytime after the trial concludes.

____ 11. A new witness may be called to testify to an appellate court.

____ 12. The appellant is the party appealing the decision; the appellee is the party against whom the appeal is taken.

____ 13. An appellate court can affirm, reverse, remand, and modify a lower court's decision.

____ 14. An appellate court is always required to review cases.

____ 15. Any property owned by a debtor can be seized and sold to satisfy a court judgment.

Fill-in Questions

Before trial, a legal assistant gathers and organizes all evidence and materials in a ________________ (trial notebook / subpoena). Jury selection includes questioning individuals through a process called ________________ (remand/*voir dire*). During this process, jurors may be excluded from the pool through ________________ (challenges/motions *in limine*). Challenges for cause are ________________ (limited/unlimited). Peremptory challenges are ________________ (limited/unlimited).

The trial begins with ________________ (charge to the jury/opening statements). The initial questioning of witnesses is referred to as ________________ (direct examination/cross-examination). The opposing attorney's questioning of a witness is referred to as ________________ (direct examination/cross-examination).

At the conclusion of the trial, the attorneys summarize the case to the jury during ________________ (closing arguments/charge to the jury). The jury then retires and deliberates and returns with a ________________ (verdict/judgment).

Multiple-Choice Questions

____ 1. An order issued by the court clerk directing a person to appear in court is called:
A. Charge
B. Subpoena
C. Remand
D. *Voir dire*

____ 2. A trial notebook should include all of the following except:
A. Copies of pleadings
B. Copies of interrogatories
C. Copies of deposition transcripts and summaries
D. Original exhibits

____ 3. A motion requesting the judge to order that certain types of evidence not be brought out at trial is a:
A. Motion for a new trial
B. Motion for judgment as a matter of law
C. Motion for judgment notwithstanding the verdict
D. Motion *in limine*

____ 4. An opening statement:
A. Is a summary of the story that will unfold during trial
B. Is the first question directed at an eye witness
C. Is a question directed at a prospective juror to determine if the juror is biased
D. Is a question that leads to a particular desired response

____ 5. Leading questions:
A. Are permitted during direct examination
B. Are asked during opening statements
C. May distort the testimony by discouraging witnesses from telling their stories in their own words
D. May be asked by the judge

____ 6. The order of a questioning a witness is as follows:
A. Direct examination; redirect examination; cross-examination; recross-examination
B. Cross-examination; direct examination; recross-examination; redirect examination
C. Direct examination; cross-examination; redirect examination; recross-examination
D. Direct examination; cross-examination; recross-examination; redirect examination

____ 7. A motion claiming that insufficient evidence has been offered in support of a claim is a:
A. Motion for a new trial
B. Motion for directed verdict
C. Motion for judgment notwithstanding the verdict
D. Motion *in limine*

____ 8. In closing arguments:
A. Attorneys summarize their presentations and argue in their clients' favor
B. Debate with each other before the jury
C. Debate with the judge about evidentiary rulings
D. Request the dismissal of jurors

____ 9. A charge is:
A. The monetary amount requested by a juror for his attendance at trial
B. A request for judgment notwithstanding the verdict
C. The judge's instructions to the jurors of the rules of law applicable to the issues
D. That which follows the jury's announcement of the verdict

____ 10. A motion requesting judgment because the jury's verdict was unreasonable and erroneous is a:
A. Motion for a new trial
B. Motion for judgment as a matter of law
C. Motion for judgment notwithstanding the verdict
D. Motion *in limine*

____ 11. A motion claiming that the trial was fundamentally flawed is a:
A. Motion for a new trial
B. Motion for judgment as a matter of law
C. Motion for judgment notwithstanding the verdict
D. Motion *in limine*

____ 12. All of the following are involved in an appeal except:
A. Opening statement
B. Appellant and appellee
C. Record on appeal
D. Panel of judges

____ 13. An order directing the sheriff to seize and sell assets is a:
A. Subpoena
B. Writ of execution
C. Remand
D. Motion *in limine*

____ 14. One who has obtained a court judgment against a debtor is:
A. An appellant
B. An appellee
C. An alternate juror
D. A judgment creditor

____ 15. Many disputes are settled out of court because:
A. It is difficult to enforce court judgments
B. The cost of litigation, including attorneys' fees and court costs, is high
C. The litigants' time is costly
D. All of the above

PRACTICE QUESTIONS

1. Assume the facts given in this chapter's Practice Question and Assignment 4, except that your firm represents the doctor who prescribed the weight-control pills. The only evidence presented during the plaintiff's case is that the pharmaceutical company failed to provide warnings of the dangers of the pill for those persons whose blood types were incompatible with the pill and that the plaintiff's daughter suffered from a congenital heart condition that would, in all probability, have shortened her life span. Draft an appropriate motion for filing with the court prior to presentation of any evidence on behalf of the doctor.
2. Assume the facts given in this Chapter's Practice Question and Assignment 4. Your firm represents the plaintiff. Prepare a subpoena for Dr. Albert Brown, the plaintiff's expert witness, who has prepared a report concerning the decedent's physical condition. Dr. Brown's office is located at One Renaissance Tower, Fifth Floor, Detroit, Michigan. What other items may need to be included with the subpoena before service?

QUESTIONS FOR CRITICAL ANALYSIS

1. Assume that you are assisting an attorney handling a personal-injury lawsuit tried to a jury. Your firm, representing the plaintiff, has presented all the evidence on behalf of your client, and the defendant has called one witness. The trial will resume tomorrow. You are having dinner at a local restaurant and notice the defendant's witness dining with two other people. During the course of your dinner, you see one of the jurors pass by the witness's table and stop and talk to him. You hear the juror ask the witness some questions about the testimony given by him that day. The witness responds to those questions. The next day you tell your supervising attorney about the dinner events. What might the firm consider filing?

ETHICAL QUESTIONS

1. During the lunch break in the course of a breach-of-contract trial, Helen Hatcher, a paralegal, was in the cafeteria line next to one of the jurors. The juror recognized Helen from the courtroom and said, "I don't understand the elements needed to form a contract. Can you explain them to me?" How should Helen respond?
2. One evening during the course of a personal-injury trial, Marjorie Mavens, a paralegal, is having dinner in a local restaurant. Marjorie overhears a conversation from the next booth and recognizes the speakers as two jurors from the trial. Not realizing Marjorie is in the next booth, one juror said, "I tend to believe the plaintiff in this case. If he would just make it clear he had no prior medical problem, I know he would win his case." The jurors leave the restaurant without seeing Marjorie. Marjorie works for the plaintiff's attorney. Should she have made her presence known? What should Marjorie do now?
3. Before trial begins for the day, Donna Smith, a paralegal, is calling witnesses to remind them of the times they are due at the courthouse. One witness, Jerry Suder, asks her how to answer a particular question if asked by the other side. How should Donna answer this question?

Technology and Today's Paralegal

Does your state or federal jurisdiction allow the use of state-of-the-art trial technology in the courtroom? Using the following suggested sites, research this question. Be aware that, as of June 1998, the following states do not have their statutes on the Internet: Hawaii, Illinois, Louisiana, Maryland, Michigan, North Carolina, North Dakota, South Dakota, Tennessee, and West Virginia.

LLRX Litigator's Resource Guide
http://www.llrx.com/columns/litigat.htm

State Legal Research
http://www.law.du.edu/library/pubs/states/htm

Cornell Law Library
http://www.law.cornell.edu

FindLaw
http://www.findlaw.com

Hieros Gamos
http://www.hg.org

ANSWERS

True-False Questions

1. F
2. F
3. T
4. T
5. F
6. F
7. T
8. F
9. F
10. F
11. F
12. T
13. T
14. F
15. F

Fill-in Questions

trial notebook; *voir dire;* challenges; unlimited; limited

opening statements; direct examination; cross-examination; closing argument; verdict

Multiple-Choice Questions

1. B
2. D
3. D
4. A
5. C
6. C
7. B
8. A
9. C
10. C
11. A
12. A
13. B
14. D
15. D

Practice Questions

1. The firm may consider filing a motion for directed verdict or motion for judgment as a matter of law, as the court has been presented with insufficient evidence in support of a medical-malpractice suit.

[Caption—Court Title and Cause]

The Defendant at the close of Plaintiff's case moves the court to withdraw the evidence from the consideration of the jury and to find the Defendant not liable.

As grounds for this motion, Defendant states that:

(1) No evidence has been offered or received during the trial of the above-entitled cause of action to sustain the allegations of medical-malpractice contained in Plaintiff's complaint.

(2) No evidence has been offered or received during the trial proving or tending to prove that Defendant was guilty of any medical-malpractice.

Date:____________________

____
Attorney for the Defendant

2. Subpoena form from 11-7a. See Exhibit 11.2 in the text.

The court clerk should be contacted to find out if there are any fees necessary for service upon the witness.

Questions for Critical Analysis

1. Because the firm may fear that the juror's conduct may be prejudicial and that the information will be conveyed to the other jurors, the firm may file a motion for a new trial, claiming that the trial is fundamentally flawed. The motion could reflect jury misconduct, resulting from the encounter between the juror and witness. The information elicited in response to the juror's questions may result in a miscarriage of justice; to avoid any taint of prejudice, the firm should request a new trial.

Ethical Questions

1. Attorneys, paralegals, and parties are not ethically permitted to discuss any aspect of the case with jurors. Helen should politely, but firmly, inform the juror of this and break off all conversation regarding the trial with the juror. Further, she should immediately report the incident to her attorney.
2. This is an ethical question that is not so easily answered. Marjorie is not ethically permitted to discuss any aspect of the case with a juror. In this case, she merely overheard their conversation. To prevent the ethical "appearance of impropriety," Marjorie probably should have made her presence known immediately once the jurors began to discuss the trial. Since she did not, Marjorie should inform her attorney of the incident. The attorney will decide if it is appropriate for Marjorie to disclose the nature of the jurors' conversation.
3. Discussing legal strategy or possible legal responses to questions at trial is giving legal advice. Paralegals are not ethically permitted to give legal advice. Donna should explain this to Jerry and tell him she will convey his question to her attorney. She should then do so and either call Jerry back with the attorney's answer or give Jerry the attorney's answer when he arrives at the courthouse.

CHAPTER 12

CRIMINAL LAW AND PROCEDURES

CHAPTER OBJECTIVES

After completing this chapter, you should be able to:

- Discuss the difference between crimes and other wrongful acts.
- List the elements that are required for criminal liability.
- Name some of the more common defenses that are raised when defending against criminal charges.
- Understand the constitutional rights of persons accused of crimes.
- Identify the basic steps involved in criminal procedure from the time a crime is reported to when the case is resolved.
- Explain why a criminal suspect may be released and the case dismissed prior to trial.
- Recognize how and why criminal litigation procedures differ from civil litigation procedures.

Chapter Outline

I. INTRODUCTION

II. WHAT IS A CRIME?
- A. Classifications of Crimes
  - 1. Felonies
    - a. A felony is a serious crime that may be punished by imprisonment for more than one year or death.
    - b. Felonies are classified by degree.
  - 2. Misdemeanors
    - a. Misdemeanors are less serious crimes such as prostitution, disturbing the peace, and public intoxication.
    - b. The penalty for a misdemeanor may include imprisonment for up to a year.
  - 3. Petty Offenses
    - a. In criminal law, a petty offense, or infraction, is considered the least serious kind of wrong.
- B. The Variety of Criminal Acts
  - 1. A variety of acts have been defined as crimes.
  - 2. Acts that violate rules and regulations of government agencies may be crimes.

III. ELEMENTS OF CRIMINAL LIABILITY
- A. The Criminal Act
  - 1. For a person to be convicted of a crime, the performance of a criminal act must exist simultaneously with the specified state of mind, or intent.
  - 2. A criminal act is known as the *actus reus,* or guilty act.
  - 3. Most crimes require that a person *do* something in order to be accused of a crime.
  - 4. In some cases, an act of *omission* can be a crime, but only when a person has a legal duty to perform the omitted act.
- B. State of Mind
  - 1. For a person to be convicted of a crime, the required state of mind, also known as *mens rea* (or wrongful mental state), must exist simultaneously with the performance of a criminal act.
  - 2. How a crime is defined and punished depends on the degree of wrongfulness of the defendant's state of mind.
  - 3. Proving lack of required mental state is necessary to convict someone of a crime.
- C. Defenses to Criminal Liability
  - 1. The Required Mental State Is Lacking
  - 2. Protection of Persons or Property
    - a. *Self-defense* is the legally recognized privilege to protect oneself or one's property against injury by another.
    - b. *Defense of others* is the reasonable use of force to protect others from harm.
    - c. *Defense of property* means the amount of reasonable force used to protect one's property from harm threatened by another. Deadly force is not normally allowed.
  - 3. Statutes of Limitations
    - a. In a criminal case, the action must be prosecuted within a certain number of years.
  - 4. Other Defenses
    - a. Mistaken identity or other defenses may be used.
    - b. The defendant may offer an alibi as a defense.
    - c. Other defenses to criminal liability have to do with violations of procedural law.

IV. CONSTITUTIONAL SAFEGUARDS
- A. The *Miranda* Rule
  - 1. The *Miranda* decision established the rule that individuals who are arrested and taken into custody must be informed of certain constitutional rights.

2. The Fifth Amendment to the U.S. Constitution guarantees the privilege against compulsory self-incrimination.
3. Any evidence or confession obtained in violation of the suspect's rights will normally not be admissible in court under the exclusionary rule.

B. The Erosion of the *Miranda* Rule
1. Omnibus Crime Control and Safe Streets Act, passed by Congress in 1968, provided that in cases of federal crimes a voluntary confession could be used as evidence even if the accused had not been informed of his or her rights.
2. The need to protect the public may warrant the admissibility of statements made by the defendant, and these statements may be admissible even when the defendant was not informed of his or her *Miranda* rights.
3. Statements made by the defendant to police in obtaining biographical data may be admissible.
4. The biographical data must be necessary to complete booking or pretrial services.

V. CRIMINAL PROCEDURES PRIOR TO PROSECUTION

A. Arrest
1. Probable Cause
   a. Before an individual can be arrested, the requirement of probable cause must be met.
   b. There must be a substantial likelihood that a crime was committed and that the individual committed the crime for probable cause to exist.
2. Arrest Warrants
   a. An arrest order is a written order, based on probable cause and issued by a judge, commanding that the person named can be arrested by the police.

B. Booking
1. After the arrest, the police take the suspect to some holding facility where booking occurs.
2. Booking takes place when an officer enters the suspect's name, offense, and time of arrival on the police log, or blotter.

C. Investigation after the Arrest
1. In some cases, where the suspect is caught in the act, the police may not have to undertake much of an investigation.
2. In other cases, the police must find and interview witnesses and conduct searches to collect evidence.

VI. THE PROSECUTION BEGINS

A. Filing the Complaint
1. Criminal litigation against a suspect begins when the prosecutor decides to prosecute the case and files a complaint.
2. The complaint includes a statement of the charges that are being brought against the suspect.
3. Once the complaint is filed, the suspect becomes a criminal defendant.

B. Initial Appearance
1. In most jurisdictions, defendants are taken before a magistrate within twenty-four hours of arrest.
2. The magistrate does the following:
   a. Makes sure the person presented is the person named in the complaint.
   b. Informs the defendant of the charges made in the complaint.
   c. Explains to the defendant his or her constitutional rights.
   d. Appoints an attorney if the defendant cannot afford one.
   e. Releases the defendant on certain conditions, such as the posting of bail.

C. Preliminary Hearing
1. The defendant again appears before a magistrate or judge at a preliminary hearing.
2. The magistrate or judge determines whether the evidence presented is sufficient to establish probable cause.

3. If the evidence is insufficient to establish probable cause, the charges are reduced or dropped.
4. If the magistrate believes probable cause exists, the prosecutor issues an information, and the defendant is bound over for trial.

D. Grand Jury Review
1. The grand jury is a group of citizens called to decide whether probable cause exists.
2. A prosecutor may call a grand jury to evaluate the evidence against a suspect.
3. Taking the case to the grand jury may indicate to the prosecutor the relative strength or weakness of the case.
4. The federal government and some states require a grand jury to decide if a case should go to trial.
5. If the grand jury finds probable cause exists, it issues an indictment against the defendant called a true bill.
6. The indictment is filed with the trial court and becomes the formal charge against the defendant.

E. Arraignment
1. Based on the information or the indictment filed, the prosecutor submits a motion to the court ordering the defendant to appear for arraignment.
2. At the arraignment, the defendant is informed of the charges against him or her and is offered an opportunity to respond to the charges.
3. At the arraignment, the defendant may plead:
   a. Guilty.
   b. Not guilty.
   c. *Nolo contendere* (no contest).
4. The defendant may agree on a plea as a result of plea bargaining between the prosecutor and defendant.

F. Pretrial Motions
1. Prior to the trial, the defendant's attorney may file pretrial motions requesting the court to dismiss the case for various reasons.
2. A pretrial motion may:
   a. Challenge the sufficiency of the evidence.
   b. Assert that certain key evidence was obtained illegally.
   c. Argue that for some other reason the case should be dismissed.

G. Discovery
1. Prior to the trial of a criminal case, discovery takes place.
2. The defendant in a criminal case is entitled to obtain any evidence relating to the case possessed by the prosecution.
3. Evidence obtained through discovery may include the following:
   a. Documents.
   b. Statements previously made by the defendant.
   c. Objects.
   d. Reports of tests or examinations.

VII. THE TRIAL

A. Special Features of Criminal Trials
1. A "Speedy and Public" Trial
   a. The Sixth Amendment of the U.S. Constitution requires a speedy and public trial for criminal prosecutions but does not specify what is meant by the term "speedy."
2. The Role of the Jury
   a. In all felony cases, the defendant is entitled to a jury trial.
   b. In most jurisdictions, jury verdicts in criminal cases must be unanimous for acquittal or conviction.

3. The Presumption of a Defendant's Innocence
   a. A defendant is innocent until proven guilty.
   b. The burden of proving guilt falls on the public prosecutor.
4. A Strict Standard of Proof
   a. The state must prove the defendant's guilt beyond a reasonable doubt.
5. The Privilege against Self-Incrimination
   a. The Fifth Amendment of the U.S. Constitution states that no person can be forced to give testimony that might be self-incriminating.
   b. Defendants and witnesses in a criminal trial may refuse to testify on this ground.
6. Rules of Evidence
   a. Criminal courts have rules of evidence that regulate what types of evidence may be presented and how the evidence may be brought out in criminal cases, especially in jury trials.
   b. These rules are designed to ensure that the evidence presented in the case is relevant, reliable, and not unfairly prejudicial to the defendant.

B. Sentencing
1. At the conclusion of trial, a defendant who has been found guilty is sentenced by the judge.
2. The sentence may involve one or more of the following:
   a. Imprisonment.
   b. Death (in some states).
   c. Probation, house arrest, or other form of supervised release.
   d. Financial penalties.

C. Appeal
1. If the defendant loses at trial, he or she may appeal the case to a higher court.
2. Only a minority of decisions are reversed on appeal.
3. If a conviction is overturned on appeal, the defendant may or may not be tried again.

QUESTIONS FOR REVIEW

TRUE-FALSE QUESTIONS

____ 1. Every defendant accused of a crime has a right to counsel.

____ 2. Criminal law is intended to compensate the injured party; civil law is intended to punish in an attempt to deter others from similar actions.

____ 3. The same act can give rise to both a crime and a tort.

____ 4. A criminal act always involves a victim.

____ 5. Federal jurisdiction is limited to felonies.

____ 6. If a criminal act has been committed *actus reus,* the accused may be convicted of a crime.

____ 7. The punishment for a crime is dependent on the degree of wrongfulness or intention.

____ 8. The right to self-defense is absolute.

____ 9. In order to admit evidence obtained in violation of a defendant's constitutional rights, it is necessary to file a motion *in limine.*

____ 10. Probable cause exists if there is a possibility that a crime was committed and that the individual committed the crime.

____ 11. Once bail has been set, the amount cannot be changed.

____ 12. Evidence in the prosecutor's possession is not available to defendant.

____ 13. Evidence in the prosecutor's possession may be inadmissible at trial.

____ 14. In most jurisdictions, a unanimous jury is only necessary for a conviction.

____ 15. The jury sentences the defendant.

Fill-in Questions

A suspect can be arrested if a police officer believes ____________________ (there is probable cause/beyond a reasonable doubt). Once arrested, the suspect is ____________________ (booked/arraigned). The suspect is informed of the charges at the ____________________ (initial appearance/preliminary hearing). The suspect is asked to enter a plea at the ____________________ (preliminary hearing/arraignment). The defendant may avoid criminal liability because he lacked the requisite ____________________ (*mens rea*/personal jurisdiction). Generally, a trial by jury will be used if the suspect is charged with a ____________________ (misdemeanor/felony). A jury is generally composed of ____________________ (six/twelve) jurors). The verdict must be agreed upon by ____________________ (a majority/all). If the defendant is found not guilty, the prosecution ____________________ (may/may not) appeal the verdict. If the defendant is found guilty, the ____________________ (prosecution/judge) sentences the defendant.

Multiple-Choice Questions

____ 1. Public prosecutors include all of the following except:
A. U.S. Attorney
B. District attorney
C. Grand jury
D. Prosecuting attorney

____ 2. Criminal law is:
A. Primarily based on statutory law
B. Prosecuted by injured parties
C. Generally punished by imposition of a judgment for money damages
D. Referred to as felonies

____ 3. Which of the following choices lists, in order, a felony, a misdemeanor, and a petty offense:
A. Prostitution; rape; building code violation
B. Rape; prostitution; building code violation
C. Building code violation; rape; prostitution
D. Building code violation; prostitution; rape

____ 4. The necessary elements for conviction of a crime include:
A. Indictment and arrest
B. *Mens rea* and *actus reus*
C. Arraignment and arrest
D. Booking and bail

____ 5. Defenses to criminal liability include all of the following except:
A. Defense of self
B. Defense of others
C. Statute of limitations
D. All of the above represent possible defenses

____ 6. Due process means:
A. That the government must follow a set of reasonable, fair, and standard procedures
B. That an accused may not be tried twice for the same criminal offense
C. That an accused may not be compelled to be a witness against himself
D. That a speedy trial must be guaranteed

____ 7. Informing an accused who has been taken into custody of certain constitutional rights is called:
A. Probable cause
B. Miranda rights
C. Booking
D. Citation

____ 8. The instructions given to a defendant to appear in court at some later date to respond to the charges is called:
A. Arrest
B. Citation
C. Booking
D. Bail

____ 9. Entering the suspect's name, offense, and time of arrival on the police log is called:
A. Arrest
B. Citation
C. Booking
D. Bail

____ 10. An amount of money paid by the defendant to the court and retained by the court until the defendant returns for further proceedings is called:
A. Arrest
B. Citation
C. Booking
D. Bail

____ 11. The procedural steps in a criminal case, in order is:
A. Booking; preliminary hearing; plea bargaining; arraignment; trial
B. Arrest; booking; preliminary hearing; plea bargain; arraignment; trial
C. Arrest; initial appearance; booking; preliminary hearing; trial
D. Arrest; booking; initial appearance; preliminary hearing; trial

____ 12. A pretrial motion claiming that there was insufficient evidence to establish probable cause is called:
A. Motion *in limine*
B. Motion to dismiss
C. Motion challenging the sufficiency of the indictment
D. Motion to suppress

____ 13. Beyond a reasonable doubt is the standard imposed:
A. Upon the defendant in establishing his or her innocence
B. Upon the prosecution
C. Upon the jury in verifying its unanimity
D. Upon the judge in a bench trial

____ 14. A witness need not testify at trial because:
A. The U.S. Constitution guarantees a right against self-incrimination
B. The U.S. Constitution guarantees a right to a speedy trial
C. A witness has a right to defend himself or herself
D. A witness lacks the prerequisite *mens rea*

____ 15. A sentence may be all of the following except:
A. Bail
B. Imprisonment
C. Probation
D. Restitution

Practice Questions

1. Assume defendant Jim Moore is charged with check kiting and that your firm has been retained to represent him. He informs you that certain ledger books were taken from his automobile prior to his arrest while his automobile was parked at a grocery store. Draft an appropriate pretrial motion.
2. Assume defendant Patrick C. Duffy, mentioned in this Chapter's Practice Question and Assignment 10, was indicted for murdering an FBI officer, Larry Row. Prepare an indictment.
3. Based on the following facts, prepare a Waiver of Trial by Jury on behalf of Helen Benson.

   Helen Benson, the defendant, was indicted by indictment number 123456-93 for tax evasion in violation of 28 U.S.C. 6604. The indictment was filed on February 22, 1995. The defendant knows that the U.S. attorney has all of her tax files, including both her personal returns and those of her business from 1990 to the present date, as well as all of her business and personal financial records for those dates. The defendant knows that these records are in the possession of the U.S. attorney, because she was served with a search warrant on July 9, 1993, which required her to turn over all of these records to the U.S. attorney. All of these records are necessary to the preparation of the defendant's defense, because without the records, she has insufficient knowledge and recollection of her finances and the returns she filed with the Internal Revenue Service.

Questions for Critical Analysis

1. Assume that Tom shot Dick. However, assume that another individual had been stalking Tom and his family. As a result of this stalking, Tom purchased a gun and stored it, loaded, in his foyer closet. On the night of the murder, Tom heard something in his front yard and noticed the stalker's car parked down the street. Tom took out his gun, and when he noticed a shadow on the patio, he shot who he thought was the stalker; instead it was Dick. Assume that Tom has been charged with murder. What possible defenses may be asserted in Tom's defense.
2. Assume the facts given in Questions for Critical Analysis 1 above and that Tom has been taken into custody, although no Miranda rights were read or explained. Assume that on the way to the police station, the police officers question Tom about the incident, and Tom responds to these questions. Furthermore, assume that his wife calls their family attorney, but the attorney fails to make contact with Tom until after the initial appearance, at which bail was denied. Bail was denied even though Tom told the court he was a life-long resident of the community, that he is self-employed and has no other source of income, and that his three children are currently enrolled in the local school. What constitutional rights of Tom may have been violated?

Ethical Questions

1. Janis Hernandez is a litigation paralegal working for a medium-sized law firm. In preparing for trial, Janis' supervising attorney asks her to make sure the witnesses are in court at the proper time. Janis has prepared subpoenas and had them served, and she made telephone calls to remind the witnesses of the date and time they are to appear. On the day of trial, a key witness does not appear. The trial judge is very unhappy with Janis' supervising attorney who, in turn, is extremely upset with Janis. What should Janis do?
2. Harry Rude is a legal assistant working to prepare exhibits for trial. Harry's law firm represents the plaintiff, who is seeking damages from a breached contract. Harry is making a chart illustrating unpaid invoice amounts. While Harry has put in the accurate amount for each invoice, he deliberately adds $10,000 to the actual total on the chart. Has Harry done anything wrong?

Technology and Today's Paralegal

Another way to find sites on the Internet that discuss crimes perpetrated on the Internet is to do a search using a search engine (such as *hotbot.com.*) and perform a search for "electronic or online crime."

Another site that provides a wealth of information on the subject of electronic crime is *http:isleauth.com/crime.htm.* This site allows you to search the Bureau of Alcohol, Tobacco, and Firearms; the Bureau of Justice Statistics; the FBI; the National Archive of Criminal Justice Data; the National Criminal Justice Reference Service; the Office of International Crimes; and Organized Crime.

Answers

True-False Questions

1. T
2. F
3. F
4. F
5. F
6. F
7. T
8. F
9. F
10. F
11. F
12. F
13. T
14. F
15. F

Fill-in Questions

there is probable cause; booked; initial appearance, arraignment; *mens rea;* felony; twelve; all; may not; judge

Multiple-Choice Questions

1. C
2. A
3. B
4. B
5. D
6. A
7. B
8. B
9. C
10. D
11. D
12. C
13. B
14. A
15. A

Practice Questions

1.

IN THE UNITED STATES DISTRICT COURT
FOR THE ______ DISTRICT OF _____
__________ DIVISION

United States of America	)	
Plaintiff	)	
v.	)	No. ________
Jim Moore	)	
Defendant	)	Judge May Smythe

MOTION TO SUPPRESS EVIDENCE

Defendant Jim Moore, by and through his attorney, ________, states that he has information from which he believes the United States of America has in its possession and intends to use as evidence in the trial of this cause certain physical evidence which was obtained by ___________ on ___________, 19____ during a search of defendant's home and premises. The defendant moves this Court to suppress such evidence and to bar the United States of America from using said evidence in this cause for the reason that the evidence was seized unlawfully, unreasonably and contrary to the Statutes and Constitution of the United States. In support of his motion, defendant would state to the Court the following:

(1) The said evidence was obtained by means of searches and seizures without any warrant or other lawful authority;

(2) Said evidence was not obtained as an instant of a lawful arrest of defendant, but was obtained by means of searches and seizures which occurred before an arrest without any warrant or other lawful authority;

(3) Defendant's arrest and the searches and seizures were unlawful, unreasonable, and violative of the following provisions of the United States Constitution:

(a) The prohibition against unreasonable searches and seizures as guaranteed by the 4th and 14th Amendments to the United States Constitution;

(b) Prohibition against defendant being compelled to be a witness and to testify against himself as guaranteed by the 5th and 14th Amendments to the United States Constitution;

(c) The prohibition against depriving any person, including the defendant, of liberty or property without due process of law as guaranteed by the 5th and 14th Amendments to the United States Constitution;

(d) The prohibition against depriving any person, including the defendant, of his natural right to liberty, the pursuit of happiness, and the enjoyment of the gains of his own industry, of equal rights and opportunity under the laws, and of the equal protection of the laws, as guaranteed by the 14th Amendment to the United States Constitution;

WHEREFORE, for all the above-mentioned reasons, defendant respectfully requests that this Honorable Court enter an Order suppressing any and all evidence seized in connection with this case and barring the government from using or referring to such evidence in any way in the trial of the above-entitled cause.

Respectfully submitted,

____

2.

IN THE UNITED STATES DISTRICT COURT
FOR THE ________ DISTRICT
OF _______, _________ DIVISION

United States of America	)	
Plaintiff	)	No. ________
v.	)	(18 U.S.C. §§ 1111, 1114)
Patrick C. Duffy	)	
Defendant	)	

The Grand Jury charges that:

On or about the ____________ day of ____________, 19____, in the ____________ District of ____________, Patrick C. Duffy with premeditation and by means of shooting murdered Larry Row who was then an officer of the Federal Bureau of Investigation of the Department of Justice engaged in the performance of his official duties.

A TRUE BILL

____
Foreperson

____
United States Attorney

3.

IN THE UNITED STATES DISTRICT COURT
FOR THE ________ DISTRICT
OF ________, ________ DIVISION

United States of America)
Plaintiff) No. ________
v.)
Helen Benson)
Defendant)

Helen Benson in the above styled cause of action in open court waives the right of trial by a jury and elects to be tried before the court.

This ____________ day of ________, 19_____.

____
Defendant

Waiver of trial by jury concurred in:

____
Attorney for Defendant

Witnesses:

____

____

In open court filed _____________, 19_____.

Approved by the Court.

____
Clerk

Questions for Critical Analysis

1. Tom may allege that he lacked the requisite mental state, intent to kill. Because of the prior stalking incidents, he may allege that he did not intend to kill but merely to ward-off. Obviously, he did not intend to kill Dick. Additionally, Tom may claim that he was acting in self-defense. Given the prior stalkings, he may have felt threatened and was, again, attempting to ward-off the perceived stalker. Accordingly, Tom could assert defense of others, his family. Finally, Tom may assert defense of property; the individual on the patio was there without Tom's permission and was, thus, trespassing. However, the degree of force in all of these situations may be unreasonable.
2. Initially, the police officers failed to inform Tom of his Miranda rights. Thus, Tom need not have responded to the officers' questions on the way to the police station. Additionally, Tom may not have known that he had a right to speak with an attorney or have his attorney present during the questioning. Tom may also argue that denial of bail, given his circumstances, was in violation of the Eighth Amendment. Since he believed he was being stalked and because he had ties to the community, denial of bail may be considered excessive and cruel and unusual punishment.

Ethical Questions

1. If Janis has kept meticulous documentation, her professional reputation and that of her supervising attorney should be protected with the trial judge. Janis should show her attorney any notes she made regarding the witness' willingness to testify. Janis should also show the attorney the copy of the subpoena that was served. As a result of Janis' careful documentation, her supervising attorney should not be exposed to any potential liability brought by the client for malpractice.
2. Harry has engaged in unethical conduct and has also made it possible for his supervising attorney to be charged with unethical conduct. Harry has prepared an exhibit that is inaccurate and misleading. Harry has jeopardized his supervising attorney's professional reputation by causing the attorney to breach a professional duty.

CHAPTER 13

CONDUCTING INTERVIEWS AND INVESTIGATIONS

CHAPTER OBJECTIVES

After completing this chapter, you should be able to:

- Understand how to prepare for an interview.
- Describe the skills needed in the interview process.
- Identify the common types of client and witness interviews.
- Explain how to create an investigation plan.
- Recognize the variety of sources used to locate information or witnesses.
- List the rules governing what types of evidence that are admissible.
- Explain how to summarize investigation results.

Chapter Outline

I. INTRODUCTION

II. PLANNING THE INTERVIEW
- A. Know What Information You Want to Obtain
  1. Before an interview, you should know what kinds of questions you want to ask.
- B. Recording the Interview
  1. Always obtain permission to tape-record the interview.
  2. When using a tape recorder, you should state the following information at the beginning of the tape:
     - a. The name of the interviewee and any other relevant information about that person.
     - b. The name of the person conducting the interview.
     - c. The names of other persons present during the interview.
     - d. The date, time, and place of the interview.
     - e. The interviewee's consent to tape-record the interview.
  3. There are advantages and disadvantages to tape-recording an interview.

III. INTERVIEWING SKILLS
- A. Interpersonal Skills
  1. Your primary goal is to obtain information from the person being interviewed.
  2. The paralegal must establish a rapport with the interviewee and put him at ease.
  3. Paralegals should use language that is familiar to the interviewee.
  4. The paralegal should avoid using legal terminology unless she clearly defines the terms for the interviewee.
- B. Questioning Skills
  1. Open-ended Questions
     - a. An open-ended question is a broad, exploratory question that invites any number of possible responses.
     - b. Use open-ended questions when you want the interviewee to talk at some length about a given subject.
     - c. Open-ended questions are useful when interviewing clients or friendly witnesses.
  2. Closed-ended Questions
     - a. A closed-ended question is intended to elicit a "yes" or "no" response.
     - b. Closed-ended questions are useful in eliciting information from adverse witnesses or in relaxing an interviewee in preparation for more difficult questions.
  3. Hypothetical Questions
     - a. Hypothetical questions are often used when questioning an expert witness.
     - b. This type of question allows you obtain an answer to an important question without revealing the facts and confidences of your client's case.
  4. Pressure Questions
     - a. Pressure questions are intended to make the interviewee feel uncomfortable and to induce that person to respond emotionally.
     - b. This type of question should only be used as a last resort.
  5. Leading Questions
     - a. A leading question suggests to the listener the answer to the question.
     - b. Leading questions may lead to distorted answers.
- C. Listening Skills
  1. Good listening skills are essential for the interviewer.
  2. Keep interruptions and distractions to a minimum so you can concentrate on the subject being discussed.
  3. Active listening requires the listener to pay close attention to what the speaker is saying.
  4. You should be constantly analyzing your interviewees' responses.

IV. INTERVIEWING CLIENTS

A. The Initial Client Interview
   1. The initial interview is usually conducted by the attorney but often is attended by the paralegal.
   2. Paralegals must indicate their nonattorney status to the client if the attorney does not do so.
   3. A follow-up letter should be sent to the client after the interview stating whether or not the attorney has decided to accept the case.

B. Subsequent Client Interviews
   1. If the firm accepts the case, paralegals are often asked to conduct additional interviews with the client.
   2. When scheduling the interview, the paralegal should tell the client what kinds of documents or information the client should bring to the interview.
   3. When conducting any kind of interview, the paralegal should always disclose his or her nonlawyer status.

C. The Informational Interview
   1. In the informational interview, the client is brought in to discuss upcoming legal proceedings.
   2. In this interview, the client is updated on the following:
      a. Case progress.
      b. Procedures.
      c. Trial dates.
      d. Other information the paralegal is authorized to convey to the client.

D. Summarizing the Interview
   1. The paralegal should summarize the interview as soon as possible after it is concluded.
   2. The interview should be summarized in a written memorandum.

V. INTERVIEWING WITNESSES

A. Types of Witnesses
   1. Expert Witnesses
      a. An expert witness is someone who has professional training, advanced knowledge, or substantial experience in a specialized area and who can give an educated opinion on facts and issues related to the case.
   2. Lay Witnesses
      a. A lay witness has no particular skill or expertise relating to the case; rather, this is someone who observed or has factual knowledge about an event related to the case.
   3. Eyewitnesses
      a. Eyewitnesses are lay witnesses who have witnessed an event and may testify in court as to what they observed.
   4. Friendly Witnesses
      a. A friendly witness is someone who knows the client and who wants to be helpful in volunteering information.
   5. Hostile Witnesses
      a. A hostile witness is someone who is prejudiced against your client or friendly to the opposing side in the lawsuit.
      b. Contact and interview hostile witnesses early in your investigation.

B. Questioning Witnesses
   1. Phrase questions so that they lead to the most complete answers possible.

C. Checking the Witness's Qualifications
   1. Each witness who is interviewed should be considered as a potential court witness.
   2. Investigate to make sure that the witness is competent to testify.
   3. Investigate the witness's possible biases.

D. Witness Statements
   1. A witness statement is a written statement setting forth what the witness said during the interview.
   2. Statutes and court rules vary as to the value of witness statements as evidence.
   3. Witness statements can also be used to refresh a witness's memory.

VI. PLANNING AND CONDUCTING INVESTIGATIONS

A. Where Do You Start?
   1. Your logical point of departure in undertaking your investigation is the information already acquired about the legal claim or problem.
   2. By using common sense and a little imagination, you can map out a fairly thorough investigation plan based on this information.

B. Creating an Investigation Plan
   1. An investigation plan is a step-by-step list of tasks that you plan to take to verify or obtain factual information relating to a legal problem.
   2. Contacting the Police Department
      a. If applicable, this should be the first step in your investigation plan.
   3. Contacting and Interviewing Witnesses
      a. The next step is to contact and interview any known witnesses and document their descriptions of the event that is the basis for the lawsuit.
   4. Obtaining Medical and Employment Records
      a. To justify a claim for personal-injury damages, you must determine the nature of the injuries sustained as a result of the accident, the medical expenses incurred, and the income or wages lost as a result of the accident.
      b. To verify this information, you must obtain copies of the injured person's medical and employment records.
      c. The injured person must sign a release that will allow you to obtain these records.
   5. Contacting the National Weather Service
      a. Weather conditions at the time of an accident could have an important bearing on the case.
   6. Obtaining Vehicle Title and Registration Records
      a. To verify the owner of a vehicle involved in an accident, obtain title and registration records.
      b. Often, these records can be located at the state department of motor vehicles or the state's secretary of state.
   7. Contacting the Insurance Company
      a. When dealing with an automobile-accident case, you can find the insurance company for the involved vehicles on the police report.
   8. Using a Professional Investigator's Services
      a. Some firms routinely use professional investigators for certain difficult and time-consuming tasks.

C. Locating Witnesses
   1. Telephone and City Directories
      a. Telephone and city directories are good potential sources of information.
   2. Other Information Sources
      a. Other sources include media reports; court records; deeds to property; birth, marriage, and death certificates; voter registration lists; the post office; credit bureaus; the tax assessor's office; and city utilities.

D. Accessing Government Information
   1. Records and files acquired and stored by government offices and agencies can aid you in your investigation.
   2. Public records are available in local government buildings or offices.
   3. The Freedom of Information Act (FOIA) enacted by Congress in 1966 requires the federal government to disclose certain records to any person on request.

E. Investigation and the Rules of Evidence
   1. Direct versus Circumstantial Evidence
      a. Direct evidence is any evidence that, if believed, establishes the truth of the fact in question.
      b. Circumstantial evidence is indirect evidence that, even if believed, does not establish the fact in question but only the degree of the likelihood of that fact.
   2. Relevance
      a. Relevant evidence is that which tends to prove or disprove the fact in question.
      b. Relevant evidence might not be admitted in court if its probative value is substantially outweighed by other important considerations.

3. Authentication of Evidence
   a. One way evidence is authenticated is for the attorney to lay the proper foundation for introduction of the evidence and to demonstrate to the court that the evidence is what the attorney claims.
   b. Commonly, evidence is authenticated by the testimony of witnesses.
   c. The rules of evidence require authentication as a safeguard against the introduction of nonverified evidence that may strongly influence the outcome of the case.
   d. The Federal Rules of Evidence provide for self-authentication of certain kinds of evidence.
4. Hearsay
   a. Hearsay is defined as any testimony given in court about a statement made by someone else. It is literally what someone heard someone else say.
   b. There are exceptions to the hearsay rule.

F. Summarizing Your Results
1. Overall Summary
   a. This summary should thoroughly describe all the facts that have been gathered about the case.
2. Source-by-Source Summaries
   a. Create a list of information sources, including witnesses, and summarize the facts obtained from each source.
   b. Each section should contain all the information gathered from that source, including direct quotes and your personal comments.
3. General Conclusions and Recommendations
   a. In the final section, present your overall conclusions about the investigation, as well as your suggestions for further development of the case.

QUESTIONS FOR REVIEW

TRUE-FALSE QUESTIONS

____ 1. The person asking questions of a witness is referred to as the interviewee.

____ 2. A minute or two chatting pleasantly with a client or witness is time well spent.

____ 3. Relevant evidence tends to prove or disprove the fact in question.

____ 4. In interviewing a witness, a legal assistant need only be concerned with gathering facts supportive of the client's position.

____ 5. Open-ended questions are useful in interviewing clients or friendly witnesses.

____ 6. Closed-ended questions may be useful in relaxing the interviewee or keeping the witness on track.

____ 7. Hypothetical questions are frequently used with lay witnesses.

____ 8. A legal assistant must assess the interviewee's verbal and nonverbal responses.

____ 9. Active listening requires the listener to pay close attention to what the speaker is saying and requires the legal assistant to ask the interviewee to repeat any missed information.

____ 10. The interviewee's responses will direct the legal assistant in further questioning.

____ 11. Assessment of an interviewee's nonverbal communication is necessary for determining that witness's effectiveness to the client's case.

____ 12. In contacting and interviewing witnesses, a paralegal must inform the client or witness that he or she is not an attorney.

____ 13. All hearsay is inadmissible.

____ 14. Checklists can be relied upon exclusively in conducting an interview.

____ 15. A legal assistant may tape-record an interview without obtaining the interviewee's permission.

Fill-in Questions

Paralegals ____________ (often/occasionally) interview ____________ (clients/clients and witnesses). The ____________ (initial/informational) interview is usually conducted by the attorney. Additional information may be elicited during a(n) ____________ (subsequent/informational) interview, often conducted by the ____________ (paralegal/attorney). The client is updated on the case progress and procedures during a(n) ____________ (subsequent/informational) interview.

The paralegal should prepare a document that identifies the witness and the details of the interview in a ____________ (witness statement/attestation clause). The document should also include the witness' signature evidencing that the information was given by the witness, contained in an ____________ (witness statement/attestation clause).

To obtain client records, such as medical records, the client must ____________ (authenticate the injuries/execute release forms). If the client your firm is representing was involved in an automobile accident, it may be necessary to verify the ____________ (weather conditions/witness statement). The investigative plan should be ____________ (used only by the paralegal/submitted for the supervising attorney's review and evaluation). The objective of an investigation is to obtain information and verify facts for eventual introduction as ____________ (witness statements/evidence at trial).

Multiple-Choice Questions

____ 1. An investigator's job is to:
   A. Gather only those facts in support of the client's position
   B. Judge the facts in the light most favorable to the client
   C. Remain neutral
   D. Gather only those facts in support of the opponent's position

____ 2. The primary goal of any interview is:
   A. To obtain factual information
   B. To demonstrate a legal assistant's knowledge of legal concepts
   C. To pressure the witness
   D. To create a hostile witness

____ 3. Instilling confidence in the client or a witness can be accomplished by:
   A. Avoiding unnecessary interruptions and affording the interviewee the legal assistant's full attention
   B. Asking questions that slant the facts
   C. Exhibiting facial gestures in relation to responses
   D. All of the above

____ 4. The open-ended question:
   A. Is a broad, exploratory question that invites any number of possible responses
   B. Is intended to elicit a "yes" or "no"
   C. Allows an answer to an important question without giving away the facts of the client's case
   D. Is intended to make the interviewee respond emotionally

____ 5. The closed-ended question:
   A. Is a broad, exploratory question that invites any number of possible responses
   B. Is intended to elicit a "yes" or "no"
   C. Allows an answer to an important question without giving away the facts of the client's case
   D. Is intended to make the interviewee respond emotionally

____ 6. The hypothetical question:
A. Is a broad, exploratory question that invites any number of possible responses
B. Is intended to elicit a "yes" or "no"
C. Allows an answer to an important question without giving away the facts of the client's case
D. Is intended to make the interviewee respond emotionally

____ 7. The pressure question:
A. Is a broad, exploratory question that invites any number of possible responses
B. Is intended to elicit a "yes" or "no"
C. Allows an answer to an important question without giving away the facts of the client's case
D. Is intended to make the interviewee respond emotionally

____ 8. Leading questions:
A. Suggest to the listener the answer to the question
B. Are effective for drawing information out of eyewitnesses or clients when they are reluctant to disclose information
C. May lead to distorted answers because the client or witness may tailor the answer to fit the perception of what the interviewer wants to know
D. All of the above

____ 9. The rules of evidence:
A. Ensure evidence presented to the court is fair and reliable
B. Govern the drafting of a witness statement
C. Lists the introduction of facts in a logical progression
D. Generally admit hearsay

____ 10. Direct evidence is:
A. Any evidence that, if believed, establishes the truth of the fact in question
B. Indirect evidence that, even if believed, does not establish the fact in question but only the degree of likelihood of the fact
C. An out-of-court statement later offered in court
D. Establishing the genuineness of an item that is to be introduced at trial

____ 11. Circumstantial evidence is:
A. Any evidence that, if believed, establishes the truth of the fact in question
B. Indirect evidence that, even if believed, does not establish the fact in question but only the degree of likelihood of the fact
C. An out-of-court statement later offered in court
D. Establishing the genuineness of an item that is to be introduced at trial

____ 12. A tape-recording of an interview should include, at the beginning of the tape, which of the following:
A. The name of the interviewee, date, time, and place
B. The name of the individual conducting the interview
C. The names of other persons that are present
D. All of the above

____ 13. An expert witness:
A. Is an individual who has professional training, advanced knowledge, or substantial experience in a specialized area
B. Does not possess any particular skill
C. Has first-hand knowledge about the event
D. Wants to be helpful in volunteering information

____ 14. A lay witness:
A. Is an individual who has professional training, advanced knowledge, or substantial experience in a specialized area
B. Does not possess any particular skill
C. Has first-hand knowledge about the event
D. Wants to be helpful in volunteering information

____ 15. An eyewitness:
A. Is an individual who has professional training, advanced knowledge, or substantial experience in a specialized area
B. Does not possess any particular skill
C. Has first-hand knowledge about the event
D. Wants to be helpful in volunteering information

____ 16. Authentication is:
A. Any evidence that, if believed, establishes the truth of the fact in question
B. Indirect evidence that, even if believed, does not establish the fact in question but only the degree of likelihood of the fact
C. An out-of-court statement later offered in court
D. Establishing the genuineness of an item that is to be introduced at trial

____ 17. Hearsay is:
A. Any evidence that, if believed, establishes the truth of the fact in question
B. Indirect evidence that, even if believed, does not establish the fact in question but only the degree of likelihood of the fact
C. An out-of-court statement later offered in court
D. Establishing the genuineness of an item that is to be introduced at trial

____ 18. Evidence, although having probative value, may not be admissible in court if:
A. The fact at issue has already been sufficiently proved or disproved by prior evidence
B. It is distracting to the jury
C. It would cause the jury to decide the issue on an emotional basis
D. All of the above

____ 19. Exceptions to the hearsay rule:
A. Except that evidence from being introduced at trial
B. Are based upon the witness's own knowledge
C. Allow hearsay to be considered as evidence at trial
D. Are circumstantial evidence

____ 20. Reliable and relevant evidence may be excluded if it is:
A. Authenticated
B. Privileged
C. Circumstantial
D. Direct

PRACTICE QUESTIONS

1. Assume a hypothetical scenario involving a barroom fight in which one party is suing another for assault and battery. Draft sample questions that you would ask the eyewitnesses when interviewing them about the fight. Phrase at least one question in each of the question formats discussed in this chapter.
2. Phillip Leane was grocery shopping at the Neighborhood Market on January 17, 1995. He turned a corner to go down an aisle and was looking at the vegetable oils to make a selection. He did not notice that there was a broken container with oil on the floor and slipped and broke his hip. He was taken to an emergency room and was treated for the injury. However, he was forced to take a leave of absence from his job at a reduced salary. In addition to his medical expenses, he has expended a considerable amount of money in therapy in order to regain strength and movement in that joint. Phillip has come to the firm for which you work, Gamson & Soren, 500 East Avenue, Southville, New Mexico 54321, inquiring about the possibility of suing to recover his lost wages and medical and therapy expenses. Draft an investigation plan.
3. Using the factual background presented in Practice Question 2 above, draft an "Authorization to Release Employment Information" letter for Phillip Leane to sign. His full name and address are Phillip A. Leane, 120 South Street, Southville, New Mexico 54321. His employer is Tiny City Botanical Laboratory, Tiny City, NM 53241.

Questions for Critical Analysis

1. Assume Jane is a legal assistant who is interviewing Bob, a neighbor and friend of the firm's client, who purportedly saw the automobile accident in which the client was involved. Can Jane be sure that the neighbor's information is accurate? If not, discuss alternatives for determining the neighbor's knowledge.
2. Assume you are interviewing an adverse witness that is reluctant to give any information. Explain alternatives to this scenario.

Ethical Questions

1. Jim Barnes' supervising attorney asks him to attend an initial client interview in a bankruptcy case. The supervising attorney fails to introduce Jim to the client. Later, when Jim is conducting a subsequent interview with the client, the client asks Jim for legal advice on whether or not to include a particular asset in the bankruptcy. How could this situation have been avoided? What should Jim do?
2. While meeting with a client, Mary Richards takes a phone call from another client. The client wants to know when her bankruptcy case will be filed. Mary answers the client by name, indicating that the bankruptcy will be filed by the end of the week. What has Mary done wrong?

Technology and Today's Paralegal

You will find many excellent medical resources on the Internet. One resource that will link you to many other health and medical databases is MEDLINE. Its URL is *http://www.nlm.nih.gov/databases/freemedl.htm*. This site provides links to the National Library of Medicine and MEDLINE*plus,* as well as free access through Internet Grateful Med to MEDLINE, AIDSLINE, AIDSDRUGS, AIDSTRIALS, BIOETHICSLINE, chemID, DIRLINE, HealthSTAR, HISTLINE, HSRPROJ, OLDMEDLINE, POPLINE, SDILINE, SPACELINE, and TOXLINE.

Another source that you should add to your bookmarks is the site for the National Institutes of Health—*http://www.nih.gov/health*. Through this site, you will find links to PubMed, Internet Grateful Med, MEDLINE*plus,* and Healthfinder. It also contains links that provide help in spelling a medical term as well as toll-free health hotlines.

ANSWERS

True-False Questions

1. F
2. T
3. T
4. F
5. T
6. T
7. F
8. T
9. T
10. T
11. T
12. T
13. F
14. F
15. F

Fill-in Questions

often; clients and witnesses; initial; subsequent; paralegal; information

witness statement; attestation clause

execute release forms; weather conditions; submitted for the supervising attorney's review and evaluation; evidence at trial

Multiple-Choice Questions

1. C
2. A
3. A
4. C
5. B
6. C
7. D
8. D
9. A
10. A
11. B
12. D
13. A
14. B
15. C
16. D
17. C
18. D
19. C
20. B

Practice Questions

1. (a) Closed-ended questions:

   "Were you at the bar on the night in question?"
   "Did you see A and B in the bar that night?"

   (b) Leading questions:

   "Isn't it true that you were at the bar on the night in question?
   "Isn't it true that you saw A and B that night?"

   (c) Open-ended questions:

   "Where were you on the night in question?"
   "Who was there that night?"

2.

	Date Requested	Date Received
1. Contact Neighborhood Market — to determine employees working that day — to ask whether any employee had been notified of breakage — to talk with the manager — SOURCE: Neighborhood Market — METHOD: Written request by mail with Mr. Leane's release enclosed	________	________
2. Obtain Employment Records — to learn employment status and income of Mr. Leane — SOURCE: Mr. Leane's employer — METHOD: Written request by mail with Mr. Leane's release enclosed	________	________
3. Obtain Medical Records — to learn necessary information about Mr. Leane's medical treatment and costs — SOURCE: Treating hospital and therapist — METHOD: Written request by mail with Mr. Leane's release enclosed	________	________
4. Contact Neighborhood Market's Insurance Co. — to find out about insurance coverage — to check liability limits	________	________

3. TO: Tiny City Botanical Laboratory
Tiny City, NM 53241

EMPLOYEE: Phillip A. Leane
120 South Street
Southville, NM 54321

You are hereby authorized to furnish and release to my attorney, Gamson & Soren, all information and records relating to my employment. Please do not disclose information to insurance adjusters or to other persons without written authority from me. The foregoing authority shall continue in force until revoked by me in writing, but for no longer than one year following the date given below.

Date: ____________________

____
Phillip A. Leane

Please attach your invoice for any fees or photostatic copies and send it with the information requested above to my office.

Thank you,

Gamson & Soren
500 East Avenue
Southville, NM 54321

____

Notary Public State of New Mexico

____________________ County

My Commission Expires: ____________________

Questions for Critical Analysis

1. The neighbor may be considered a friendly witness. Thus, Jane should be aware of possible bias in the client's favor. She should examine closely the extent of the Bob's knowledge by asking specific questions concerning that knowledge. For example, ask Bob where he was at the time of the accident. Ask for a specific distance, or ask him to describe possible obstructions and lighting conditions. Inquire about the neighbor's other senses; for example, what did he hear or smell? Assessment of the neighbor's testimony is necessary, as any missing information will be explored during cross-examination—to the detriment of the client's case.
2. The paralegal could consider asking closed-ended questions that would permit a simple "yes/no" response. This may create a rapport with the witness, enabling the legal assistant to obtain information. If the interview appears to be unproductive, however, the paralegal should conclude the interview and note the inability to communicate with the witness for the file. The paralegal might then request that the supervising attorney suggest an alternative interview or perhaps conduct that interview himself or herself.

Ethical Questions

1. When a supervising attorney does not indicate the paralegal's nonattorney status to the client, the paralegal must do so. The client probably misunderstands Jim's role and limitations in working on the case. Jim must immediately explain his role as a paralegal, stress that he is not a lawyer, and explain that he cannot give legal advice.
2. Mary has just breached the ethical duty of confidentiality. The client in her office now knows that the other client will soon be filing bankruptcy. This could potentially have a great impact on the second client's bankruptcy case if the information was leaked to creditors before the case was filed. Mary should have asked the switchboard to hold her calls while she was in conference with a client. If this was not possible, Mary should have selected her words more carefully. At the least, she should not have identified the client by name.

CHAPTER 14

LEGAL RESEARCH

CHAPTER OBJECTIVES

After completing this chapter, you should be able to:

- Identify how primary and secondary sources of law differ.
- Know how to use primary and secondary sources in the research process.
- Understand how to use legal encyclopedias and other secondary sources to find case law relevant to your research topic.
- Discuss how court decisions are published and how to read case citations.
- Describe how federal statutes and regulations are published.
- Explain the major sources of statutory and administrative law.
- Point out what kinds of resources are available for researching the legislative history of a statute.
- Understand why finding current law is important.
- Know how to verify that your research results are up to date.

Chapter Outline

I. INTRODUCTION

II. PRIMARY AND SECONDARY SOURCES
- A. Primary sources of the law consist of all documents that establish the law.
- B. Examples of primary sources are:
  1. Court decisions.
  2. Statutes.
  3. Regulations.
  4. Constitutions.
  5. Presidential orders.
- C. Secondary sources consist of books and articles that summarize, systematize, compile, or otherwise interpret the law.
- D. Examples of secondary sources are:
  1. Legal encyclopedias.
  2. Articles in a law review.
  3. Treatises.

III. RESEARCHING CASE LAW—THE PRELIMINARY STEPS
- A. Defining the Issue
  1. The first step in the legal-research process is to identify the legal question, or issue, to be researched.
  2. Examine the facts of the case to determine the nature of the legal issue involved.
- B. Determining Your Research Goals
  1. Cases on Point
     - a. A case on point is a previous case involving fact patterns and legal issues that are similar to a case that has not yet been decided by a court.
     - b. The ideal case on point would be a case in which all four elements of the case (parties, circumstances, legal issues, and remedies sought) are very similar; such a case is called a case "on all fours."
  2. Mandatory Authorities
     - a. A mandatory authority is any source of law that a court must follow when deciding a case.
     - b. To serve as mandatory authority, a case must be on point and decided by a superior court.
     - c. A lower court is bound to follow decisions set forth by a higher court in the same jurisdiction.
     - d. When researching, look for cases on point decided by the highest court in your jurisdiction.
  3. Persuasive Authorities
     - a. A persuasive authority is not binding on a court.
     - b. Examples are as follows:
       - 1) Prior court opinions of other jurisdictions.
       - 2) Legal periodicals.
       - 3) Encyclopedias.
       - 4) Legal dictionaries.

IV. SECONDARY SOURCES OF CASE LAW
- A. Legal Encyclopedias
  1. *American Jurisprudence,* Second Edition
     - a. This legal encyclopedia offers a detailed discussion of virtually every area of American law.
     - b. The volumes are kept current through supplements called pocket parts.
     - c. Topics are organized alphabetically.
  2. *Corpus Juris Secundum*
     - a. This legal encyclopedia also offers a detailed discussion on virtually every area of American law.
     - b. *Corpus Juris Secundum (C.J.S.)* offers an explanation of contradictory court decision on an issue, if there are any, and provides the names for these cases and their citations.

   c. The volumes are kept current through supplements called pocket parts.
   d. Topics are organized alphabetically.
3. *Words and Phrases*
   a. This is a forty-six-volume encyclopedia of definitions and interpretations of legal terms and phrases.
   b. Topics are organized alphabetically.

B. Case Digests
1. The West Key-Number System
   a. In the late nineteenth century, West Publishing Company developed its key-number system of classification.
   b. All areas of American law are separated into specific categories and are arranged alphabetically.
   c. Topics are further divided into subtopics, each of which is designated by a key number.
   d. West editors provide headnotes for every area of the law discussed in each decision or opinion published in the West reporters.
   e. Every headnote is described by its topic name, which is followed by a key number indicating the specific subject discussed.
   f. This system allows West to gather all headnotes under the same topic and key number into one published work—the digest.
2. West's Federal Digests
   a. These digests cover cases from the United States Supreme Court, the U.S. courts of appeals, the U.S. district courts, and various other federal courts.
   b. There are five separate federal digests.
3. West's State and Regional Digests
   a. West provides state digests for all states except Utah, Nevada, and Delaware.
   b. West currently publishes four regional digests.
4. West's Comprehensive *American Digest System*
   a. The advantage of this digest is its vast coverage of cases from different courts.
   b. These books are also called West's decennial digests.
   c. The table of cases lists all cases included in the digest, in alphabetical order.
5. Other Digests
   a. Publishers other than West offer digests for specific jurisdictions and specialized interest areas.

C. Annotations: *American Law Reports*
1. Quick Indexes
   a. These volumes combine the topical approach and the factual-word approach in an alphabetical listing.
2. Annotations
   a. Annotations consist of articles that focus on specific issues.
3. Updating Supplements
   a. *A.L.R.* annotations are updated periodically by the addition of relevant recent cases.

D. Treatises
1. Law treatises are formal scholarly publications discussing specific legal topics or areas.
2. Treatises are written by law professors, legal scholars, and practicing attorneys.
3. Treatises are secondary materials and have no binding effect on courts.
4. Treatises do merit judicial respect and recognition when written by leading legal scholars.
5. Hornbooks are single-volume treatises that synthesize the basic principles of an area of the law.
6. Treatises are usually organized by section numbers rather than by page numbers.
7. Most treatises are updated by supplementary loose-leaf pages or pocket-part additions.

E. *Restatements of the Law*
1. Restatements are highly respected scholarly compilations of the common law that are published by the American Law Institute (ALI).

2. Restatements present an overview of the basic principles of the common law in ten specific fields:
    a. Agency law.
    b. Conflict of laws.
    c. Contracts.
    d. Foreign relations law.
    e. Judgments.
    f. Property.
    g. Restitution.
    h. Security.
    i. Torts.
    j. Trusts.
3. Restatements are not primary sources of law and are not binding on the courts.

F. Legal Periodicals
1. Legal periodicals are a source of secondary authority and, as such, are not binding.
2. Legal periodicals contain thoroughly researched information on a specific area of the law.
3. Authors are usually law professors, attorneys prominent in their fields, judges, legal scholars, or law students.

V. THE CASE REPORTING SYSTEM

A. State Court Decisions
1. State Reporters
    a. State appellate court opinions, including those of state supreme courts, are normally published in state reporters.
    b. State court decisions are usually published in both official and unofficial reporters.
    c. A few states, including New York and California, publish more than one official state reporter.
2. West's National Reporter System
    a. State court opinions appear in regional units of the National Reporter System, published by West Group.
    b. The National Reporter System divides states into geographical regions.
3. Citation Format
    a. After an appellate decision has been published, it is normally referred to by its citation.
    b. A reference to the other reporter or reporters in which the case can be found is called a parallel citation.
    c. When performing legal research, you should include citations to cases or other legal sources in your notes.
    d. The most widely used book on how to cite legal sources is *The Bluebook: A Uniform System of Citation.*

B. Federal Court Decisions
1. Federal trial court opinions are published unofficially in West's *Federal Supplement* (F.Supp.).
2. Opinions from the federal circuit courts of appeals are published unofficially in West's *Federal Reporter* (F., F.2d, or F.3d).

C. United States Supreme Court Decisions
1. The *United States Reports*
    a. The *United States Reports* is the official edition of all decisions of the United States Supreme Court.
    b. Approximately two to four weeks after the United States Supreme Court issues a decision, the official slip opinion is published as an individual pamphlet.
    c. After a number of slip opinions have been issued, they are put together into a paperback book called advance sheets.
    d. Almost all United States Supreme Court opinions, as well as the text for many statutes and treatises, are available on the Internet.
2. The *Supreme Court Reporter*
    a. United States Supreme Court opinions are also published in West's *Supreme Court Reporter* (S.Ct.).

   b. The Supreme Court Reporter is an "unofficial" reporter.
   c. The opinion is preceded by a brief syllabus and headnotes with key numbers.
3. The *Lawyers' Edition of the Supreme Court Reporter*
   a. This unofficial edition of the entire series of the Supreme Court reports contains many decisions not reported in earlier official volumes.
   b. The *Lawyers' Edition* offers research tools and provides summaries of the briefs presented by counsel.
4. Unofficial Loose-Leaf Services
   a. This service publishes United States Supreme Court decisions on the day after a decision is announced.

VI. RESEARCHING STATUTORY LAW
- A. The Publication of Federal Statutes
   1. Federal statutes are published in three forms:
      a. *Slip laws* present the text of the statutes in the form of pamphlets or single sheets.
      b. *Session laws* are collections of statutes contained in volumes and arranged by the year or legislative session in which they were enacted.
      c. *Codes* arrange statutory provisions by topic.
   2. Federal statutes are published officially in the *United States Code* (U.S.C.).
- B. The *United States Code*
   1. The *United States Code (U.S.C)* is published every six years by the U.S. government. It is also updated annually.
   2. The *U.S.C.* organizes statutes into fifty subjects, or titles.
   3. *U.S.C.* further subdivides each title into chapters (sections) and subchapters.
   4. The researcher can find a statute in the *U.S.C.* through the following methods:
      a. Searching through the topical outlines.
      b. Looking in the index.
      c. Looking under the act's popular name in the volume entitled *Popular Name Table.*
- C. Unofficial Versions of the Federal Code
   1. The *United States Code Annotated*
      a. The *United States Code Annotated (U.S.C.A.)* contains the full text of the *U.S.C.*, the U.S. Constitution, the Federal Rules of Evidence, and various other rules, including the Rules of Civil Procedure and Rules of Criminal Procedure.
      b. The *U.S.C.A.* is more current than the *U.S.C.* and provides updated statutory information through supplemental pocket parts and pamphlets many times a year.
   2. The *United States Code Service*
      a. This code is published by West Group.
      b. The research section of the *United States Code Service (U.S.C.S.)* provides references and citations to some sources that are not contained in the *U.S.C.A.*, such as *American Law Reports,* legal periodicals, and *American Jurisprudence.*
      c. Paralegals can begin statutory research in the *U.S.C.S.* by reviewing the *Subjects Index* or the *Popular Name Table.*
- D. Interpreting Statutory Law
   1. One approach to interpreting statutory law involves researching case law on the subject to find how other courts have interpreted the statute.
   2. Another approach to interpreting statutory law involves determining the legislature's intent when enacting the statute.
- E. Researching Legislative History
   1. Committee Reports
      a. Congressional committees produce reports for each bill.
      b. These reports often contain the full text of the bill, a description of its purpose, and the committee's recommendations.
      c. Committee reports are published according to a numerical series and are available through the U.S. Government Printing Office.
   2. The *Congressional Record*
      a. The *Congressional Record* contains verbatim transcripts of congressional debates and proceedings, including legislative hearings.

3. Other Sources of Legislative History
    a. The *United States Code Congressional and Administrative News* (*U.S.C.C.A.N.*) contains reprints of statutes as published in the *Statutes at Large* and sections describing the statutes' legislative history, including committee reports.
    b. The *Congressional Information Service (C.I.S.)* contains information from committee reports, hearing reports, documents from both houses, and special publications.

F. State Codes
1. State codes follow the *U.S.C.* pattern of arranging statutes by subject.
2. In many states, official codes are supplemented by annotated codes published by private publishers.

VII. RESEARCHING ADMINISTRATIVE LAW

A. The *Code of Federal Regulations*
1. The *Code of Federal Regulations (C.F.R.)* contains all federal administrative agency regulations.
2. The regulations in the *C.F.R.* are compiled from the *Federal Register.*

B. Publication of the *C.F.R.*
1. The *C.F.R.* is revised and republished four times a year.
2. A good place to start researching administrative regulations is in the index section of the *C.F.R.*'s *Index and Finding Aids* volume.

C. Finding Tools for Administrative Law
1. The *Congressional Information Service (C.I.S.)* provides an index to the *C.F.R.*, which is helpful in locating regulations by subject matter and in determining the geographical area affected by the regulation.
2. The *American Digest System* provides coverage of court cases dealing with administrative questions but does not contain agency rulings.
3. Other certain loose-leaf services provide administrative decisions for particular specialty fields.

VIII. FINDING CONSTITUTIONAL LAW

A. Constitutions are primary sources of the law.
B. The U.S. Constitution can be found in a number of publications, including the extensively annotated official publication, which is available through the Library of Congress.
C. Annotated versions of state constitutions are also available.

IX. UPDATING THE LAW—LEARNING TO USE CITATORS

A. Case Law
1. The Organization of *Shepard's Citations*
    a. The researcher first finds the appropriate citator that corresponds with the researched case's citation.
    b. Then the researcher finds the pages covering the relevant volume of the researched case's citation.
    c. Next the researcher locates the page on which the case begins.
    d. Parallel citations to other reporters are listed in parentheses with the case.
    e. Following the other reporters is a listing of citations of any higher courts that have reviewed the case.
    f. Then comes a listing of cases that have cited the main case.
2. Types of Information Provided by *Shepard's Citations*
    a. *Shepard's Citations* allows the researcher to verify whether a case or statutes represent current law by indicating whether:
        1) Other cases have cited your main, or cited, case.
        2) A case has been overruled or reversed.
        3) A statute has been repealed or amended.
        4) An agency regulation has been voided or superseded.

B. Statutory and Constitutional Law
   1. *Shepard's* citators for constitutions and statutes are similar to the case citators.
   2. *Shepard's* can serve as a valuable tool in constitutional and statutory research by identifying other sources that have discussed the researched provision.
   3. *Shepard's* can also provide information on the status of the provision.

C. Administrative Regulations
   1. *Shepard's Code of Federal Regulations Citations* provides citations to federal and state administrative law decisions.
   2. *C.F.R. Shepard's* uses a system of abbreviations to indicate the impact that a court decision has had on the cited regulation.

D. Legal Periodicals
   1. *Shepard's Law Review Citations* includes citations to approximately two hundred legal periodicals and law reviews.
   2. Researchers can use this source to locate references to law-review articles mentioned in court decisions and other legal services.

E. Online Citators
   1. Online citators, include:
      a. Lexis®.
      b. Westlaw®.
   2. These online citators enable the researcher to access recent cases, statutes, or regulations.
   3. Online citators enable the researcher to ensure that research results are as up to date as possible.

QUESTIONS FOR REVIEW

TRUE-FALSE QUESTIONS

____ 1. Secondary sources are finding tools in that they assist a researcher in finding primary sources.

____ 2. Customers invited onto a business' premises are referred to as business invitees.

____ 3. A case on "all fours" refers to a case in which the parties, the circumstances, the legal issues involved, and the court are all similar.

____ 4. Mandatory authority must be a case on point and decided by an inferior court.

____ 5. Annotations are comments or explanatory notes added to a written document.

____ 6. Publications containing the actual texts of court cases are referred to as headnotes.

____ 7. The table of cases lists all of the cases included in the digest in alphabetical order.

____ 8. Hornbooks are single-volume treatises that synthesize the basic principles of an area of the law.

____ 9. A case may have two citations; that is, a parallel citation may be available.

____ 10. A syllabus is a summary of the case.

____ 11. A citator provides a list of legal references that have cited or interpreted the case or law.

____ 12. *Shepard's* provides a means to verify the history of a case.

____ 13. *Shepard's* lists parallel citations in italics.

____ 14. Unofficial loose-leaf services publish Supreme Court decisions the day after a decision is announced.

Fill-in Questions

The first task in legal research is to ______________________ (define the issue/consult secondary sources). The researcher should then ________________________ (consult primary sources/determine the goal of the research project). After all relevant research materials have been consulted, a researcher should __________________ (begin writing/synthesize and summarize research results).

When researching, the cases that carry the most weight are those decided by the __________________ (trial/highest) court. A higher court __________________ (is/is never) required to follow an opinion written by a lower court in the same jurisdiction. Persuasive authority may assist a court in deciding a case __________________ (of first impression/about business invitee).

American Jurisprudence is an example of a(n) __________________ (encyclopedia/hornbook) that a researcher may consult to obtain background information. Another source of general background information is found in the ________________ (*Restatements of the Law*/annotations). Legal periodicals, such as __________ (headnotes/law reviews) contain thoroughly researched information on a specific area of the law.

West publishes cases in regional units referred to as the ____________________ (National Reporter System/Key-Number System).

Multiple-Choice Questions

____ 1. Primary sources include:
A. Legislative enactments
B. Administrative agencies' rules and regulations
C. Presidential orders
D. All of the above

____ 2. Secondary sources include:
A. Legislative enactments
B. Administrative agencies' rules and regulations
C. Books and articles that summarize, systematize, or interpret the law
D. All of the above

____ 3. A previous case involving fact patterns and legal issues similar to a case that has not yet been decided by a court is referred to as a:
A. Case on point
B. Mandatory authority
C. Persuasive authority
D. Parallel citation

____ 4. Authority that the court must rely on in its determination of the issue is referred to as a:
A. Case on point
B. Mandatory authority
C. Persuasive authority
D. Parallel citation

____ 5. Authority that a court is not required to following in making its decision is referred to as a:
A. Case on point
B. Mandatory authority
C. Persuasive authority
D. Parallel citation

____ 6. Legal encyclopedias are kept current through supplements called:
A. Digests
B. Citators
C. Pocket parts
D. Hornbooks

____ 7. Which of the following is true regarding digests:
A. They provide indexes to case law
B. They arrange topics alphabetically
C. They provide information to help locate referenced cases
D. All of the above

____ 8. West Group designates its subtopics by:
A. Key numbers
B. Citators
C. Slip opinions
D. Reporters

____ 9. A formal scholarly work that treats a given subject systematically and in detail is referred to as a:
A. Digest
B. Code
C. Hornbook
D. Treatise

____ 10. A citation includes:
A. The name of the case
B. The volume number
C. The abbreviated name and page number of the reporter
D. All of the above

____ 11. The first authoritative text of an opinion, printed as an individual pamphlet, is referred to as a:
A. Key number
B. Citator
C. Slip opinion
D. Reporter

____ 12. The first publication of a statute's text is referred to as a:
A. Slip law
B. Public law number
C. Session law
D. Code

____ 13. The number assigned to each statute upon completion of the legislative process is referred to as a:
A. Slip law
B. Public law number
C. Session law
D. Code

____ 14. Collections of statutes contained in volumes and arranged by the year or legislative sessions are referred to as:
A. Slip laws
B. Public law numbers
C. Session laws
D. Codes

____ 15. Statutory compilations arranged by topics are referred to as:
A. Slip laws
B. Public law numbers
C. Session laws
D. Codes

Practice Questions

1. Assume the facts presented in this chapter's Practice Question and Assignment 5 and the following:
   A. That your research has led you to two cases on point—one decided by the court in which Mr. Consumer's lawsuit is pending and one by the state's highest court. Which case should you cite as mandatory authority?
   B. That the case you wish to cite is a United States Supreme Court case in which Robert D. Brown was the plaintiff and Roberta E. Black was the defendant. The case is printed at volume 607 of the United States Reports, page 510. The year of decision is 1995. How would you cite this case?
   C. That you wish to include parallel citations to the United States case. What unofficial publications exist for the United States Supreme Court?
2. Assume in the example above that the *Brown v. Black* case has a headnote on all fours with your case. Should your research end there? Why or why not?

Question for Critical Analysis

1. What is the syllabus? Why is it useful?

ETHICAL QUESTIONS

1. Wilma Morris has been recently hired by Boggs & Black. This is Wilma's first paralegal job after graduation. One of Wilma's first assignments is to do the legal research for a brief her supervising attorney will soon be filing. Because Wilma does not have a great deal of experience, she approaches her research assignment in a haphazard fashion. She does not have a clear idea of her research task and does not ask her attorney for clarification. She also forgets to keep proper notes as her research progresses. As a result, Wilma spends extra time researching issues not appropriate to the case at hand. She also must retrace her steps in the law library to relocate a source again and obtain the citation. What ethical concern should Wilma and her supervising attorney have?
2. Rose Dunlap is a paralegal doing legal research on an issue important to the success of a client's case. Rose researched the issue about a month ago for a case very similar to the case currently being litigated. Rose has checked the relevant printed volume of *Shepard's Citations* and finds no recent cases or modifications that affect her research. Has Rose done everything she can to ensure the earlier research is still valid?

TECHNOLOGY AND TODAY'S PARALEGAL

One of the best online sources for researching legislative history is Thomas—Legislative Information on the Internet—*http://thomas.loc.gov.*

This site is a current source of legislative information, including floor activities of Congress, major legislation, legislative histories, congressional record text, and historical documents. It also has links to other congressional Internet services.

Answers

True-False Questions

1. T
2. T
3. F
4. F
5. T
6. F
7. T
8. T
9. T
10. T
11. T
12. T
13. F
14. T

Fill-in Questions

define the issue; determine the goal of the research project; synthesize and summarize research results

highest; is never; of first impression

encyclopedia; *Restatement of the Law;* law reviews

National Reporter System

Multiple-Choice Questions

1. D
2. C
3. A
4. B
5. C
6. C
7. D
8. A
9. D
10. D
11. C
12. A
13. B
14. C
15. D

Practice Questions

1. A. The most superior court's opinion should be cited.
   B. *Brown v. Black,* 607 U.S. 510 (1995).
   C. West Group's *Supreme Court Reporter* (S.Ct.) and *Lawyer's Edition of the Supreme Court Reports* (L.Ed.)
2. Headnotes are not primary authority; this represents West's method of arranging legal and factual issues by subject matters. The actual text of the opinion is the primary authority, which represents the goals of the researcher.

Question for Critical Analysis

1. The syllabus is a summary of the case, which is generally provided by the court. It permits a quick view of the case to determine its relevance to the issue being researched and also facilitates access to the body of the opinion in which that particular issue is being discussed by the court. In short, it saves a researcher time in evaluating the relevancy of a case.

Ethical Questions

1. Time is a valuable resource for the attorney and a costly one for the client. First, the attorney may have needed Wilma's assistance on other cases. Second, the client has a right to expect to be charged a reasonable fee. By not minimizing the number of hours spent on this legal research and by failing to keep proper research notes, Wilma has not been efficient in her research. If the client is charged for the entire time Wilma completed her research, that would not constitute a reasonable fee. This would be an ethical violation, as attorneys have a duty to charge their clients reasonable fees.
2. No, Rose has not made absolutely certain her earlier research results are still valid. She should use an online citator to ensure no recent statutes or regulations affect the prior research. The failure to update her research may seriously harm the client's success in this litigation. Therefore, the client's interests have not been properly served.

CHAPTER 15

COMPUTER-ASSISTED LEGAL RESEARCH

CHAPTER OBJECTIVES

After completing this chapter, you should be able to:

- Explain how CD-ROMs and legal-research services provided by Westlaw® and Lexis® help legal professionals in computer-assisted legal research (CALR)
- Understand what the Internet is and how it can be accessed and navigated.
- Describe strategies for planning and conducting research on the Internet.
- Explain how you can find people and investigate companies using Internet search tools and databases.
- Understand how to find some of the best legal resources available on the Internet.

Chapter Outline

I. INTRODUCTION

II. CD-ROMS AND LEGAL RESEARCH

A. Advantages of Using CD-ROMs

1. CD-ROMs are far less costly to purchase and require much less space than their printed counterparts.
2. A CD-ROM holds the equivalent of over 600 megabytes of data, which means that one CD-ROM can store approximately 300,000 pages or over one hundred volumes of legal reference materials.
3. CD-ROMs are easily transported.
4. Searches of materials on CD-ROMs can be conducted more easily and quickly than when using printed reference materials.
5. You can copy segments of a case or statute directly to your computer.

B. Disadvantages of Using CD-ROMs

1. CD-ROMs can become outdated.
2. Even the most recently issued CD-ROM version of legal references may be somewhat outdated because of the time it takes to create and distribute the CD-ROM.

III. WESTLAW® AND LEXIS®

A. Accessing Westlaw® or Lexis®

1. Traditionally, a subscriber accessed Westlaw® or Lexis® by using the subscriber's computer to access the database through a modem connection over a telephone line.
2. Today, both Westlaw® and Lexis® can be accessed online through the Internet; special software is no longer needed.
3. The advantage of accessing these services on the Web is that research is done easily with a standard browser and without the extensive training needed for the proprietary software.
4. The disadvantage of accessing these services through the Web is that users do not have the accompanying user manuals on how to use these services.
5. Another disadvantage for Lexis® users is that only a portion of the Lexis® databases are included on the Internet.
6. On Westlaw® or Lexis®, you can retrieve documents by citation, check citations, or search databases for cases, statutes, or other documents and legal resources on a given topic or issue.

B. Retrieving a Document By Citation

1. To find a document, enter the citation for a document, such as a case or statute.

C. Checking a Citation

1. Westlaw® and Lexis® both offer online citators.
2. Online citators are more up to date than printed citators.
3. The tools on Westlaw® and Lexis® allow you to update the law within seconds.
4. Making sure that your research results reflect current law is a crucial step in legal research.

D. Selecting a Database

1. Both Westlaw® and Lexis® have databases for cases, statutes, and other legal authorities and reference materials that relate to certain topics or legal issues.
2. Once you become familiar with the database identifiers for Westlaw® and Lexis®, you can access that database more directly.

E. Searching a Database

1. The Terms and Connectors Method
    a. To conduct a search using terms and connectors, you use numerical and grammatical connectors to specify the relationship between your terms or phrases.
    b. A list of terms and connectors can be found in the instruction manuals provided to Westlaw® and Lexis® subscribers.
    c. When drafting search queries, you want to make sure that your query is not too broad or too narrow.
2. The Natural Language Method

a. The natural language method is called "Freestyle" on Lexis® and "WIN" on Westlaw®.
b. This type of search allows you to type a description of an issue in plain English to retrieve relevant documents.

F. Browser Enhancements
1. There are internal browsing tools in both Westlaw® and Lexis® that help you to pinpoint your search more precisely.
2. When browsing through your search results, remember that the time you spend online using the service is costly.

IV. GOING ONLINE—INTERNET BASICS

A. What Is the Internet?
1. The Internet is a global communication network of interconnected computers.

B. Internet Tools
1. Uniform Resource Locators
a. A uniform resource locator (URL) is an Internet "address."
b. The basic format for a URL is "service://directorypath/filename."
c. The letters "http" stand for hypertext transfer protocol.
d. Hypertext is a database system by which disparate objects (such as text or graphics) can be linked to each other.
e. The letters "www" stand for the World Wide Web, which is a hypertext-based service through which data is made available on the Internet.
f. To enter a URL on a browser, it is not usually necessary to type "http" or "www." The browser will enter these terms automatically.
2. E-Mail
a. This is one of the most common uses for the Internet.
b. E-mail addresses are often included in letterhead stationary and business cards.
3. File Transfer Protocol
a. File transfer protocol (ftp) is a very basic interface that connects one computer with another to copy files.
b. To find files that are available from ftp servers, researchers use an online index called "Archie."
4. World Wide Web
a. The Web is a data service on the Internet that is accessed through a browser.
b. Web pages, or sites, usually contain links in boldface, underlined, or colored text.
c. By selecting or clicking on a link, the user is transported to other pages or sites.

C. Accessing the Internet
1. Commercial Online Services
a. Some small businesses and many individuals access the Internet through commercial online services, such as America Online.
b. These services have advantages and disadvantages.
2. Internet Service Providers
a. An Internet Service Provider (ISP) is a service that provides dedicated access to the Internet.
b. An ISP is less consumer oriented than a commercial online service.
c. An ISP normally does not have the same volume of users as a commercial service and can deliver data faster.

D. Navigating the Internet
1. Browsers
a. A browser is software that allows a computer to roam the Web.
b. Although each browser has its own features, all browsers perform the same basic functions.
c. Browsers make it possible to copy text from Web sites and paste it into a word-processing document.
d. Browsers allow you to download images, software, and documents to your computer.
e. With browsers, you can search a single document that appears in your window.

2. Guides and Directories
   a. Lists of Web sites categorized by subject are organized into guides and directories, which can be accessed on the Web.
   b. These sites provide menus of topics that are usually subdivided into narrower subtopics, which are further subdivided until a list of URLs is reached.
3. Search Engines
   a. Next to browsers, search engines are the most important tool for conducting research on the Web.
   b. A search engine scans the Web and indexes the contents of pages into a database.
   c. Search engines vary in size and scope of services.
   d. The use of connectors with search engines is limited to connectors such as "and," "or," and "not."
   e. Search engines often list sources that are not relevant to your search.
   f. To get the best results, a researcher should know the features of each search engine and how to focus queries to take advantage of those features most effectively.
   g. There are two basic types of searches: by key word or by concept.
4. Meta Search Engines
   a. Meta search engines run Internet searches on more than one search engine simultaneously.
   b. Even though they are the best tools for searching the most Web space possible, nothing searches the entire Web.

V. CONDUCTING ONLINE RESEARCH

A. A Threshold Question: Is the Internet the Right Research Tool for Your Project?
1. Conducting Legal Research on the Internet
   a. Many primary sources of law are now available on the Internet.
   b. The availability of secondary sources on the Internet varies.
   c. Many law firms provide background material for their sites on the Internet.
2. The Limited Scope of Online Legal Sources
   a. Although numerous legal materials are available on the Internet, their scope is limited.
   b. For serious, in-depth legal research, the free Web sites on the Internet are not excellent resources.
   c. The expense of data compilation and storage limits the availability of what is accessible on the Internet.
   d. The limited facility of browsers and search engines also detracts from the usefulness of the free resources on the Internet.
3. Conducting Fact-Based Research on the Internet
   a. The Internet is very useful when researching peripheral materials and information, such as scientific, technical, technological, or other types of research.
   b. The Internet is an excellent and speedy tool for locating people, investigating companies, and conducting other practical, fact-based research.

B. Plan Ahead—Analyze the Facts and Identify the Issues
1. State your objectives clearly, and be sure that you understand your goals.
2. Determine which sources are most likely to lead you to the desired results.

C. Starting Points
1. Research sessions can begin with online directories or guides.
2. A search engine or a meta search engine may be used to compile a list of Web sites that contain certain key words.
3. Different search engines yield different results.
4. Many sites include their own links to other sources that may be helpful.

D. Discovering What Resources are Available
1. Your initial research goal may be to find out the extent of what is available online, with your ultimate goal being to locate more precise results.
2. Many libraries provide access to their catalogues online, which are searched the same as you would search them in a library.

3. A listserv list is a list of e-mail addresses of persons who are interested in a particular topic. They provide more anonymity than newsgroups.
4. A newsgroup is a forum that resembles a community bulletin board.

E. Browsing the Links
1. Traveling around the Internet to locate sites and information is known as "surfing the Web."
2. A browser "Favorite" (Explorer) or "Bookmark" (Netscape) is a way to create an automatic link to any point on the Web and return to it any time.
3. A slow browser can be the result of, for example, an outmoded browser, bad telephone lines, your service provider's problems, the limits of equipment, or quirks in the weather.
4. If traffic is heavy at a particular site, look for a mirror site with the same data.
5. Avoid downloading or uploading large files at a site's busy times.

F. Narrowing Your Focus
1. Many sites on the Internet provide links to text and graphics.
2. Some sites include internal search utilities that allow you to look for specific information.
3. Using your browser's "find" tool, you can also search an individual Web page.

G. Evaluating What You Find
1. Once you locate the information for which you are searching, you should evaluate its reliability.
2. To evaluate the credibility of a source, determine whether the source is a primary, secondary, or a tertiary source.
3. Primary sources include experts, persons with firsthand knowledge, and publicly filed documents.
4. Secondary sources include books and periodicals.
5. Tertiary sources are any other sources that might be used in research.
6. Determine whether the online information is outdated and whether the source is reputable.

H. Updating Your Results
1. Confirm whether your research results represent the most recent data available by going to relevant Web sites.

VI. LOCATING PEOPLE AND INVESTIGATING COMPANIES

A. Finding People
1. Broad Searches
   a. A research can run a broad search on the Internet with a general search engine or Internet telephone directories.
2. Narrow Searches
   a. If something is known about a person, the Web can be a good source for locating him or her.
3. Locating Expert Witnesses
   a. There are several sites on the Internet specifically listing expert witnesses.
   b. If it is available, search the directory of a school or business firm to find a certain professor at a particular university or an employee at a certain company.
4. Searches Based on Specific Characteristics
   a. A search can be based on such characteristics as a person's professional status or where he or she went to school.
   b. It is possible to search to verify a person's business license, to locate a veteran, to access information about a federal prison inmate, or to find a federal employee, among other things.
5. Fee-Based Searches
   a. Some commercial services provide access to their databases only for a price.

B. Investigating Companies
1. Finding Company Names and Addresses
   a. A researcher can find a company's name and address by running a search with a telephone number or through the help of an online directory that searches by industry and state.

2. Uncovering Detailed Information about Public Companies
   a. In-depth research is necessary to discover more than the company name and address.
   b. Most companies maintain their own Web sites.
   c. Information may be available through the Web sites for government agencies.
   d. Some states have put their corporate records online.
   e. Other information about public companies can be found at other free sites or fee-based sites.
3. Learning about Private Companies
   a. Data about private companies is more difficult to find because they are not subject to the SEC's disclosure requirements.

VII. SOME OF THE BEST LEGAL-RESOURCE SITES ON THE INTERNET

A. Basic Resources
   1. Almanacs and Nonlegal Encyclopedias.
   2. Area Codes.
   3. Case Citation Guide.
   4. Dictionaries.
   5. E-Mail Addresses.
   6. Internet Directories.
   7. Internet Search Tools.
   8. Internet Service Provides.
   9. Legal Dictionaries.
   10. Legal Ethics.
   11. Library Catalogues.
   12. Maps.
   13. Multiple Dictionaries.
   14. Specialized Dictionaries.
   15. Telephone Directories.
   16. Thesauri.
   17. Zip Codes.

B. University Sites
   1. Law-Related Starting Points.
   2. Government Resources Listings.
   3. Law-Related Discussion Groups.
   4. Web Site Evaluations.

C. Government Sites
   1. Law-Related Starting Points.
   2. Business and Economic Information.
   3. Information about Public Companies.
   4. Government Publications.
   5. Discussion Group.

D. Sites for Associations and Organizations
   1. Associations.
   2. Professional Organizations.
   3. Nonprofit Organizations.

E. Free Commercial Sites
   1. All-Purpose Starting Points.
   2. Law-Related Starting Points.
   3. Media Directory.

QUESTIONS FOR REVIEW

TRUE-FALSE QUESTIONS

____ 1. CD-ROMs are more costly to purchase and require much more space than their printed counterparts.

____ 2. Terms and connectors can only be used on Westlaw® and Lexis®.

____ 3. The Internet is a global communication network of interconnected computers.

____ 4. An URL means your computer has crashed.

____ 5. An "ISP" is a service that provides dedicated access to the Internet.

____ 6. Online citators are extremely useful to legal researchers because they are more up to date than printed citators.

____ 7. When you draft queries, make sure they are not too broad or too narrow.

____ 8. E-mail is not used as a research tool.

____ 9. File transfer protocol is used by a computer to access the World Wide Web.

____ 10. Everything on the World Wide Web has been cataloged and indexed.

____ 11. A search run by a search engine on the Internet is always better than anything you will find on Westlaw® and Lexis®.

____ 12. Meta search engines run searches on more than one search engine simultaneously.

____ 13. All information found on the Internet is accurate and up to date.

____ 14. One of the great benefits of computer technology for the legal field is CALR (computer-assisted legal research), which includes Westlaw® and Lexis®.

____ 15. Westlaw® and Lexis® are less current than printed sources, and it is necessary that research results reflect current law.

FILL-IN QUESTIONS

(Terms and connectors/Natural language) ____________________ are numerical and grammatical connectors to specify the relationship between the key words or phrases. A (URL/database) is an address to a site on the Internet. Use a ____________________ (browser/e-mail) to copy text from Web sites and paste it into word-processing documents.

(Primary/Secondary) ____________________ sources of law on the Internet include the United States Constitution, the United States Supreme Court decisions, and the United States Code. The Internet works best in conducting (in-depth legal/factual) ____________________ searches.

A (listserv/newsgroup) ____________________ is a forum that resembles a community bulletin board. A list of e-mail addresses of persons who are interested in a particular topic or area is called a (listserv/newsgroup) ____________________.

Multiple-Choice Questions

____ 1. Software that allows a computer to roam the World Wide Web is called:
A. An Internet Service Provider
B. A search engine
C. A browser
D. A meta search engine

____ 2. ____________________ allow(s) you to scan the documents retrieved by your search result for terms that were not included in your query.
A. Terms and connectors
B. Locate
C. Natural language
D. Browsers

____ 3. ____________________ is the system of formats and rules that enable two computers to communicate.
A. Protocol
B. Http
C. World Wide Web
D. Internet Service Provider

____ 4. Next to browsers, the most important tools for conducting research on the Internet are:
A. Terms and connectors
B. URLs
C. Westlaw® and Lexis®
D. Search engines

____ 5. If you are looking for a certain person on the Internet and you also have some good background information on that person, you should perform what kind of search:
A. Narrow
B. Broad
C. Terms and connectors
D. Natural language

____ 6. Data on private companies is more difficult to find, because these firms:
A. Are not listed on Dun and Bradstreet
B. Are not subject to the SEC's disclosure requirements
C. Are not listed on the Internet
D. Want to remain secret

____ 7. Which of the following is false regarding CD-ROMS:
A. One CD-ROM can store 300,000 pages of reference material
B. It is accessed through a disk drive
C. It can be used to store data
D. All of the above are true

____ 8. ____________________ are Internet service providers that, for a fee, allow their subscribers access to resources that are otherwise restricted.
A. Commercial online services
B. Westlaw®
C. Lexis®
D. Listservs

____ 9. The main page of a Web site is called a:
A. Hypertext transfer protocol
B. CALR
C. Mirror site
D. Home page

____ 10. A Web site that duplicates an already existing site is called:
A. Hypertext transfer protocol
B. CALR
C. A mirror site
D. A home page

____ 11. A command through which one document links to another on the Web is called a:
A. FTP
B. http
C. ISP
D. URL

____ 12. One major disadvantage of CD-ROMs is that:
A. They are too expensive
B. They take up too much space
C. They become outdated
D. They need special software to run

____ 13. Commercial online services are considered to be a ____________________ on the Internet.
A. Mirror site
B. URL
C. Gateway
D. Hyperlink

____ 14. Automatic links to Internet sites are called:
A. Bookmarks
B. Browsers
C. Hyperlinks
D. Mirror sites

____ 15. Which are the best tools for searching the most Web space possible:
A. Directories
B. Search engines
C. Commercial online services
D. Meta search engines

Practice Questions

1. Viagra, the new anti-impotence pill from Pfizer Pharmaceutical, is not being covered by at last two of the largest HMOs in the United States, because the HMOs have decided that the drug is unnecessary and too expensive.

   Using the search engine Excite, find the names of as many HMOs as you can who have refused to cover Viagra, and find out how much Viagra costs *per pill.*

2. Using the meta search engine, DogPile, and Internet connectors (also called custom commands by some search engines), attempt to locate information about your paralegal program or another paralegal program in your area or state. List the first five search engines or directories that DogPile returned. What did you find?

Questions for Critical Analysis

1. You know that your search words on the Internet can contain Boolean operators to allow you to search for documents that contain exactly the words you want. These operators include AND, NOT, OR, the parentheses, and quotation marks, among others.

   Each search engine has its own tricks—operators—for getting the best results from your search. To find these operators, click on hyperlinks such as "search tips," "power search," or "advanced search." It is always a good idea to read any tips or suggestions for devising a search query; doing so will save you time in the long run. Once you become well acquainted with a certain search engine, you will no longer need to check the search tips before you begin.

   Consider the following problem:

   Individuals have begun to win lawsuits against the tobacco industry for failing to warn of the dangers of cigarette smoking and nicotine addiction. Locate cases in which the individual prevailed against the tobacco industry, and identify the name of the case, the year of the decision, and the state from which the case originated.

   Follow these instructions when running your search query:

   Run a search query on at least five different engines for the above problem. Before you run your search, click on the "search tips" for that search engine, and become acquainted with that search engine's operators. After you have run your search once, do it several more times using different operators for the same search terms. Write down your search queries, the search engine you used, and how your search was impacted by using different operators.

2. Assume you are performing a search on a CALR service like Westlaw® or Lexis® and that you were called away from the terminal as a result of an emergency, and you fail to sign-off. These systems generally will automatically sign-off after the expiration of a certain amount of time. What should you do after you realize your failure?

3. Not all sites on the Internet contain accurate information. When can you assume that the information you have retrieved from the Internet is credible?

Ethical Questions

1. The NFPA has rendered an Informal Ethics and Disciplinary Opinion on the ethical implications, if any, concerning client confidentiality of paralegals communicating in cyberspace. Locate this opinion on the Internet.

   Based on this opinion, if a paralegal e-mails a message to the client and the message contains a discussion of confidential information, what ethical duty, if any, has the paralegal violated? Explain why.

2. The NFPA has rendered an Informal Ethics and Disciplinary Opinion on the ethical implications, if any, concerning the unauthorized practice of law as it relates to paralegals communicating in cyberspace. Locate this opinion on the Internet.

   Based on this opinion, if a paralegal communicates with another person in cyberspace, explain how a paralegal avoids engaging in the unauthorized practice of law.

Technology and Today's Paralegal

There are many directories available to help you find a certain person or expert witness. To find a certain person, check out the following:

American Directory Assistance

http://www.lookupusa.com

http://www.lycos.com/peoplefind/

http://www.isleuth.com

http://bigfoot.com

http://www.usa.com

http://www.whowhere.com

For reverse telephone searches, try the following:

http://www.555-1212.com/whte_us.htm

http://www.peoplefind.lycos.lycos/reverse.htm

http://www.theultimate.com/white/

http://www.switchboard.com

For zip-code lookup and address information, try the following:

http://www1.bigyellow.com/

http://www.usps.gov/ncsc/

To find a lawyer, search the following:

Lawyer Finder
http://www.lawyerfinder.com/search.asp

ABA Network Lawyer Locator
http://www.abanet.org/martindale.html

Martindale-Hubbell Lawyer Search
http://lawyers.martindale.com/marhub

Lawyer Finder
http://www.law.tulane.edu/

To locate expert witnesses, search the following:

http://www.spk@indsource.net

http://www.expertpages.com/

http://www.expertwitness.com

http://www.lawInfo.com/biz/expertwitness.html

American Medical Association
http://www.ama.assn.org

American Psychological Association
http://www.apo.org

CyberAttorney's Experts Online
http://www.cyberatty.com/experts

Legal Research Network
http://www.witness.net

National Directory of Expert Witnesses
http://www.claims

Technical Network Consulting Service
http://www.techmedexperts.com

Answers

True-False Questions

1. F
2. F
3. T
4. F
5. T
6. T
7. T
8. F
9. F
10. F
11. F
12. T
13. F
14. T
15. F

Fill-in Questions

terms and connectors; URL; browser

primary; factual

newsgroup; listserv

Multiple-Choice Questions

1. C
2. B
3. A
4. D
5. A
6. B
7. D
8. A
9. D
10. C
11. B
12. C
13. C
14. A
15. D

Practice Questions

1. Search strategy: Viagra AND HMO
   Search Engine: Excite
   Names of HMOs (at the time of this publication): Cigna and HealthCare
   How much Viagra costs per pill (at the time of this publication): $7 per pill
2. The answer to this problem will vary depending on the area or state in which you live or go to school. The important thing is to learn how to use a meta search engine and to become familiar with the results it can obtain for you.

Questions for Critical Analysis

1. Regardless of which search engine you chose, you should have located the special search tips hyperlink on the home or first page.

   For example, with **Yahoo!**, you would have seen that + and – could be used to either require or prohibit words from appearing in the search results. Attaching one of the operators "t:" or "u:" to the front of your search will restrict the search to certain document sections. By typing a "*" at the end of a keyword, you can search for the word with multiple endings.

   AltaVista has two sections containing information about the search engine—the help and advanced options. AltaVista is a somewhat sophisticated search engine. Its features include the NEAR connector, asterisk (*) wildcard, and a Refine feature to narrow your search. If you want to search for an exact phrase, use double quotation marks around the phrase when you enter the words in the search box. The Refine button (located next to the Search button in the search box) dynamically sorts your results into different topics to help you become more exact with your search keywords. You can continue to refine the search as many times as you wish.

   Excite searches in one of three ways. The first option is by Excite Search, which taps into the traditional search engine listings created from crawling the Web. The second search option is by Channels by Excite, which lists sites by topics. Third, you can use Excite News Tracker. This allows you to search only listings generated by crawling specialty news sites.

   Like most search engines, Excite looks for documents containing the exact words you entered into the query box, but it also goes further by looking for ideas closely related to your query. Use the + sign for words that your results must contain. Use the – sign to tell the search engine that your results should not contain a certain word. Search for exact phrases using double quotation marks. Use Boolean operators, such as AND, OR, NOT, and parentheses. These operators must appear in all caps with a space on each side to work.

   HotBot scores each document that matches the requirements of a search. HotBot considers these factors when computing these scores: (1) word frequency in a document, (2) search words in the title, (3) search words in keywords, (4) document length, and (5) "spoofing."

   Spoofing means that someone has maliciously "spoofed" search engines into returning pages that are not relevant to the search at hand or that rank higher than their relevance and content warrant.

   HotBot's pull-down menus and buttons let you modify or refine your search. Use these tools to narrow your search by placing more conditions on your query. Ask better questions, and you can dramatically improve your search results. Be specific and pick words that are unique to the topic you are investigating.

   Try **SuperSearch**, a powerful but easy-to-understand extension of the HotBot search interface. In SuperSearch, you can use drop-down lists to filter out certain words, limit results within a specific date range, and have the results contain certain types of media located within that page.

   Infoseek has a directory, as well as a search engine. The directory lists sites by topics. Some sites are listed with red check marks, which means that these are Infoseek Select Sites. These sites have been reviewed and recommended by Infoseek.

   With Infoseek, a search for tobacco litigation will return pages containing tobacco and/or litigation, with the phrase tobacco litigation. "Tobacco litigation" will return pages with the word "tobacco" next to the word "litigation." The search "+tobacco litigation" will return pages with tobacco and possibly litigation. The query "+tobacco +litigation" will retrieve both tobacco and litigation in the document, but not necessarily next to each other. If you are using a plus (+) or minus (–) search operator, there is a space before the operator but no space between the operator and the search term.

   Use the pipe(|) search option when you want to narrow your search from a broad topic to a specific topic. (You can do the same thing by clicking "search within these results.") Example: law | litigation | tobacco. A field search can be performed on a link, site, URL, title, or ALT. The field name should be in lower case and should be immediately followed by a colon (for example, url:cats).

FindLaw is a search engine you should add to your Bookmarks or Favorites. Search for any word or phrase by typing the word or phrase into a query form and clicking the search button. Searches produce a list of files that contain the word or phrase regardless of where they appear in the text.

There are specific rules for formulating queries in FindLaw. Queries are case-insensitive, so you can type in uppercase or lowercase. To use specially treated characters—such as &, |, ^, #, @, $, ()—in a query, enclose the query in quotation marks. You can use Boolean operators (AND, OR, NOT, and NEAR) to specify additional search information. The wildcard character (*) can match words with a given prefix. The query "esc*" matches the terms "ESC," "escape," and so on.

2. Because the computer-assisted legal research systems are normally charged by the minute and are expensed to the client, you should inform your supervising attorney of your failure to sign-off. The attorney may review that expense specifically upon the office's receipt of that charge.
3. Sites constructed by individuals with no known credentials about the subject discussed on the site have dubious credibility. Some sites are constructed merely for amusement and should not be taken as a credible source for information. You can trust data obtained from municipal, state, and federal government sites, professional directories, and sites sponsored by national or professional organizations or associations, such as the American Medical Association.

Ethical Questions

1. The address for the NFPA is *http://www.paralegals.org*. Once you reach this site, click on the button for Ethics. (The site is *http://www.paralegals.org/Development/*). The number of the opinion is 96–1.

   The paralegal has violated the duty to preserve client confidences and secrets. Even if the paralegal carefully prepares an electronic communication (such as an e-mail, listserv, bulletin board, World Wide Web forum, Internet Relay Chat, usenet and newsgroup), it is possible, although illegal, to intercept that communication. It is also possible for electronic communications to be inadvertently delivered to an unintended party.

   According to NFPA's opinion, the risk of communicating over the Internet is summarized as:

   A. The lack of a final judicial determination about the confidentiality and privilege.
   B. The possibility that confidential communications may be retained and subject to discovery or inadvertent disclosure.
   C. That inadvertent disclosure may occur because of the way information is transmitted within the Internet.
   D. The risk that the communication may be construed to be consent to disclosure and, thus, waivers of confidentiality.

2. The address for the NFPA is *http://www.paralegals.org*. Once you reach this site, click on the button for Ethics. (The site is *http://www.paralegals.org/Development/*). The number of the opinion is 96–2.

   A paralegal can avoid misunderstandings and miscommunications about the paralegal's role and responsibilities by disclosing the paralegal's title in each cybercommunication. In addition, the paralegal's jurisdiction (state in which he or she is located) should be disclosed.

   According to NFPA's opinion, there is no agreement about what constitutes the unauthorized practice of law (UPL) nor the practice of law. "Generally, it has been held that paralegals may not set or negotiate a client's fee; sign a legal document; represent a client in court or before a tribunal; and give legal advice. One of the largest areas of debate about giving legal advice which is relevant to cybercommunications is that involving providing legal information and legal forms. . . ." (NFPA Ethics Opinion, 96–2). Adding disclaimers to cybercommunications is another method to avoid allegations that a paralegal's cybercommunications are considered engaging in the unauthorized practice of law or giving legal advice. In addition, to avoid violating the UPL statutes, you can avoid giving legal advice even if it is permitted in your jurisdiction. Finally, you can avoid giving legal advice that is tailored to particular facts.

CHAPTER 16

LEGAL ANALYSIS AND WRITING

CHAPTER OBJECTIVES

After completing this chapter, you should be able to:

- Read and analyze case law.
- Recognize some techniques for reading statutory law and guidelines traditionally used for interpreting statutory law.
- Understand the factors you should consider before undertaking a legal-writing assignment.
- Discuss the factors you should consider when drafting a legal document.
- Explain the purpose and format of the most common types of legal letters.
- Prepare a legal memorandum.
- Prepare an appellate brief.

Chapter Outline

I. INTRODUCTION

II. ANALYZING CASE LAW
   A. The Components of a Case
      1. Citation and Case Title
         a. The citation indicates the name, volume number, and page number of the reporter series in which the case appears.
      2. Docket Number
         a. The docket number is assigned by the court clerk when a case is initially filed.
         b. It serves as an identifier for all papers submitted in connection with the case.
         c. This number may serve as a valuable tool in obtaining background information about the case.
      3. Dates Argued and Decided
         a. Usually these dates immediately follow the docket number.
      4. Syllabus
         a. A syllabus is a brief synopsis of the facts of the case, the issues analyzed by the court, and the court's conclusion.
         b. This is usually prepared by the courts in official reporters and by the publisher's editors in unofficial reporters.
         c. Reading the syllabus is not a substitute for reading the case.
      5. Headnotes
         a. Headnotes are short paragraphs that follow the general syllabus and highlight and summarize the specific rules of law mentioned in the case.
         b. In reporters published by West Group, headnotes are correlated to West's key-number system.
      6. Names of Counsel
         a. These are the names of the lawyers who represented the parties.
      7. Name of Judge or Justice Authoring the Opinion
         a. The name of the judge or justice who authored the opinion appears just before the court's opinion.
         b. In some cases, the decision will be authored *per curiam,* which means that the opinion is that of the whole court and not of any one judge or justice.
      8. Opinion
         a. The formal opinion of the court contains the analysis and decision of the court that heard and decided the case.
         b. Most opinions contain a brief statement of the facts of the case, a summary of the legal issues raised by the facts, and the remedies sought by the parties.
      9. The Court's Conclusion
         a. At the end of the opinion, the conclusions presented within the opinion will be briefly reiterated and summarized. If no conclusions were yet presented, they will be presented in the concluding section of the opinion.
   B. Analyzing Cases
      1. In analyzing case law, it is essential to understand the significance of the various components of the case.
      2. The syllabus and headnotes are often helpful in giving you an overview of the issues involved.
      3. Some opinions are easier to understand than others, because some judges write more clearly and logically than others.
      4. Identify *dicta* (nonbinding views expressed in the opinion) and distinguish it from the holding (the legally binding principle to be drawn from the court's decision).
   C. Summarizing and Briefing Cases
      1. Legal professionals often use an analytical technique called case briefing to reduce the content of the case to its essentials.

   2. A typical case brief will contain the case citation, the key facts of the case, the case's procedural history, a statement of the issue(s) raised in the case, the court's holding, the court's rationale, and the court's judgment.
   3. Knowing how to read, analyze, and brief cases makes it easier to compare and synthesize case research accurately and efficiently.
- D. Synthesizing Your Research Results
   1. Through synthesizing research results, you extract the most important rules of law, issues, and defenses.
   2. This synthesis is incorporated into whatever legal document you need to draft.
   3. You can synthesize results in three different ways by grouping cases according to:
      - a. Rules of law.
      - b. Issues.
      - c. Defenses raised.

III. ANALYZING STATUTORY LAW

- A. Reading Statutory Law
   1. Coverage and Effective Date
      - a. You should first find out whether the statute is applicable to the client's case.
      - b. Each statute indicates the date on which it will become legally effective.
   2. Definitions
      - a. Normally, at the beginning of a statute or at the beginning of a major section, there is a list of terms followed by their definitions.
   3. Subdivisions
      - a. Statutes often indicate subsections by letters or numbers.
      - b. Statutes frequently contain even more levels of subsections, which you may need to diagram to discern the interrelationship of various subsections.
   4. *And* versus *or*
      - a. When reading a statute, you should pay careful attention to the words *and* and *or* in the text.
      - b. Consciously looking for these connectors can help to clarify the meaning of a statutory provision.
- B. Interpreting Statutory Law
   1. Rules of Construction
      - a. These are the rules that control the judicial interpretation of the statutes.
      - b. Specific provisions are given greater weight than general provisions when there is a conflict between the two.
      - c. Recent provisions are given greater weight than earlier provisions when there is a conflict between the two.
      - d. Masculine pronouns refer both to males and females.
      - e. Singular nouns also include the plural forms of the nouns.
   2. The Plain-Meaning Rule
      - a. Under this rule, the words chosen by the legislature must be understood according to their common meanings.
   3. Previous Judicial Interpretation
      - a. Courts are obligated to follow the precedents set by higher courts in their jurisdictions.
   4. Legislative Intent
      - a. A court relying on legislative intent determines the meaning of the statute by attempting to find out why the legislators chose to phrase the statute in that particular language or what the legislators sought to accomplish by enacting the law.

IV. LEGAL WRITING—THE PRELIMINARIES

- A. Understanding the Assignment
   1. Upon receiving a writing assignment, the paralegal should make sure that he or she clearly understands the following:
      - a. The nature of the assignment.

        b. When the assignment should be completed.
        c. What approach should be used.
    2. A paralegal should never equate asking questions with incompetence, but instead with executing a task as efficiently as possible.
B. Time Constraints and Flexibility
    1. When receiving a writing assignment, a paralegal needs to understand clearly when it must be completed.
    2. If little time is given for completion of a project, a paralegal must decide what information is crucial and what can be omitted.
C. Writing Approaches
    1. Determine if a writing assignment requires:
        a. *Objective analysis*—which either focuses on facts or discusses fairly both sides of a legal matter.
        b. *Advocacy*—which involves presenting the facts and issues in a light most favorable to the client.
    2. No matter which writing approach is needed, attorneys have a duty of candor, even if it is adverse to the client's position.

V. THE IMPORTANCE OF GOOD WRITING SKILLS

A. Organize and Outline Your Presentation
    1. Choice of Format
        a. Documents to be filed with the court must conform to the procedural rules of the particular jurisdiction.
        b. Most law firms adopt special types of formats for other documents.
    2. Structural Devices
        a. When writing about complex and numerous issues, divide your presentation into several sections, with each section addressing one issue.
        b. Include descriptive headings and subheadings in your document so the reader never gets lost.
        c. A chronologically structured discussion can sometimes be easier for the reader to follow.
B. Write to Your Audience
    1. The writing should be tailored for the intended audience.
    2. The ultimate goal of legal writing is to communicate information or ideas to the reader.
C. Avoid Legalese
    1. The writing should avoid legalese.
    2. Eliminate legal jargon, or those terms used by legal professionals but unknown to most people outside the legal profession.
    3. When translating legalese into plain English, make sure that you correctly understand the intent of the legal phrase.
D. Be Brief and to the Point
    1. The writing should be brief and to the point.
    2. Generally, do not use words that are not essential to the point you are making.
E. Writing Basics: Sentences
    1. The writing should present well-constructed sentences.
    2. Use short, concrete sentences with active, dynamic verbs.
    3. Write in the active voice rather than the passive voice.
    4. Use correct grammar, spelling, and punctuation.
F. Writing Basics: Paragraphs and Transitions
    1. The writing should present well-constructed paragraphs.
    2. Each paragraph should begin with a topic sentence.
    3. Use transitional sentences to relate paragraphs.
G. Be Alert for Sexist Language
    1. The writing should use gender-neutral language.
    2. Avoid using masculine pronouns when the gender of the referent is unknown.

H. Proofread and Revise Your Document
   1. The writing should be free of typographical errors, misspelled words, and other flaws.
   2. A good portion of the time creating a polished document should be spent in proofreading and revising the written work product.

VI. PLEADINGS AND DISCOVERY

A. Always become familiar with the rules of court where the documents are being filed.
B. Use the proper format of that particular court.

VII. GENERAL LEGAL CORRESPONDENCE

A. General Format for Legal Correspondence
   1. Date
      a. All legal correspondence must be dated.
      b. The date of a letter may be important in matters involving legal notice of a particular event.
   2. Method of Delivery and Address Block
      a. The method of delivery indicates how the letter was sent (if other than by U.S. mail).
      b. The address block indicates to whom the letter is addressed.
   3. Reference Line and Salutation
      a. The reference line identifies the matter discussed in the letter.
      b. The salutation is the formal greeting to the addressee and is placed just below the reference line.
   4. Body and Closing
      a. The main part of the letter is the letter's body.
      b. The body of the letter should be formal and should effectively communicate information to the reader.
      c. The closing is the final comment in a letter that is placed above the signature, such as "Sincerely" or "Very truly yours."

B. Types of Legal Letters
   1. Informative Letters
      a. These are letters that convey information.
   2. Confirmation Letters
      a. Confirmation letters state the substance of a previously conducted verbal discussion to provide a permanent record of the oral conversation.
   3. Opinion Letters
      a. This type of letter conveys advice or a legal opinion to a client and is based on a detailed analysis of the law.
      b. Opinion letters must always be signed by attorneys.
   4. Demand Letters
      a. A demand letter is adversarial in nature.
      b. This kind of letter attempts to persuade the reader that he or she should accept a position that is favorable to the writer's client by demanding that the reader do or not do a certain thing.

VIII. THE INTERNAL MEMORANDUM

A. Heading
   1. The heading contains the date on which the memo is submitted, the name of the person submitting the memo, the name of the person to whom the memo is addressed, and a brief description of the matter, usually in the form of a reference line.

B. Statement of the Facts
   1. The statement of the facts introduces the legal issues by describing the factual elements of the dispute.
   2. Only relevant facts are included.
   3. The facts presented must not be slanted in favor of the client.
   4. Never omit facts that are unfavorable to your client.
   5. The statement of the facts should contain a logical and concise description of the events surrounding the conflict.

C. Questions Presented
   1. The questions presented address the legal issues to be addressed by the memorandum.
   2. This section may involve just one simple issue or a number of complex issues.

D. Brief Conclusion
   1. This is sometimes called the short answer or brief answer.
   2. This section states succinct responses to the questions presented.
   3. This section may vary in length, but each conclusion should be limited to no more than one paragraph.

E. Discussion and Analysis
   1. This section contains the discussion and analysis of each legal issue to be resolved.
   2. If legal memorandums address multiple issues, as they often do, they should be organized into separate parts so that each legal issue can be analyzed in the discussion separately.
   3. The discussion is the core of the legal memorandum.
   4. Points of law should be identified and supported with proper citations.
   5. When quoting from a case or other legal authority, remember that the attorney for whom the memorandum is prepared wants to see your analysis, not a reiteration of a court's opinion.

F. Conclusion
   1. The conclusion is the culmination of the legal memo, and it is your opinion of how the issues discussed may be resolved.
   2. The conclusion may inform the attorney that more information is needed or may demonstrate that a certain issue should be evaluated further.

IX. THE APPELLATE BRIEF

A. Types of Appellate Briefs
   1. Appellant's Brief
      a. The appellant is the party appealing the case.
      b. The appellant's brief is the first brief filed with the court; it establishes the issues to be addressed.
      c. The purpose of this brief is to convince the appellate court that the lower court's decision was erroneous.
   2. Appellee's Brief
      a. The appellee is the party who prevailed in the lower court and against whom the appeal is brought.
      b. The appellee's brief discusses the issues raised by the appellant's brief and is filed as a direct response to the claims made by the appellant.
      c. The purpose of this brief is to rebut any arguments made in the appellant's brief and to emphasize the lower court's judgment rendered in the appellee's favor.
   3. Reply Brief
      a. The reply brief is filed by the appellant in response to the appellee's brief.
      b. The reply brief is narrow in scope.
   4. *Amicus Curiae* Brief
      a. This brief is filed with the court by a party not directly involved in the lawsuit.
      b. The purpose of this brief is to convince the court to rule in favor of one of the parties because not to do so would affect a broad interest of society.

B. Writing an Effective Appellate Brief
   1. Title Page
      a. This is the front cover of an appellate brief, which provides certain information about the case on appeal.
      b. Courts often have rules specifying the format and colors to be used for the covers of appellate briefs.
   2. Table of Contents
      a. The table of contents lists the sections of the appellate brief and gives the page number where each section begins.
      b. It functions as an index and also outlines the points made in the argument.

3. Table of Authorities
   a. This provides the reader with page references for all authorities cited in the brief.
   b. These authorities are arranged in a particular order.
   c. This is one of the last sections completed in an appellate brief.
   d. Accuracy is extremely important.
4. Statement of Jurisdiction
   a. This section indicates the source of authority for the appellate court's jurisdiction over the dispute.
5. Questions Presented
   a. This section sets out the legal issues that will be argued by the parties to the dispute.
   b. These questions should be framed in such a way that they lead to a response in the client's favor.

C. Statement of the Claim
1. This section usually contains a preliminary statement dealing with the procedural background of the case and a statement of the relevant facts.
2. The facts are not presented objectively.
3. The facts are limited to the facts that appear in the appellate record.
4. The author must cite the part of the record from which the fact was obtained.

D. Summary of the Argument
1. This is a condensed version of the developed argument made in the main text of the brief.
2. This section of the brief is relied upon heavily by those who have not had an opportunity to review the argument section.
3. It is not necessary to include citations in the summary.

E. Argument
1. Point Headings and Subheadings
   a. Point headings are brief recapitulations of the argument.
   b. Effective point headings enhance the argument's presentation.
   c. Subheadings help to clarify the structure of the presentation.
   d. There should not be too many subheadings under any point heading.
2. The Body of the Argument
   a. This section develops the reasons why the court should decide in favor of your client.
   b. Detailed arguments are contained in this section, and each argument must thoroughly analyze the legal and factual aspects of the case.
   c. This section must be well organized and fully supported by law.

F. Conclusion
1. The conclusion follows the argument.
2. The conclusion is not a summary of the argument but a claim for relief based on the arguments.

QUESTIONS FOR REVIEW

TRUE-FALSE QUESTIONS

____ 1. An appellate brief is an attorney's written argument setting forth the legal reasons why the court should rule in favor of the attorney's client.

____ 2. A docket number is assigned to a case after it has been decided by the court.

____ 3. The date on which a case was decided by a court is unimportant in analyzing case law.

____ 4. *Dicta* is the legal principle to be drawn from the court's decision.

____ 5. Legal professionals often use case briefing to reduce the content of a case to its bare essentials.

____ 6. It is helpful in analyzing statutes to consider certain rules of interpretation referred to as rules of construction.

____ 7. The plain-meaning rule used in interpreting statutory language refers to according words their common meaning.

____ 8. Documents to be filed with a court must conform to the procedural rules of the particular jurisdiction.

____ 9. Arranging events, especially facts leading to a lawsuit, in a chronological fashion may be helpful to the reader.

____ 10. The audience of a document is a necessary consideration in drafting the document; for example, a writer should avoid legalese in a letter to a client.

____ 11. Generally, it is unnecessary to confirm in writing what was discussed orally to clients.

____ 12. A date should always be included in correspondence.

____ 13. A title such as "Paralegal" or "Legal Assistant" should always follow the name of the paralegal writing correspondence on behalf of a firm.

____ 14. A paralegal can sign any type of letter: informative, demand, opinion, or confirmation.

____ 15. Demand letters are adversarial in nature and seek to advance the client's interests.

FILL-IN QUESTIONS

The full citation of a case is necessary, ____________________ (including/not including) parallel citations.

Researching statutory law ____________________ (does/does not) include researching case law.

Comparison of two rental agreements requires ____________________ (advocacy skills/objective analysis). Assertion of a client's position requires ____________________ (advocacy skills/objective analysis).

Facts presented in a legal memorandum ____________________ (must/must not) be slanted. The legal issues should be specific and straightforward and set out in the ____________________ (questions presented/conclusion). Each brief conclusion should ____________________ (include discussion/be limited to one paragraph). The core of a legal memorandum is the discussion and should provide a thorough ____________________ (analysis of the law/conclusion). The conclusion is ____________________ (the court's reasoning/your opinion) of the issues.

MULTIPLE-CHOICE QUESTIONS

____ 1. The case citation indicates the following information about the reporter series in which the case appears:
A. Name
B. Volume number
C. Page number
D. All of the above

____ 2. Which of the following is false regarding a syllabus:
A. It provides a clear overview of the case and points out legal issues discussed by the court
B. In official reporters, the courts usually prepare the syllabi
C. It can be cited as authority
D. In unofficial reporters, the publishers of the reporters usually prepare the syllabi

____ 3. The formal opinion of the court contains:
A. The names of counsel
B. The headnotes
C. The key numbers
D. The analysis and decision of the judge(s) that heard and decided the case

____ 4. Legally binding statements of a court are referred to as the:
A. Holding
B. *Dicta*
C. Closing
D. Opinion

____ 5. The docket number for a case is assigned by:
A. The paralegal
B. The judge
C. The supervising attorney
D. The court clerk

____ 6. Synthesizing research results can best be accomplished by grouping cases according to:
A. Their rules of law
B. Their issues
C. The defenses
D. All of the above are acceptable

____ 7. To discern the intent of the legislators who drafted a particular law, legislative history may need to be investigated by reviewing:
A. Committee reports
B. Records of congressional hearings
C. Other relevant documents
D. All of the above

____ 8. Each paragraph should begin with a sentence that indicates what the paragraph is about, referred to as a:
A. Salutation
B. Topic sentence
C. Closing
D. Reference line

____ 9. Proofreading a document includes reviewing it for:
A. Organizational coherence
B. Sexist language
C. Word choice
D. All of the above

____ 10. The address block:
A. Tells to whom the letter is addressed
B. Tells to whom the letter is addressed and how it was sent
C. Indicates the matter discussed in the letter
D. Greets the addressee

____ 11. A reference line may:
A. Identify the matter discussed in the letter
B. Contain the name of the case
C. Contain the case file
D. All of the above

____ 12. A letter that conveys information to another party is a(n):
A. Informative letter
B. Confirmation letter
C. Demand letter
D. Advisory letter

____ 13. A letter that puts into written form the contents of an oral discussion is a(n):
A. Informative letter
B. Confirmation letter
C. Demand letter
D. Advisory letter

____ 14. A letter that provides a detailed analysis of the law, giving a legal opinion is a(n):
A. Informative letter
B. Confirmation letter
C. Demand letter
D. Advisory letter

____ 15. The goal in drafting a legal memorandum is to:
A. Inform, explain, and evaluate the client's claim or defense
B. Argue persuasively in support of the client's claim
C. Advance arguments of the opponent
D. Discuss settlement terms

Practice Questions

1. State whether the following sentences are written in the active or passive voice:
   A. Plaintiff received severe lacerations.
   B. The car was driven by the defendant.
   C. The defendant purchased the murder weapon on Friday.
   D. The victim was stalked by the defendant for two years.
2. Analyze the construction of the following paragraphs. How could they be improved?

   Murder can be intentional. Murder can be accidental. There are two forms of murder.

   She voluntarily subjected herself to the dangers when she enrolled in that course. She knew that karate could result in injuries. The plaintiff knew of the dangers involved.
3. Rewrite the following paragraph.

   Plaintiff sliped and feel on the side walk. She hd ben drinkng ll aafternoon. She called his moter but left bfore she arrved to pik her up. She, in fac, contrbuted to her oinw injries.

Questions for Critical Analysis

1. Why are court opinions difficult to read and understand at times?
2. Why is it important to consider your audience in drafting various legal documents and correspondence?

Ethical Questions

1. Jan Jones is employed with a large law firm, primarily working in the area of workers' compensation. Jan's supervising attorney has assigned her to a case involving a client who lost several fingers on the job while operating a punch press. The client is not only seeking workers' compensation but has also asked the law firm to evaluate a possible personal-injury case. After evaluating the medical records and the client's version of the facts, Jan writes an opinion letter to the client. Jan does not indicate her status as a paralegal. Has Jan done anything wrong?
2. While writing an internal memorandum, Barry Simms, a paralegal, minimizes the importance of a recent supreme court case in his state. Although the facts in that case were very similar to the facts in the current case, Barry does not think the court would decide the current case in the same way. Has Barry used objectivity in writing this memorandum?

Technology and Today's Paralegal

Legalese—the bane of the legal profession. Will Rogers once said, "The minute you read something and you can't understand it, you can be sure it was written by a lawyer." Legalese is not required by case precedent, by statute, or any other excuse.

Your text suggests that you do a keyword search on the Internet for "plain language" and "plain English." If those phrases do not yield the results you want, try a keyword search for "legal writing" using your favorite search engine.

Some other sites you might wish to add to your Bookmarks are:

The Plain Language Network—National Partnership for Reinventing Government
http://plainlanguage.gov/main.htm

Plain Language Online—Bibliography
http://plainlanguage.com/biblio.htm
This site contains links to and information about numerous books on writing in plain English.

Plain Legal Language
http://www.plainlanguage.com/legal/index.htm

Answers

True-False Questions

1. T
2. F
3. F
4. F
5. T
6. T
7. T
8. T
9. T
10. T
11. F
12. T
13. T
14. F
15. T

Fill-in Questions

including

does

objective analysis; advocacy skills

must not; questions presented; be limited to one paragraph; analysis of the law; your opinion

Multiple-Choice Questions

1. D
2. C
3. D
4. A
5. D
6. D
7. D
8. B
9. D
10. B
11. D
12. A
13. B
14. D
15. A

Practice Questions

1. A. Active
   B. Passive
   C. Active
   D. Passive
2. There are two forms of murder. Murder can be intentional. Murder can be accidental.
   The plaintiff knew of the dangers involved. She knew that karate could result in injuries. She voluntarily subjected herself to the dangers when she enrolled in that course.
3. Plaintiff slipped and fell on the sidewalk. She had been drinking all afternoon. She called her mother but left before she arrived to pick her up. She, in fact, contributed to her own injuries.

Questions for Critical Analysis

1. Many times the opinions involve various complex issues. It may be necessary to have some background knowledge about the particular issues being researched in order to understand the court's analysis. Furthermore, each court has its own writing style and format; adapting to each requires patience and skill.
2. If your audience is the firm's client, it is necessary to adequately inform the client by writing in an easily readable and easily understandable style. If the document contains legal terms beyond the client's understanding, it may alienate or infuriate the client.
   If your audience is the court, it is necessary to provide an articulate, well-versed document that reflects the confidence and competence of the firm, supporting the client's position. The court must be convinced that the position is supported by the facts and the law, not just an opinion of an expected result.

Ethical Questions

1. To avoid liability for the unauthorized practice of law, Jan should not have signed an opinion letter with her own name. This letter should have been signed by the attorney. The attorney is the legal professional authorized to give legal advice. Even if Jan had permission from the attorney to communicate the information directly to the client, she should have indicated her status below her name at the end of the letter.
2. No, Barry has not written an objective memorandum. In deciding whether the client should sue, the attorney needs to make an informed judgment. The attorney is relying on the paralegal to supply objective information. The attorney must be made aware of all potential arguments of opposing counsel, whether the paralegal believes they will apply or not.